AN INTRODUCTION TO REGIONAL PLANNING

AN INTRODUCTION TO REGIONAL PLANNING

Concepts, Theory and Practice

JOHN GLASSON

*Senior Lecturer, Department of Town Planning,
Oxford Polytechnic*

 HUTCHINSON EDUCATIONAL

To Carol and Rebecca

Hutchinson Educational Ltd
3 Fitzroy Square, London W1

London Melbourne Sydney Auckland
Wellington Johannesburg Cape Town
and agencies throughout the world

First published 1974
© J. Glasson 1974

Set in Monotype Garamond
Printed in Great Britain by
R. J. Acford Ltd, Chichester, Sussex

ISBN (cased) 0 09 116770 1
       (paper) 0 09 116771 X

Contents

Preface   ix

Acknowledgements   xiii

Part One: The Conceptual Basis of Regional Planning

1: THE CONTEXT OF REGIONAL PLANNING   3
  1. Why plan?   3
  2. What is planning?   4
  3. Levels of planning   7
  4. The need for regional planning   10
  5. 'Inter' and 'intra' regional planning   11
  6. Summary   15

2: THE REGION IN REGIONAL PLANNING   18
  1. The concept of the region   18
  2. Regionalisation and the delineation of regions   23
  3. Regionalism and the administration of regions   32
  4. Summary: planning regions and regional planning   39

Part Two: The Analysis of Regions

A. Inter-Regional Analysis   45

3: THE REGIONAL FRAMEWORK   45
  1. The adequacy of the UK regional data base   46
  2. Regional accounts   48
  3. Descriptive regional input-output tables   51
  4. Summary   59

4: REGIONAL CHANGE—SHORT RUN   62

1. Economic base theory   63
2. Inter-regional trade multipliers   69
3. Regional input-output analysis   74
4. A compromise approach   80
5. Summary   81

5: REGIONAL GROWTH—LONG RUN   84

1. Aggregate growth models   85
2. A disaggregated approach—industrial structure analysis   91
3. Regional Growth—convergence or divergence?   97
4. Summary   99

B. *Intra-Regional Analysis*   102

6: THE LOCATION OF INDUSTRY   102

1. Location of industry: theory and practice   102
2. Industrial location theory   103
3. Industrial location in practice   113
4. Summary   120

7: THE SPATIAL STRUCTURE OF REGIONS   125

1. Central place theory   126
2. The validity of central place theory   135
3. Central place theory and regional planning   139
4. Summary   141

8: GROWTH POLE THEORY   145

1. Basic concepts of growth pole theory   146
2. Growth pole theory and regional planning   154
3. Models of spatial interaction   156
4. Summary   160

Part Three: The Practice of Regional Planning

9: INTER-REGIONAL PLANNING IN THE UNITED KINGDOM   165

1. The identification of UK problem regions—how many nations?   167
2. The case for intervention—goals and objectives   172

3. A choice of strategy—labour migration or industrial location? 175
4. The tactics of UK inter-regional planning 178
5. The effectiveness of UK policy 194
6. An appraisal of the tactics 203
7. Summary 210

10: INTRA-REGIONAL PLANNING IN THE UNITED KINGDOM 214

1. The aims of intra-regional planning 214
2. The evolution of intra-regional planning 216
3. The regional planning process 225
4. Growth centre policies 231
5. Regional planning in the metropolitan South East 236
6. Regional planning in the industrial North West 247
7. Summary 255

11: UK REGIONAL PLANNING—
AN ADMINISTRATIVE PROBLEM 258

1. The reorganisation of local government 259
2. Regional economic planning councils and boards 268
3. Reform at the regional/provincial scale 272
4. Regional reform and national administration 280
5. Summary 282

12: REGIONAL PLANNING IN A EUROPEAN CONTEXT 284

1. Regional planning in France 284
2. Dutch regional planning 299
3. Regional planning in a European Community 307
4. Summary 316

CONCLUSION: RETROSPECT AND PROSPECT 319

Appendices 323

Preface

Regional planning means many things to many men. For some, regional planning has an economic bias and is primarily concerned with the centrally directed allocation of resources between regions to achieve certain regional and national objectives. For others, regional planning involves the physical, economic and social planning of development within regions and sub-regions and has more of a land use content. Not surprisingly it tends to be something of an enigma and is often regarded as an intruder in the planning fraternity. Nevertheless it has given rise to a diverse literature in many countries although much of this tends to be rather specialised covering only narrow areas of the wider field.

This book is intended as a general and introductory text in regional planning, particularly oriented to the United Kingdom context. It seeks to provide an insight into the nebulous subject, attempting to integrate the various aspects into a systematic framework. As such, the aim is to avoid the narrow specialist approach yet provide sufficient depth into regional analysis and practice necessary for a meaningful understanding of the subject area.

It has been designed and written with the requirements of undergraduate education in mind but it may also prove useful to certain postgraduate courses. It is hoped that it will be of particular use to students in urban and regional planning, geography, economics, business and other related subjects such

ix

as surveying and architecture. It is also designed to form a survey of the subject for those involved professionally, either directly or peripherally, as well as for the interested layman.

The book is subdivided into three major parts—the Conceptual Basis of Regional Planning, the Analysis or Anatomy of Regions and Regional Planning in Practice. Of course the wide scope of the subject means that argument may be compressed in places. For example, the text does not attempt to provide a comprehensive guide to the regional planning process, nor indeed a detailed examination of specific regional plans and strategies. In such cases it is hoped that the references will help to fill the gaps.

In Part One a distinction is made between inter- and intra-regional planning. This simple taxonomic device provides the framework for the discussion of the regional analysis and the practice of regional planning in Parts Two and Three. It must be noted at the outset however that there is a considerable overlap and interrelationship between inter- and intra-regional analysis and likewise between inter- and intra-regional planning—both of which may be involved in the development of a region.

Of course, regional planning, involving an interference with the existing patterns of activity within a region, requires some knowledge of the 'laws' that underlie their structure and growth. Part Two examines the anatomy of regions, critically discussing the various regional theories. Chapters 3 to 5 adopt an inter-regional approach, seeking to explain the differences between regions, taking regions as a whole. The following Chapters, 6 to 8, examine the theories of the internal structure of regions. The former, concerned with growth and change, draw heavily on economic concepts, and the latter, concerned with locational analysis, derive much from the geographer's spatial theories. All the theories serve the basic descriptive function providing an aid to the understanding, comparison and further analysis of a variety of unique regions. Several also have useful predictive and prescriptive attributes and these are discussed.

Regional science is one of the popular names given to this study of the regional anatomy. It is not a pure discipline, drawing heavily on the theories of regional economics—perhaps the parent discipline—geography, mathematics, physics and more recently certain socio-political concepts. However, as yet, the body of theory is still rather indeterminate, as aptly illustrated by Hilhorst

'regional planners have set to work openly confessing that although they knew more about their profession than others, they still have not mastered their trade, if only because no adequate theory of regional development exists.'*

There have been several important developments in the practice of regional planning over the last few years. These are discussed in Part Three with particular reference to the United Kingdom but with a limited discussion of some European practice of relevance to the British situation. Of course, in such a rapidly evolving area this should be seen as part of an ongoing discussion and indeed new developments are imminent, notably in the field of regional administration and European regional policy. Thus before too long—hopefully—we should have the report of the Commission on the Constitution, set up to examine the administrative and other relationships between the various parts of the United Kingdom, and by 1974 there should be available the new European Economic Community regional policy called for by the 1972 EEC Summit Conference.

*J. G. M. Hilhorst, *Regional Planning*, Rotterdam University Press (1971).

Acknowledgements

My grateful thanks are due to the many people in practice, teaching and research who have introduced me to the field of regional planning. I am particularly grateful to my colleagues at Oxford Polytechnic who have helped me to develop my interest and to my students who have critically tested many of my ideas. But above all I owe a special debt of thanks to my wife. She has typed and retyped the manuscript and provided me with that most valuable of commodities, time. Without her help and encouragement the book would never have been produced.

PART ONE
The Conceptual Basis of Regional Planning

1 The context of regional planning

Regional planning has tended to be somewhat of an intruder in the planning fraternity for several reasons. Its rôle in the planning framework is not very clearly defined, nor are its aims fully worked out or generally agreed. Comprehension is further complicated by the very flexibility of the actual concept of the 'region'. Thus there is a need to set regional planning in its planning context, and this will be considered in the first chapter; the actual concept of the region will be left open until the second chapter. The placing of regional planning in its context involves asking certain very basic questions. Why in fact is there a need to plan at all? What is 'planning', and how does regional planning fit in? Why is there a need for regional planning and what form does it take?

1 Why Plan?

Planning has been going on throughout history and it is tempting to explain it away by merely stating that man has a natural urge to plan, it is part of his organisational make-up. This could be the psychologist's approach, setting 'planning' up as one of the basic 'social drives' of society—a drive which is not biologically inborn, but which is learned in society, and upon the satisfaction of which rests the survival of society.

Although relevant, this does not explain the rapid increase in planning over the last 100 years. There has been a rapid evolution from a society dominated by *laissez-faire* principles to one where

3

state intervention is accepted to varying degrees in many aspects of everyday life. But why this increase in planning? It has been demonstrated over time that the normal interplay of private action and market forces often results in situations which the nation is not willing to tolerate and which can only be improved by means of a control mechanism—planning. Such an explanation is applicable at most scales and in most contexts; thus the lack of family planning and the problems of oversize families, the lack of national economic planning and the problem of oversize dole queues.

Particular problems of the *laissez-faire* approach are the inequalities of income distribution between groups and regions, as evidenced, for example, by the income gaps between old-age pensioners and motor-workers and between South East England and Northern Ireland in the United Kingdom. Another problem is the divergence between the voluntary private costs and benefits and the involuntary social costs and benefits of private actions. The limited provision of 'public goods' such as open space and fresh air; the wastes of competition and the dangers of monopoly; and the problems of economic instability—in particular, the problem of unemployment, are also synonymous with the *laissez-faire* approach. More recently, the rapid rise in population (especially urban population), increasing affluence and rampant technology have all increased the need for planning; but what is this control mechanism called planning?

2 What is planning?

Individual definitions of planning are abundant, but a general theory of planning has not yet been written. Indeed, with a subject which is so obviously evolutionary and responsive to its own history of development and to the wider developments taking place in society as a whole, it is perhaps too much to expect a final statement on what constitutes 'planning', and this will certainly not be attempted here. However, certain features of planning in general, features common to all types of planning, can be identified. In addition, certain alternative types of planning of some relevance to the regional form can be identified within this general framework.

Major features of general planning include a sequence of actions which are designed to solve problems in the future. The planning problems vary but tend to be primarily economic and social; the planning period, the time horizon of 'the future', also varies according to the type and level of planning; but all planning involves a sequential process which can be conceptualised into a number of stages, such as:

the identification of the problem;

the formulation of general goals and more specific and
   measurable objectives relating to the problem;

the identification of possible constraints;

the projection of the future situation;

the generation and evaluation of alternative courses of action;

and the production of a preferred plan, which in its generic
   form may include any policy statement or strategy as well
   as a definitive plan.

This process is relevant to the whole spectrum of planning problems—how can I get from London to Manchester as quickly as possible? How can an extra 2 000 000 people be accommodated in South East England over the period 1971–91? How can the British economy achieve a growth rate of 4% per annum? Summing up in Friedman's words:

'planning is primarily a way of thinking about social and economic problems, planning is oriented predominantly toward the future, is deeply concerned with the relation of goals to collective decisions and strives for comprehensiveness in policy and program. Wherever these modes of thought are applied, there is a presumption that planning is being done.'[1]

Within this general planning framework, there are a wide variety of types of planning. Certain basic distinctions between the various types are particularly useful in our analysis of regional planning. The first and perhaps most fundamental distinction— and one which has been a constant source of confusion in regional planning—is that between *physical planning* and *economic planning*. Physical planning is the planning of an area's physical structure —land use, communications, utilities and so on, and has its origins in the regulation and control of town development, which outstripped the ability of the market mechanism to cope. Economic planning is concerned more with the economic structure of an area and its overall level of prosperity. It works more through the market mechanism than physical planning which relies heavily on direct controls. Unfortunately many see this physical/economic division as absolute, which is misconceived because physical planning is an important means in the implementation of plans and vice versa.[2]

A second distinction is between *allocative* and *innovative planning*.[3] These are the names given to two instrumental models of planning divided according to 'function' or 'area of concern'. Allocative planning is concerned with co-ordination, the resolution of conflicts ensuring that the existing system is ticking over efficiently through time in accordance with evolving policies. Hence it is sometimes known as regulatory planning. In the context of a small firm, it would involve the planning of the deliveries of inputs of raw materials and labour and the distribution of the final goods. In the context of the national economy, it would involve the month-to-month regulation of the economy using fiscal and monetary policy. Innovative planning, on the other hand, is not merely concerned with planning for the efficient functioning of existing systems, but is more concerned with improving/developing the system as a whole, introducing new aims and attempting to mould change on a large scale. For this reason, it is sometimes known as development planning. In our small-firm example, the marketing of a new product or the opening of a factory extension within a specific period of time, would involve innovative planning. Of course, as with physical and economic planning, there is a great deal of overlap between the two and any planning action may involve both allocative and innovative elements.

A third distinction is between *multi* or *single objective planning*. Whatever its type or form, planning has certain aims, or in the planner's jargon, goals and objectives. The distinction between the latter is clearly made by Young[4]: 'a goal is an ideal and should be expressed in abstract terms' (for example, 'to improve the standard of living in Scotland'); 'an objective is capable of both attainment and measurement, its inherent purpose is explicit rather than implicit' (for example, 'to improve all the houses in

6

Glasgow to Parker Morris standards'). Planning may have single or multiple goals and objectives. A local authority may plan to build a new road to improve internal accessibility, but also to attract new firms and to widen its shopping hinterland. Similarly an individual may plan to build an extension to his house to accommodate his growing family, gain more privacy from his neighbours and increase the market value of his property. Goals and objectives are usually social and/or economic in nature. This raises another distinction, that between 'manifest' and 'latent' aims. Manifest aims are obvious and explicit, latent aims are less obvious and quite often unconsciously pursued.

The final distinction between *indicative* and *imperative planning* relates to the method of implementation of planning. Indicative planning merely lays down general guidelines and is advisory in nature, imperative or command planning involves specific directives. The distinction can clearly be seen at a national level by comparing the indicative UK *National Plan* (1965)[5] with the imperative USSR seven year plans, or at an individual level by comparing the approaches to family planning in different countries.

This planning typology is particularly relevant at the regional level. Regional planning usually involves both physical and economic planning. Some regional plans may be purely allocative, but the majority include certain innovative elements—an extreme example being that of the Dutch Polders Scheme. In addition, regional planning is invariably multi-objective, but the method of implementation may vary greatly between the 'advisory' British regional plans and the 'command' Eastern European and Russian versions.

3 Levels of planning

Regional planning is thus similar to other types of planning in that it possesses the same basic features and may be a combination of the variety of alternative forms already outlined. But it is also distinct from other types of planning in that it is planning for a region. In general terms, a region is a flexible concept, referring to a continuous and localised area intermediate between national and urban levels. As such, regional planning can be seen as fitting into a continuum of planning—'regional planning is the process of formulating and clarifying social objectives in the ordering of activities in supra-urban space.'[6] For some, this arbitrary division into levels would seem to contradict the essentially comprehensive and theoretically indivisible nature of planning, while others would argue that there is no natural continuum, and merely disparate existence. However, from a practical viewpoint, some sub-division is necessary to allow an understanding of such a comprehensive subject and as a basis for administration.

In the United Kingdom, planning is most clearly identified at the national and local levels. This obviously reflects in part the government and administrative systems, which in contrast to countries with strong federal systems, are clearly polarised at these levels.

Planning at the *national level of government* tends to be strongly economic in content. This certainly is the case in Britain although other countries do have a system of national physical planning. National economic planning can be subdivided into the short-run allocative form concerned with the stabilisation of the 'ups and downs' of the economy, and the long-run innovative form concerned primarily with the achievement of certain rates of economic growth. The UK *National Plan* (1965) and the various post-war French five-year plans, are examples of the long-run form. The plans are multi-objective, and differ in implementation according to the ideology of the country involved. The medium/long-run form of national planning is not well developed in this country. Both the 1965 Labour national plan and the earlier Conservative proposals[7] came to ignominious ends, owing to a combination of reasons. The plans were weak in methodology and hurriedly produced; they were over-ambitious in the light of the prevailing economic climates; and being of an indicative form, carried little weight and were difficult to implement. This lack of an effective national planning framework of course has important implications for the lower levels of planning. In contrast, in France, there is a long history of successful national planning, with the production and fulfilment of five plans since the War and the sixth currently in progress.

Planning in Britain is particularly well developed at the *local authority level*. Here, town and country planning has played a more

8

dominant rôle resulting in a more land-use orientated approach. The Town and Country Planning Act (1971) provides for two tiers of plans, with the preparation of structure plans—setting out the local authority's policy and general proposals in respect of the development and other use of land, including measures for the improvement of the physical environment and the management of traffic; and local plans—formulating in detail the ways in which the policy and general proposals are to be worked through.

However over the last few decades, the need to plan for an *intermediate level* has gained momentum in many countries, including Britain. The *regional level* of planning straddles the national-local gap. It is concerned with the planning for an area with distinctive economic and social characteristics, opportunities and problems—setting it apart from other regions. Economic factors are again of major importance when dealing with areas at this level, such as the North West and Northern Ireland; but there are of course also fundamental physical problems, as in the South East. Hence, as noted earlier, the introduction of a physical/economic split into the continuum must be kept in perspective, as physical and economic elements are generally present to varying degrees at all levels. Indeed, at the regional and sub-regional levels, economic and physical elements would appear to be inextricably woven together.[8] The *sub-regional level* is perhaps the most difficult to define. It is something of a 'hybrid', relating to a part of a larger region, and although it may not be too clearly definable, it has a certain logic in practical terms. In Britain, the sub-region may overlap local authority boundaries relating more to specific problems than administrative convenience. It is a more localised area with its own particular structure, problems and potential. There is more emphasis on physical elements at this level, and the sub-region can be regarded as the highest level at which physical elements are major components of the plan.

Of course, not all these levels may be present in any one country at any particular time. In some small countries, the national and regional levels may be collapsed into one, in others, there may be little distinction between regional and sub-regional. In Britain, the regional-sub-regional distinction can be misleading and the concepts and analysis of later chapters are certainly assumed to be

9

relevant to both these levels. Perhaps at this point we should switch from this rather arbitrary continuum to a consideration of why in fact there is a need for regional planning. Indeed, for reasons already outlined, the levels approach should not be over-emphasised.

4 The need for regional planning

Pressure for governmental action for the regional level, may come from a variety of sources. Originally, the existence of separate regional cultures and political identities may have produced the necessary pressure, with regional planning being a response to regionalism. To some extent, this may still be a major factor in a country such as France, or even in the Celtic fringes of the United Kingdom—Scotland, Wales and Northern Ireland. More recently however, in the United Kingdom and several other countries, regional planning has arisen in response to certain functional problems—the problems of urban regions arising from rapid population growth, increasing urbanisation and increasing standards of living and personal mobility; and the problems of depressed industrial and rural regions suffering from 'economic malaise'. Unfortunately, because of these two distinct origins, regional planning, certainly in the UK, has been dichotomised throughout its history.

The first problem, that of congested urban regions, has resulted in an aspect of regional planning that is more physical or environmental in nature. It grew up in Britain during the late nineteenth century and its original motivations were largely social stressing the health hazards of living in congested, smoky, noisy, dirty cities as compared with the delights of garden suburbs, or later, new towns. In essence, it is a land-use planning approach evolved through the early Health Acts with the aim of improving living conditions and creating a better environment. It is primarily physical based involving the location of land uses within the region. Although, originally concerned with the major conurbations, it is equally of concern to other smaller 'urban regions' based on smaller towns and cities.

The second problem, that of depressed industrial and rural regions, has resulted in an aspect of regional planning that is primarily economic. It developed virtually independently of the physical aspect, germinating in the depression years of the 1920's/ 1930's but only really coming to the fore in the 1960's. It is derived from social welfare and seeks to find solutions to the economic inequalities between regions. In Britain, this inequality or regional imbalance can be clearly illustrated by drawing a line from the Humber to the Exe, and comparing the 'divided nation' with the prosperous regions to the east and south and problem industrial and rural regions to the west and north. Mackinder in his classic text *Britain and the British Seas*, called these two areas Metropolitan England and Industrial England. It is interesting to note that even before Mackinder in 1902 novelists such as Mrs. Gaskell and Disraeli were drawing attention to the 'two nations'.

The actual stimulus to action may come directly from within the regional level—congested urban region or depressed industrial region—as already outlined; or indirectly from either of the adjacent national and urban levels. There is now general agreement that overall national planning should take into account the problem of the inter-regional allocation of resources. Further, regional information is a major element in the formulation of national plans and policies, and regional policies are of some importance in their implementation. At the other end of the scale, it is recognised that a city or large urban centre cannot be planned in isolation from its hinterland. For physical, economic and social reasons, it must be seen and planned in its regional context.

5 'Inter' and 'intra' regional planning

The primary rôle of regional planning is to deal directly with the functional problems of the regional level. This has given rise to two approaches clearly outlined in the following quotation from the *Strategic Plan for the South East*.

'The rôle of regional planning . . . On the one hand it is an extension of local planning, dealing particularly with those matters—the movement and distribution of population and employment, the complex interaction of social and economic needs, the provision of major recreational facilities and the main communications network, for example—which can only be decided for areas much larger than the areas of existing local planning authorities.

'On the other hand it is concerned with inter-regional flows of population and employment, with the availability and use of resources, and with long term economic prospects which cannot properly be considered except in the context of the balance to be achieved between growth in one region and growth requirements in other parts of the country, on which only the Government can decide.'[9]

This quotation reflects the planning response to the specific problems previously outlined. The problems of the urban region resulting from factors such as population growth and urbanisation, and increasing personal mobility have given rise to a land-use planning approach. This can be regarded as *intra-regional* planning—that is, planning within regions, but at a level higher than the local authority. The prime aim of intra-regional planning is to achieve a satisfactory relationship between people, jobs and the environment within the region. More specifically, social objectives concerned with factors such as the provision of housing, social, cultural and recreational facilities; economic objectives relating to the control of the diseconomies of the congested cities and the distribution of new investment; and aesthetic objectives relating to issues such as the quality of urban form and the prevention of urban sprawl, can be identified. Obviously, with such multiple objectives, there may be conflict, for example, socially desirable housing distribution may conflict with the preservation of areas of attractive landscape, and a ranking of priorities and trade-off between them may be necessary.

Examples of intra-regional planning in Britain date back to the proposals around the turn of the century for 'garden cities' to deal with the problems of the overcrowded city. More recently, in the 1940's, Abercrombie prepared a series of regional plans for some of the major conurbations of the country. During the 1960's and early 1970's, this trickle of planning has turned into a flood with plans, studies and strategies being produced at both the regional and sub-regional levels.

The problems of economic malaise in certain areas have given rise to a more economic planning approach concerned with the inter-regional allocation of resources. This can be regarded as *inter-regional planning*—that is, planning between regions. The prime aim is obviously more economic in nature, relating to the achievement of a satisfactory relationship between people and jobs.

As with its intra-regional counterpart, it is also multi-objective, drawing in particular on the national economic objectives of economic growth, full employment and social equity, and giving them a spatial dimension. Economic growth involves the efficient utilisation of resources to achieve a higher rate of output, yet some regions may have high levels of unemployment and under-utilised capital assets. The injection of investment into such regions, in the form of new infrastructure or industry, may provide the necessary catalyst for regional economic growth, thereby also aiding national economic growth. The former UK Department of Economic Affairs can be quoted as saying that for them 'regional planning is an integral part of the steps being taken to implement, the National Plan and to raise industrial efficiency.'[10]

Most countries are also now committed to a national economic objective of full employment. But employment and unemployment have a spatial as well as a time dimension, and the eradication of major inequalities in regional unemployment has been the major factor behind inter-regional planning. Related to this full employment objective is that of social equity, which is often equated with the reduction in inter-regional differences in *per capita* incomes. Unfortunately there may also be conflict between these regional economic objectives. Time horizons are important here, especially in the allocation of investment between 'strong' and 'weak' regions. Allocation of preferential investment to the 'weak' regions on equity grounds may limit economic growth in the short run, by failing to take advantage of the economies of scale of the 'strong' regions. However, in the long run, the situation may be quite different, for with the removal of barriers to growth in the 'weak' regions and the prevention of possible diseconomies in the 'strong' regions, the various objectives may be consistent with one another.

The terms 'balanced growth' and 'regional balance' have often been explicitly linked with, or implicitly implied in, discussion of the above objectives. The achievement of a regional balance between people, jobs and the environment is fine rhetoric, but the term 'balance' is somewhat confusing and has been given a variety of meanings. For instance, what is really meant by the term 'balanced growth'? It could mean that poorer regions should grow faster than rich ones so that income levels tend to equalise; in this context, 'balance' means 'convergence'. Another interpretation could mean that the rate of growth in the poor regions should keep pace with that in the prosperous regions. In this case, the nation and the constituent regions would grow at the same rate, but a consequence of this would be a widening of the absolute income differentials between rich and poor regions.

But what of the second of these grandiose terms, 'regional balance'—a term that has been referred to as 'the most secret and unexamined of sacred cows'?[11] Is it the same as the first or something much wider? In the UK, the term was first widely used by the Barlow Commission in 1940, but since they failed to define it adequately at that time, it has since been, as Hall puts it, 'flung around as an all-purpose phrase in lieu of thought'.[12] It could be interpreted as equal population density in each part of the country, or zero net migration between regions with the distribution of activities and people remaining for ever the same as it is now. It is worth considering that if such rules had been followed in the eighteenth century there would have been no industrial revolution in Britain. A more acceptable interpretation might be that the government should use a combination of policies to ensure that the level of economic activity is the same in each region. But is this the meaning of 'balance'? 'Balance', in the regional context, does not imply equality, uniformity or conformity. It does however imply equality of opportunity for each region to redress demographic, economic, social and environmental weaknesses and to achieve its full potential, thus ensuring that the 'quality of life' is not a function of the area of the country in which people happen to live and work.

In the United Kingdom, the origins of inter-regional planning date back to the inter-war depression years. This period saw the introduction of the 'Special Areas' and the development of a variety of measures to deal with their problems, ranging from labour migration schemes to the building of trading estates. Following the 1940 Barlow Report,[13] the immediate post-war

14

years saw a vigorous development of inter-regional planning with the advent of many policies—such as the designation of Development Areas and the use of controls on industrial location—which have persisted to the present day. But this was quickly followed by a decade of 'freewheeling' in the 1950's. Since 1960 however, there has been a considerable re-emphasis of policy with a widening and strengthening of the range of measures to help a wide variety of problem regions.

It is unfortunate that these two forms of regional planning have maintained strict lane discipline throughout their histories rarely purposely crossing each other's path. In fact at times there has been obvious conflict. The inter-regional pre-occupation with taking work to the areas of worst unemployment meant that new employment was often being pumped into crowded conurbations which intra-regional planning schemes were, at the same time, trying to decongest. Similarly, the difficulties of attracting industry to the depressed industrial areas were often increased by the obvious preference of businessmen for the attractive overspill sites in the South East and the West Midlands. This is not to deny that there have also been some notable examples of harmony. The Barlow Report in the 1940's and the 'growth area' philosophy of the 1960's represent occasions when the two aspects did come together, although even then their stated aims were often in contention.

In addition to the primary rôle of dealing with functional problems on an inter-regional and intra-regional basis, regional planning has other secondary rôles. It can be seen as providing an information and regional basis for national planning showing, in more detail than would be possible in a national plan, what the region can contribute to national economic and social objectives. It can also be seen as providing a basis for co-ordinating urban and local plans so that inconsistencies can be reconciled and each locality can make a better contribution to the region's objectives and thus to those of the nation.

6 Summary

The regional level can be viewed as an intermediate level between national and local. At this level, particular functional problems of growing urban regions and depressed industrial and rural regions have given rise to the need for an intermediate level of planning. Yet despite the urgency and convincing nature of the reasons for and aims of regional planning, its rôle has remained imprecise and capable of a variety of interpretations. For the purposes of this text, a simple taxonomic approach is adopted dividing regional planning into 'inter' and 'intra' forms.

To conclude with a more general definition of regional planning, Mr. Claudius Petit, one of the pioneers of regional planning and for many years French Minister for Reconstruction, commented that 'regional planning really means the planning of our society'.[14] There could be no better way of summing up in a few words the vital importance of the problem facing many governments, and certainly most European governments, today.

References

1 Friedman, J., Regional Planning as a Field of Study, in Friedman, J. and Alonso W., *Regional Development and Planning*, page 61, MIT Press, Cambridge, Mass. (1964).
2 For a discussion of the interrelationship of physical and economic planning, see: Robertson, D. J., The Relationship between Physical and Economic Planning, a Paper delivered to the *Town and Country Planning School, St. Andrews* (1965).
3 Friedman, J., A Conceptual Model for the Analysis of Planning, *Administrative Science Quarterly,* **12,** 12 (1967).
4 Young, R. C., Goals and Goal Setting, *Journal of the American Institute of Planners,* pages 76–85, **32** (1966).
5 *The National Plan,* Cmnd. 1764, HMSO (1965).
6 Friedman, J., Regional Planning as a Field of Study, *op cit,* page 64.
7 *Growth of the UK Economy to 1966,* NEDC, HMSO; *Conditions Favourable to Faster Growth,* NEDC, HMSO (1963).
8 Robertson, D. J., *op cit.*
   Also Lichfield, N., Scope of the Regional Plan, *Regional Studies,* page 15, **1,** 1 (1967).
9 South East Joint Planning Team, *Strategic Plan for the South East,* HMSO, page 4 (1970).
10 Rodgers, W. T., The Future of Regional Planning, *Journal of the Town Planning Institute,* June 1966.

11 Ash, M., Realism and Regionalism, *Town and Country Planning*, **36**, 4 (1968).
12 Hall, P., Regional Balance, *Town and Country Planning*, June 1968.
13 *Report of the Royal Commission on the Distribution of Industrial Population,* Cmnd. 6153, HMSO (1940).
14 Council of Europe, *Regional Planning: A European Problem* (1968).

2 The Region in Regional Planning

Planning has been identified as a future-oriented problem-solving process, which may be classified in a variety of ways. Regional planning fits into this general classification, but differs from other forms of planning in that it is specifically concerned with the regional level. This level lies somewhere between the national and local levels, and the region is a continuous and localised area at this level. But this is all very vague and provides little insight into the actual concept of the region. The idea of the region has been much used and abused over the years and there have been numerous controversies and disagreements over its meaning, perhaps reflecting the variety of disciplines involved in regional studies. To some, the region is a real entity that can be positively identified—a 'natural region'; to others, it is merely a product of the imagination, a method of classification. This chapter seeks to clarify the concept of the region, outlining alternative forms and discussing their relevance as planning regions.

1 The concept of the region

THE REGION: FACT OR FALLACY?

A first step in an outline of the concept of the region is to examine whether regions are natural phenomena or merely mental constructions. There are two divergent views—one objective, the other subjective. The subjective view sees a region as a means to an end, simply an idea, a model, to help in the study of the world. It is a method of classification, a device to segregate areal features, with the only 'natural' region being the surface of the earth on which man finds his home. The objective view adopts an opposite stance, seeing the region as an end in itself, a real entity, an organism, that can be identified and mapped.

The *subjective view* is now generally accepted. Hartshorne[1] wrote that attempts to see the region as a unitary concrete object 'have passed into history'. Regions are seen as descriptive tools, defined according to particular criteria, for a particular purpose—there being as many regions as there are criteria to define them. In this context they perform a particularly useful function, avoiding the extremes of description. Without the regional concept, for example, a description of Britain would either be so general as to be meaningless—'an industrial nation, with a cool climate, capital London'—or so complex as to be incomprehensible, cataloguing every single feature of the local landscape.

The *objective view* that regions actually exist was held by many academics in the early twentieth century, and was linked with the search for the elusive 'natural' region. The famous Oxford geographer, A. J. Herbertson,[2] adopting an analytical approach, divided the world into 'natural regions' on the basis of four criteria—land configuration, climate, vegetation and population density, but with climate as the dominant factor. Numerous followers applied his analytical approach at more local levels. Unstead,[3] on the other hand, approached the problem from the other end of the scale. He adopted a synthetic approach building up a series of British regions based on physical factors, extending outwards from the centre of a region until the periphery no longer shared the characteristics of the centre. Vidal de la Blache adopted a similar approach in France, although he used population as the basic criteria and starting point for his identification of *pays*. All these approaches have obvious geographical determinism undertones with the physical factors determining the human environment. In the words of de la Blache 'man and nature have become moulded to one another over the years rather like a snail and its shell'.[4]

However, most academics have now come round to the

19

subjective way of thinking, although there are important exceptions. There is an important East/West ideological split with many Russian geographers repeatedly stating that economic regions objectively exist.[5] In addition, in this country, the regionalism movement with its demands for various forms of regions for political, administrative and planning purposes could be seen as taking a more objective view of regions. The topical idea of the city region, linking a central town or city with its rural hinterland, has been put forward as much for the purpose of creating regions as for simply describing them. R. E. Dickinson,[6] a constant advocate of the city region sees it as a 'natural social unit'. Certain other recent studies could also be seen as lending limited support to the concept of the region as a 'natural' entity. Carter,[7] in an interesting analysis of *Referenda on the Sunday Opening of Licensed Premises in Wales*, correlates 'wet' and 'dry' votes with the ability to speak Welsh, and identifies a distinct 'cultural core' zone in Wales—albeit a declining zone. Perhaps this cultural core could be seen as the remainder of a natural region? In another equally fascinating study, Gould and White[8] attempt to draw the mental maps of british school leavers. These maps, based on the ranking of alternative areas in Britain as residential locations, contain a series of 'perception surfaces' with distinct 'peaks' (e.g. the Lake District) and 'troughs' (e.g. Greater London) which might also be interpreted as unique 'natural regions'.

THE REGION: FORMAL OR FUNCTIONAL

The concept of the region as a method of classification has evolved through two distinct phases reflecting the economic advance from a simple agrarian economy to a complex industrial system. The first phase saw the 'formal region'—concerned with uniformity, and defined according to homogeneity. The second phase saw the development of the 'functional region'—concerned with interdependence, the interrelationship of the parts, and defined on the basis of functional coherence.

A formal region is a geographical area which is uniform or homogeneous in terms of selected criteria. In early definitions of formal regions, the criteria were predominantly physical (such as topography, climate or vegetation), linked with the concept of geographical determinism. Later there was a shift to the use of economic criteria (such as industrial or agricultural types), and even social and political criteria (such as party political allegiance). The 'natural region' was a physical formal region. Interest in this form of region stemmed partly from the fact that physical factors are more stable than dynamic economic factors and hence much easier to study, but also from the influence of Darwin's Theory of Evolution. Following from Darwin's concept of natural selection, geographers believed that the survival of man depended on his adaptation to his environment. Hence, it was thought that the human environment could best be understood by isolating and studying the physical environment.

Economic formal regions are generally based on types of industry or agriculture (such as the South Yorkshire coal mining region or the Cotswolds sheep farming region), although there are obvious physical undertones. A traditional sub-division of Britain into economic formal regions is that by Stamp and Beaver,[9] who divided Britain into 19 agricultural regions upon which were superimposed 13 industrial regions. More recent attempts to delimit economic formal regions have been based on criteria such as income level, rate of unemployment and rate of economic growth. An interesting development of this approach is used by Smith[10] who divides the North West into several 'economic health' sub-regions using multiple socio-economic criteria.

A functional region is a geographical area which displays a certain functional coherence, an interdependence of parts, when defined on the basis of certain criteria. It is sometimes referred to as a nodal or polarised region and is composed of heterogeneous units, such as cities, towns and villages, which are functionally interrelated. The functional relationships are usually revealed in the form of flows, using socio-economic criteria such as journey-to-work trips or shopping trips linking the employment or shopping centre with subsidiary centres.

Ebeneezer Howard[11] was one of the early pioneers of the concept of the nodal region. He suggested that the solution to the problems of a large urban area such as London lay in developing a cluster of new towns linked to the central city in a functional relationship. Patrick Geddes[12] also stressed the interdependence and interrelationships of factors in a region, using his famous 'place–work–folk' diagram. It was Geddes also who coined the term 'city-region' which has come to be the most widely used form of nodal region. Rather more recently, Dickinson,[13] Smailes,[14] Green[15] and others have pioneered research into nodal regions, attempting to identify the region by deductive processes. Dickinson attempted to determine the nodal region of Leeds by analysing the distribution of the Leeds based *Yorkshire Evening Post*. Green used the frequency of bus services to determine the hinterland of urban centres. Foreign researchers, such as Christaller and Lösch have used a more inductive approach, concentrating on the hierarchical relationships between centres within the functional region.[16]

This brief analysis of the concept of the region suggests that regions are a means to an end, rather than ends in themselves. They may be formal or functional based on a single or multi-criteria. The development in Europe from vertically related primary producing economies to modern economies characterised by high levels of specialisation and horizontal relationships has tended to continue the trend towards a classification by functional regions, using mainly economic criteria. However, the formal region defined on the basis of socio-economic criteria is also useful, but the physical formal region, in particular the 'natural region' is of declining importance.

Formal or functional regions, or a combination of both, may provide a useful framework for a third type of regional classification into *planning regions*. There have been numerous definitions of planning regions. Boudeville[17] defines planning regions (or programming regions) as areas displaying some coherence or unity of economic decisions. Keeble[18] sees a planning region as an area which is large enough to enable substantial changes in distribution of population and employment to take place within its boundaries, yet which is small enough for its planning problems to be seen as a whole. Klaassen[19] believes that amongst other things, a planning region must be large enough to take investment decisions of an economic size, must be able to supply its own industry with the necessary labour, should have a homogeneous economic structure, contain at least one growth point and have a common approach to and awareness of its problems.

In the context of earlier discussion, such definitions suggest that planning regions are geographical regions suitable for the designing and implementing of development plans for dealing with the regional problems outlined earlier in Chapter 1. The problem of economic malaise displays a considerable degree of homogeneity in areas such as North East England and Central Scotland. On the basis of criteria such as unemployment levels, activity rates and migration trends, formal regions could be defined. The problem of congestion in South East England is more concerned with journey-to-work and service flows between major and subsidiary centres. Using these flows as criteria, functional regions could be defined. In practice, the formal and functional regions very rarely overlap neatly, and often vary markedly. The identification of satisfactory planning regions may therefore involve some compromise. This also assumes that the formal and functional regions can actually be delineated and that the resultant regions are administratively viable, which introduces the problems of regionalisation and regionalism.

2 Regionalisation and the delineation of regions

Regionalisation is the process of delineating regions. This process may take several forms depending on the purpose of regionalisation, the criterion/criteria to be used and data availability. Thus, as previously mentioned, a resolution of the problem of economic malaise may involve the delineation of formal regions using certain relevant criteria, and similarly the resolution of the congestion problem may involve the delineation of functional regions. In the absence of adequate data, qualitative intuitive approaches have been used, but this tends to lead to very 'misty' regional boundaries which, the more closely they are examined, the more vague they appear. Understandably, there has been a shift to a more quantitative approach to regional identification.

The delineation of formal regions involves the grouping together of local units which have similar characteristics according to certain clearly defined criteria, but which differ significantly from units outside the region on the basis of the chosen criteria. The resultant formal region will never be perfectly homogeneous, but must be homogeneous within certain clearly defined limits.*

If the criteria are simple and static, such as 'land over 500 feet', identification is relatively simple. But if there are a variety of criteria, such as unemployment rates, activity rates, and migration trends, and many of the criteria are dynamic and constantly changing, the task becomes more difficult. Several techniques have actually been used to delineate formal regions. Two of these, representing the extremes in sophistication, will now be briefly outlined.

a *The weighted index number method* has been outlined in its simplest form by Boudeville,[20] and has been developed by others into more sophisticated techniques such as cluster analysis and social area analysis. Figure 2.1 presents a very much simplified example of the method. The study area contains nine localities varying according to unemployment rates and per capita income levels. For policy reasons, there is a need to isolate the main problem region, the area of 'economic malaise'. Taking the criteria individually, it is difficult to isolate the problem region; but taken together and weighted, region B can be isolated. Problems implicit in this method are of course the choice of the original criteria, the choice of weights and the determination of acceptable homogeneity limits. Nevertheless, because of its simplicity, it is a well-used method.

b *The factor analysis method* is a more sophisticated approach to regionalisation which owes much to the pioneering work of

---

* Here, use can be made of simple statistical variation tests. For example, in the regionalisation of localities on the basis of unemployment rates, it may be decided that no unit within the region must diverge from the mean unemployment rate by > one standard deviation. Thus, if the mean $(\bar{x}) = 4\%$, and standard deviation (SD) = $\frac{1}{2}\%$, a locality with an enemployment rate of 3% would not be included in the formal unemployment region.

Berry[21] in the USA. The technical details of the method are more complex,[22] but the basic principles can be illustrated with reference to the economic health regionalisation of North West England by Smith.[23] Smith identified 14 industrial criteria on a

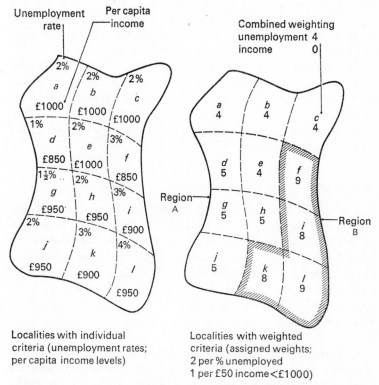

Localities with individual
criteria (unemployment rates;
per capita income levels)

Localities with weighted
criteria (assigned weights;
2 per % unemployed
1 per £50 income<£1000)

Applying a statistical variation test to the weights, Region *A* has a mean ($\bar{x}$) of 4·5 and standard deviation (SD) of 0·5, and Region *B* has ($\bar{x}$) = 8·5, (SD) = 0·5. Therefore, both regions are homogeneous within the limits ($\bar{x}$) ± 1 (SD).

Fig. 2.1   Delineation of formal regions (simple weighted-index number method)

local employment exchange area base and 14 socio-economic criteria on a local authority base. Many of these criteria were obviously interdependent, and determined by some underlying factors. The factor analysis method can be used to isolate these basic factors, and to group areas on the basis of factor loadings. A contiguity constraint can be applied to give continuous regions. In his analysis, Smith identified 'industrial change' and 'industrial structure' as major industrial factors, and 'social structure' and 'population change' as major socio-economic factors. On the basis of these factors he was able to delineate economic health regions, highlighting East Lancashire and the 'cotton–coal belt' of Central Lancashire as distinctive problem areas.

The method is of course only as good as the choice and quality of data employed. But with the rapid development of associated computer 'software' and relevant statistical techniques, such as multivariate analysis, the method would seem to have considerable potential, not only for delineating regions, but in the wider field of planning.

THE DELINEATION OF FUNCTIONAL REGIONS

The delineation of functional regions involves the grouping together of local units which display a considerable degree of interdependence. The concern is thus more with flows linked to a central point rather than with the uniformity of the region as a whole. Two basic approaches to functional regionalisation will be outlined—'flow analysis' based on actual observations of what people do, and 'gravitational analysis' based on theoretical observations of what they might do.

a Flow analysis builds up functional regions on the basis of the direction and intensity of flows between the dominant centre and surrounding satellites. Each flow will show decreasing intensity as it becomes more distant from the main centre and increasing intensity as it approaches another centre. The boundary of the sphere of influence of the dominant centre will be where the flow intensity is at a minimum. The flows may be of several types. They are often economic, categorised according to type (such as cargo or passenger, road or rail) or purpose (such as shopping or commuting). They may also be social (such as the flow of students or hospital patients); political, especially the flow of government expenditure; or information, such as telegrams, newspapers and telephone calls, which in fact may provide a good proxy indicator for the rest.

Green[24] and Carruthers[25] have attempted to delimit the sphere of influence of a centre, its functional region, using bus services as indicators of economic linkages. Green worked on the assumption that bus services were economic concerns, and would therefore choose the most economic routes which would similarly reflect the areas of greatest demand and functional linkages with the dominant centre. From bus timetables, he constructed flow diagrams of the frequency of service and from the latter he deduced the sphere of influence of centres, drawing up functional regions. The value of Green's approach is somewhat reduced by the impact of increasing competition from other forms of transport, especially the private car, and the fact that some public transport services are run on a social rather than on an economic basis.

An interesting variation of simple flow analysis is *graph theory*. This is again a very simple approach, but a more ordered and systematic way of identifying functional or nodal regions. The approach has been employed by Nystuen and Dacey,[26] and Boudeville,[27] and measures the relationships between selected groups of centres on the basis of flows between the centres. The number of telephone calls is the usual flow criteria, and provides a useful index of a wide range of economic and social relationships. The flows are plotted in matrix form, from which the primary and secondary flows into and out of each centre can be identified. The resulting hierarchy of nodes can be plotted as a simple network, providing an insight into the form and extent of functional relationships within an area. Figure 2.2. provides an example of simple graph theory, showing that D is the major centre, with B, E and G subsidiary centres. Figure 2.3 illustrates the use of both simple flow analysis and graph theory in the identification of sub-regions in South East England.

b Gravitational analysis is concerned with the theoretical forces of attraction between centres rather than the actual flows. As such, it could be regarded as a second-best approach, but if used with care it can provide a good guide to the actual flows and, perhaps more important, the potential flows between centres.

This rapidly developing field of 'social physics', as developed by Zipf, Reilly, Stewart, Stouffer and others, is based on a probability view of human interaction, and originates from the

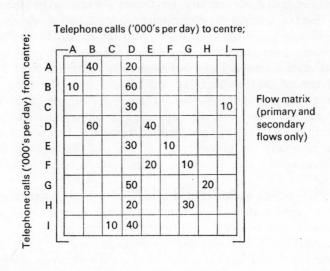

Telephone calls ('000's per day) to centre;

Telephone calls ('000's per day) from centre;

	A	B	C	D	E	F	G	H	I
A		40		20					
B	10			60					
C				30					10
D		60			40				
E				30		10			
F					20		10		
G				50				20	
H				20			30		
I			10	40					

Flow matrix (primary and secondary flows only)

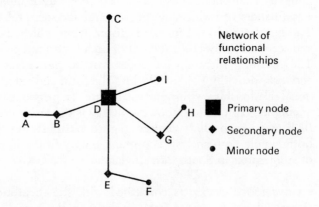

Network of functional relationships

■ Primary node

◆ Secondary node

● Minor node

Fig. 2.2 Graph theory: a simple illustration

application of analagous reasoning to Newtonian Physics.[28] Only the simple principles relevant to functional regionalisation will be discussed here, as interaction models are discussed in Chapter 8.

The simple gravity model assumes that the interaction between two centres is directly proportional to the 'mass' of the centres and inversely proportional to the 'distance' between the centres. The variables used to measure 'mass' and 'distance' depend on the problem and data availability. In recent planning developments of the model, 'mass' has been represented by such variables as population, employment, income, expenditure and retail turnover, and 'distance' in physical terms (miles), time, price and intervening opportunities. In mathematical notation:

$$T_{ij} = k \left[\frac{P_i P_j}{d^2_{ij}} \right]$$

where T_{ij} is the gravitational force between towns i and j, P_i and P_j are the masses of the two centres, d_{ij} is the distance between them, and k is a constant.

The concept of demographic or gravitational potential is a development of the original concept of particular relevance for regionalisation. The demographic potential at a centre i caused by a mass at centre j, $(_jV_i)$, is defined as:

$$_iV_j = k \left[\frac{P_j}{d_{ij}} \right]$$

If i is surrounded by a number of centres, n, the total potential at Centre i will be:

$$_iV = k \sum_{j=1}^{n} \left[\frac{P_j}{d_{ij}} \right]$$

By calculating the potential for the centres in a study area, contour lines of equal potential can be plotted on a map, illustrating the relative attractiveness, spheres of influence, of the various centres. From such lines, functional regions can be identified.

Thus, regions can be identified in practice. Indeed there are several quantitative approaches to the delineation of both formal and functional regions. However, there are problems—the first one being the invariable lack of correlation between regions defined according to different criteria. Although there may sometimes be a general resemblance, it would be a great coincidence if different functional flows, such as journey-to-work, shopping or recreation flows were spatially matched. It is even more unlikely

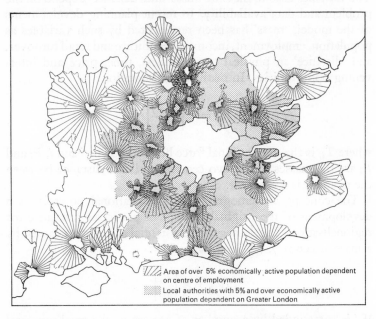

Area of over 5% economically active population dependent on centre of employment
Local authorities with 5% and over economically active population dependent on Greater London

Fig. 2.3(a) Functional sub-regions in South East England

that regional boundaries defined according to both functional and formal criteria would also be closely matched. The dynamic nature of regional activities presents a further problem. Firms are continuously expanding and contracting, with some regions becoming more prosperous, others becoming less so. The flows of functional regions and the spheres of influence of centres are also constantly changing, particularly in response to transport developments. One only needs to note the impact of the Severn Bridge on the nodal relationships of Cardiff and Bristol, or to speculate on the possible impact of a Humber Bridge or a Dee Barrage to illustrate this point.

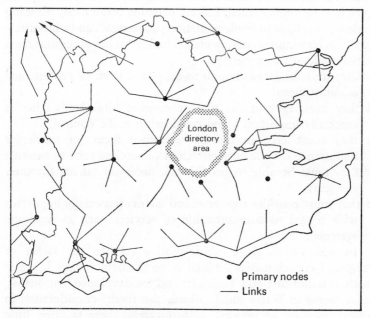

Fig. 2.3(b)   Telephone linkages, South East, 1967
Use of graph theory for identification of sub-regions

SOURCE   *Strategic Plan for the South East, Studies 4; Strategies and Evaluation*

But, in spite of these difficulties, the regional types outlined may provide a useful basis for planning regions if delineated on the basis of 'problem' criteria. Although even if regions could be defined on the basis of such criteria, there are additional problems of whether they are administratively suitable and whether they closely reflect the regional consciousness, the 'regional identity' of the areas concerned.

3 Regionalism and the administration of regions

Planning regions, however precisely defined on the criteria of formal or functional problems, may not correlate with administrative areas, and the latter are obviously important if the regional plan is to be implemented. Indeed, planning is not really planning unless it is related to implementation programmes and administration. To be administratively viable, Smith[29] believes regions must satisfy at least five criteria:

a they must be large enough to support a team of professional administrators;

b they must take in the main commuter hinterlands (this is especially important when considering traffic control);

c they must take in human catchment areas (of particular importance for the administration of services such as health);

d they must be able to provide the necessary talents for their services;

e they must consider topographical factors (especially important with regard to administration of services such as sewerage systems).

In addition to these administrative criteria, the factor of 'regional consciousness', which is particularly strong in areas such as Lancashire and Yorkshire and has developed 'nationalist' movements in Wales and Scotland, also merits consideration in the delineation of regions. Unfortunately, there is often little correlation between the problem defined regions, administrative regions and areas of regional identity, and this has been a major constraint on effective regional planning. However, there have been many suggestions and approaches to a resolution of this conflict which can be discussed under the umbrella of 'regionalism'.

REGIONALISM

'Regionalism' has been used by many people—geographers, political scientists, town planners and economists—to mean many different things. Hence, there is much confusion attached to the term. In the standard text on regionalism, Smith attempts to clarify the confusion and offers the following definition:

> 'Regionalism may thus be defined as an attempt to delimit areas usually larger than those of local government structure, with a view to making local and national government and planning more effective and efficient. Regionalism in this sense is essentially concerned with the problem of defining areas for a new, intermediate level of government and administration, rather than with the purely geographical function of delimiting areas of the earth's surface according to physical features.'[30]

The pressure behind regionalism comes from three major groups— those seeking administrative devolution from central government, those seeking local government re-organisation and those seeking a more efficient land-use planning system.

France was one of the first countries to consider regionalism. Many moves were made to replace *départements* as political units, but it was not until the 1950's, with the introduction of 22, and later 21, 'program regions', that the first steps were taken towards a nationwide system of administration and planning at the regional level. In the United Kingdom, the regionalism movement dates back to the beginning of this century, but it is only in the last few years, with the arrival of the Regional Economic Planning Councils and Boards (1965), that there has been any substantive progress.

THE EVOLUTION OF REGIONALISM IN THE UNITED KINGDOM

A review of some of the major stages in the evolution of regionalism in the United Kingdom will serve to illustrate some of the confusion associated with the term, and also clarify certain meanings relevant to regional planning. Since 1900 there have been numerous attempts to formulate an intermediate administrative level between the local and national levels and to reduce the fragmentation of administrative boundaries which initially date back to 1888 but which in shape and extent date back to 1066. Suggestions for reform have been mainly limited to England, with

Scotland, Wales and Northern Ireland already possessing some degree of regional autonomy within their 'cultural' regions. The majority of suggestions usually outlined a limited number of large regions or provinces. All tended to be rather limited being heavily weighted by the particular service(s) or policy they had in mind.

H. G. Wells in his *Anticipations* in 1902 predicted the development of urban regions or 'city regions', but it was the Fabian Society[31] in 1905 who were the first to advocate a series of large-scale regions as a basis for administrative reform. Their 'new heptarchy' was made up of seven great provinces, each incorporating several counties, and based on the major centres of Newcastle, Leeds, Liverpool, Manchester, Birmingham, Nottingham and London.

Somewhat later in 1919, the geographer, Fawcett,[32] in *The Provinces of England* divided England into 12 provinces on the basis of six principles:

1. The provincial boundaries should be so chosen as to interfere as little as possible with the ordinary activities and movements of the people.
2. There should be in each province a definite capital, which should be the real focus of its regional life. (This capital should be easily accessible from every part of the province.)
3. The least of the provinces should contain a population sufficiently numerous to justify self-government. (Fawcett suggested a figure of at least one million.)
4. No one province should be large enough to be able to dominate the others.
5. The provincial boundaries should be drawn near watersheds rather than across valleys, and very rarely along streams.
6. The grouping of areas must pay regard to local patriotism and to tradition.

Fawcett believed that this 'systematic application of geographical science to the existing conditions' provided the most practical and satisfactory delimitation of provinces. His twelve provinces are illustrated in Figure 2.4. This framework was later modified, and in 1942 he produced a revised version, the major difference being the elimination of the Peakdon province based on Sheffield.

Regionalism as a whole, however, never really came alive as a political issue in the inter-war years, and it was not until the war years of the 1940's that the movement gained a fresh impetus. To meet the war emergency, Regional Commissioners were appointed to control the affairs of nine groups of counties termed Civil Defence Regions. The various Ministries of Transport,

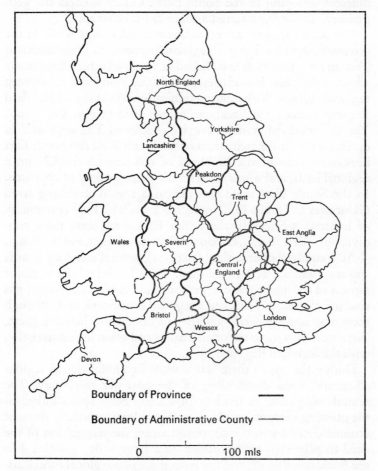

Fig. 2.4 Fawcett's original provinces

SOURCE C. B. Fawcett, *Provinces of England*, rev. edn. by W. G. East and S. W. Wooldridge. Hutchinson (1961).

Education, Labour, Agriculture and so on, had representatives and staff at the regional capitals. The validity of these regions as a basis for post-war regional administration was hotly disputed during this period. The geographer, Gilbert, made use of them in postulating his ideas for 13 provinces (the main difference from Fawcett being the subdivision of the Northern province and a different grouping in the South East). Others such as the geographer, Taylor,[33] preferred a more radical change.

The need for postwar reconstruction did in fact result in the government maintaining a regional framework. Nine Standard Treasury Regions were established in 1946 and other departments adopted the same boundaries to facilitate co-operation between regional officials. With minor modifications (in 1956) the Standard Regions formed the backbone of regionalism into the 1960's. Yet the subdivision did have its problems. The approach to dealing with the different areas of the South West and South East illustrated some of the problems of splitting up the UK on a regional basis, and displayed a certain inconsistency of approach. In the South West there was only one region stretching from Gloucester to Land's End, including areas with little community of interest; whereas in the South East there were three subdivisions—East Anglia, London and the South East, and the South.

At roughly the same time (1945–51), several statutory boards and corporations were established. These bodies related to major aspects of the life of the country, such as hospitals, railways, gas coal and electricity. Each had a regional framework, and although there was some general similarity of boundaries between them, there were also some major anomalies and often little correlation with the Standard Regions.

During the 1950's there was a wane in administrative regionalism and some dismantling of the post-war machinery. The reawakening came in the late 1950's and early 1960's linked to the growing recognition of regional problems, especially those of economic malaise in the depressed areas; the recognition of the need to plan vital infrastructure on a large scale as outlined in the Buchanan Report; and the resurgence of a regional consciousness possibly encouraged by the development of the new universities and regional TV, such as Granada and Tyne-Tees. New forms of regions were outlined, and the *Economist*,[34] for example, produced an imaginative plan for dividing up Britain into 15 regions. The culmination of this movement was the establishment of the Regional Economic Planning Regions under the new Labour Administration in 1965. (See Figure 2.5.) These regions,

Fig. 2.5   United Kingdom: economic planning regions

eight English plus Northern Ireland, Scotland and Wales are very similar to the original Standard Regions, except for the creation of a larger South East and an integrated Yorkshire and Humberside. However they are far from standard in size and Table 2.1 gives a population breakdown illustrating the regional disparity, with the population of the new South East region larger than the sum of the population of the next three regions.

Table 2.1. *UK Economic Planning Regions: Population (1970)*

Region	Population (000's)
North	3360
North West	6789
Yorkshire and Humberside	4812
West Midlands	5178
East Midlands	3363
South West	3764
South East	17316
East Anglia	1673
Scotland	5199
Wales	2734
Northern Ireland	1524

SOURCE: CSO, *Abstract of Regional Statistics,* No. 7, 1971, Table 5.

The establishment of the Economic Planning Regions each with its council and board (with special arrangements for Northern Ireland), represents the present state of affairs in UK regional administration. But this is not to suggest that a satisfactory system of administrative regions are now generally agreed and are operating effectively. The dissatisfaction with the economic planning councils and boards in their rôle of planning and co-ordination at the regional level, the electoral successes of the Scottish and Welsh Nationalists, and the creation of the Commission on the Constitution at the beginning of 1969, have all contributed to a resurgence of interest in regionalism in the late 1960's and early 1970's.

But in addition to this revival of interest in the need for a limited number of large regions, between 10 to 15, the 1960's have also witnessed growing support for a larger number, between 30 to 60, of smaller regions or sub-regions integrating town and country, based on the organic concept of the relationship between a town or a city and the surrounding area. The system of local government created in the nineteenth century with its division into administrative counties and county boroughs effected a cleavage in this organic relationship. Geographers such as Smailes[35] and Dickinson[36] sought to identify alternative 'city-regions', but it was not until 20–25 years afterwards that the concept was seriously considered as a viable administrative unit in the UK. In the mid 1960's, Senior,[37] a latter-day 'city-regionalist' revived interest in the concept. He was fortunate in that his interest coincided with the establishment of a Royal Commission on Local Government in 1966. Over the next few years, alternative frameworks were proposed for local government reform, ranging from Senior's advocacy of 30 to 35 city regions to the Maud Report[38] suggestions for approximately 60 unitary authorities.

The problem of the existing regional administrative framework and the proposals for reform at both the level of the large planning region and the smaller city region will be examined in more detail in a later chapter. Suffice it to say at this stage that these two types of regions have evolved out of the history of regionalism in the UK.

4 Summary: planning regions and regional planning

As outlined earlier, subjective and objective views can be taken of the concept of the region. The subjective view regards regions as descriptive tools, defined according to particular criteria for a particular purpose. On this basis, formal and functional regions can be identified. Such regions may provide the basis for ideal planning regions, with for example the identification of an economic planning region on the basis of homogeneity in a certain criteria such as unemployment, and the identification of city regions on the basis of functional flows. But this assumes that the regions can actually be delineated on the basis of available data. It also assumes that the regions thus identified reflect the underlying regional consciousness of the areas concerned and are administratively viable. In most cases there will undoubtedly be conflict between these criteria, and the need for compromise. As such, the region will generally be 'satisfactory' rather than 'ideal'. In practice, planning regions may be more determined by administrative expediency than by theoretical excellence.

In the United Kingdom context, there appears to be the emergence of two new intermediate levels of administration and planning region—with the large 'economic planning regions' representing a devolution from above, and the smaller 'city regions' representing scale enlargement from below. Inter-regional planning, concerned with the allocation of economic resources between regions, demands the large region with some uniformity of problem. Intra-regional planning, with rather more emphasis on land-use planning, is of relevance equally to the large regions as it is to their constituent sub-regions.

References

1 Hartshorne, R., *Perspective on the Nature of Geography,* Chicago, page 31 (1959).
2 Herbertson, A. J., The Major Natural Regions, *Geographical Journal,* XXV (1905).
3 Unstead, J. F., A synthetic method of determining geographical regions, *Geographical Journal,* XLVIII (1916).
4 De la Blache, Vidal, in Wrigley, E. A., *Changes in the Philosophy of Geography* (in Chorley, R. J. and P. Haggett, *Frontiers in Geographical Teaching,* London (1965) page 8).
5 Alampiev, P. M., The objective basis of economic regionalisation and its long range prospects, *Soviet Geography* II, pages 64–74 (1961).
6 Dickinson, R. E., *City and Region: A Geographical Interpretation,* Routledge and Kegan Paul (1964).
7 Carter, H. and Thomas, J. G., Referendum on Sunday Opening of Licensed Premises in Wales, *Regional Studies,* pages 61–71, **3,** 1 (1969).
8 Gould, P. R., and White, R. R., The mental maps of British school leavers, *Regional Studies,* pages 161–82, **2,** 2 (1968).
9 Stamp, L. D., and Beaver, S. H., *The British Isles,* Longmans (1933).
10 Smith, D. M., Identifying Grey Areas—a multivariate approach, *Regional Studies,* **2,** 2 (1968).
11 Howard, E., *Garden Cities of Tomorrow,* Faber and Faber (1945).
12 Geddes, P., *Cities in Evolution* (1915).

13 Dickinson, R. E., *op cit*.

14 Smailes, A. E., The Urban Hierarchy in England and Wales, *Geography*, pages 41–51, **29** (1944).

15 Green, F. H. W., Urban Hinterlands in England and Wales, *Geographical Journal*, **116** (1950);
also: Green, F. H. W., Urban Hinterlands: Fifteen Years On, *Geographical Journal*, **132** (1966).

16 Christaller, W., *Central Places in Southern Germany*, (Trans. C. W. Baskin), Englewood Cliffs, New Jersey (1966).

17 Boudeville, J. R., *Problems of Regional Economic Planning*, Edinburgh U.P. (1966).

18 Keeble, L., *Principles and Practice of Town and Country Planning*, 4thedition, Estates Gazette, page 47, London (1969).

19 Klaassen, L., *Area Social and Economic Redevelopment*, OECD (1965).

20 Boudeville, J. R., *op cit*.

21 Berry, B. J. L., A method for deriving multifactor uniform regions, *Przeglad Geograficzny*, pages 263–82, **33** (1961).

22 See: Bruton, M. J., An introduction to factor analysis and its application in planning, *Oxford Working Papers in Planning Education and Research*, W.P.8, Oxford Polytechnic, November 1971.

23 Smith, D. M., *op cit*;
also Spence, N. A., A multifactor uniform regionalization of British counties on the basis of employment data for 1961, *Regional Studies*, **2**, September 1968.

24 Green, F. H. W., *op cit*.

25 Carruthers, I., A classification of service centres in England and Wales, *Geographical Journal*, pages 371–85, **123** (1957).

26 Nystuen, J. D. and Dacey, M. F., A graph theory interpretation of nodal regions, *Papers and Proceedings of the Regional Science Association*, pages 29–42, **7** (1961).

27 Boudeville, J. R., *op cit*, Chapter Two.

28 For a discussion of the principles, problems and application of gravitational analysis, see: Dept. of Town Planning, Lanchester Polytechnic, Coventry, *Gravity Models in Town Planning*, October 1969.

29 Smith, B. C., *Regionalism 3: the new regional machinery*, Acton Society Trust, page 36 (1965).

30 Smith, B. C., *Regionalism 2: its nature and purpose*, Acton Society Trust, pages 22–3 (1965).

31 Sanders, W., *Municipalization by Provinces,* Fabian Society (1905) ('New Heptarchy' series).

32 Fawcett, C. B., *Provinces of England,* London (1919), revised edition, London (1961).

33 For Prof. Taylor's suggested regions, see *Geographical Journal,* page 62, **99** (1942), and those of Professor Gilbert on page 76 of the same volume.

34 *The Economist,* Federal Britain's New Frontiers, 18 May 1963.

35 Smailes, A. E., *op cit.*

36 Dickinson, R. E., *op cit.*

37 Senior, D., The City Region as an Administrative Unit, **36,** *Political Quarterly,* January–March 1965.

38 *Report of the Royal Commission on Local Government in England 1966–69* (Chairman: Lord Redcliffe-Maud), 3 Volumes, Cmnd. 4040 (1969).

PART TWO
The Analysis of Regions

A: Inter-regional Analysis

3 The regional framework

The quality of the regional data base is a major influence on regional planning. Adequate data is essential both for the initial definition of regions and for their subsequent analysis and planning. The formal and functional regional definitions of Chapter 2 and the 'inter' and 'intra' regional analysis of later chapters require a wide range of spatially aggregated and disaggregated data on people's activities (such as employment, education), land use, and flows (such as journey-to-work patterns). This chapter seeks to generally examine the British regional data base, outlining available sources, their adequacy or otherwise for regional planning and possible refinements. In particular, it is interesting to investigate whether Prof. Chester's view that the 'existence of large gaps in our statistical information about regional problems is by now well recognised as a major obstacle of realistic planning'[1] is still borne out by the facts. The possibility of establishing a framework of regional accounts including input-output tables is discussed rather more fully. Such accounts and tables are spatially aggregate, abstracting from the locational differences within the region, and looking at the region as a whole. They thus provide a valuable context for further inter-regional analysis in the following chapters.

1 The adequacy of the UK regional data base

Appendix A lists some of the major sources of regional statistics, subdividing them into *general sources* and *supplementary sources* (including both activities and land use). But are such sources adequate? There are limitations and inadequacies in all statistics which can only be clearly identified when they are required for a specific purpose. At this level of discussion of statistics for general use for regional definition, analysis and planning, only general comments on their adequacy or otherwise would appear justified. As such, adequacy will be stressed against the general criteria of availability, frequency of publication, time lag in publication comparability and overall relevance.

The range of sources in the Appendix clearly suggests that a large body of regional statistics is readily available in published form. But it must be remembered that although two series may be equally available in the objective sense that they both appear in official publications, in the subjective sense they may differ widely if one is a regular publication and the other is more obscure.

Associated with the criteria of availability is that of frequency of publication. Some of the most useful data is that which is available on a frequent and regular time series. Employment data is available at monthly intervals, housing data at three-monthly intervals, and much other useful information is available annually. However, other very important sources, such as detailed Inland Revenue data and the Censuses of Population, Production and Distribution are more infrequent with five-year and ten-year intervals, and this of course reduces their value. The decennial Population Census is particularly infrequent, although the insertion of a 10% sample census in 1966 gives some hope of improvement.

The non-comparability of the data from various sources presents another problem. This is largely due to the use of different regional boundaries. It may occur at one point in time where different statistical sources use different boundaries—for example, the non-comparability of data based on hospital, electricity board and economic planning regions. It may also occur over a period of time for one particular series of statistics. Thus the population statistics for the standard regions of the early 1960's are not directly comparable with the more recent population data based on the new economic planning regions.

46

But even if data is immediately available, published regularly and comparable in time and space, it is still useless unless it is relevant to the broad uses outlined earlier. From the list of sources, one immediately apparent inadequacy would seem to be the lack of information on land use and flows as compared with the considerable amount of published information on activities. This data is in fact normally available from a different set of sources collected on a unified basis by local surveys and censuses conducted by planning bodies. Broad national land use surveys are provided in a limited form by the Ordnance Survey and by the *National Land Utilization Surveys* of Stamp and Coleman, but it is arguable that there is a need for a more comprehensive national land use survey to complement the national population census.

With regard to this question of general relevance, another inadequacy is the limited nature of information on the regional economic structure. A knowledge of the latter is essential in assessing the problems and potential of the region, yet available information is primarily related to employment characteristics, with very infrequent censuses on production and distribution. There is a need for a more comprehensive framework with data on the internal and external interrelationships of industrial sectors in the regional economy.

Therefore in spite of a reasonable coverage of many areas of relevance to regional planning, regional statistics do have their problems. But it would probably be unfair to say that these deficiencies constitute the main obstacle to regional planning at the present time. Administrative problems may be much more fundamental here. But what of the future for regional statistics, how can the various problems be overcome? One interesting possibility is the development of data collection on a more disaggregated basis. Another is the development of regional accounts.

To be of maximum use to planning, relevant data from all agencies needs to be disaggregated to a common level of small and spatially regular units. These can then be aggregated into whatever geographical units are necessary. Aided by the rapid advances in information processing technology, many countries are now, in fact, introducing data collection based on metric grid systems. In Sweden, an information system links a basic population register (with data on income, employment, education, migration, etc. for individuals or groupings) and an enterprise register (providing data on the economic life of individual concerns) to a property register which can provide the locational element based on grid references. In Britain the 1971 Population Census collected information on a 100-metre grid square basis in many areas. This represents a major advance in British data collection, and opens up many possibilities for the future including the production of computer based census maps. The implicit problems however of extending this system to give a comprehensive statistical framework for not only regional and sub-regional planning but also for more local levels of planning should not be underestimated. How should it be organised—by a national collecting agency with an expanded census or by local collecting agencies using standardised methods or by a combination of both? How can a wide variety of agencies, some producing handwritten statistics, others producing them on magnetic tape be physically integrated into a unified system? And finally and most important, what of the cost and confidentiality aspects of obtaining this information? Many agencies, firms and private individuals, as revealed in the 1971 census, may object to the increasing intrusions of 'Big Brother'.

2 Regional accounts

A comprehensive picture of the regional economic structure is vital for regional planning. One possible approach is through the development of regional accounts. These accounts are similar to national accounts, which in the UK provide an annual picture of monetary flow, traditionally using a 'treble entry' system with Income = Expenditure = Output. However, an interesting and more recent development is the presentation of the economic interrelationships of the major sectors of the economy—households, firms, government, financial sector and rest of the world—in a series of social accounts, presented in a matrix form.

McCrone[2] believes that the development of accounts at the regional level is an essential prerequisite before regional planning can be undertaken. They have already been developed in several other countries at this level. Italy, for example, has a comprehensive set of regional accounts for the Mezzogiorno; Belgium has estimates of regional product by industry at the provincial level and France has comprehensive income data by *départements*. But enthusiasm for their development in the UK must first be qualified by an examination of their potential role in regional planning and the data and conceptual problems involved in their construction.

Besides providing a detailed picture of the interrelationships of the major sectors of the regional economy, regional accounts can also provide a valuable basis for regional policy and decision making. With information on topics such as regional income, output, investment and productivity, regional policy need no longer rely solely on political and social arguments and the dubious economic criteria of unemployment. Estimates of regional product by industry would facilitate the isolation of strengths and weaknesses in the regional economy, while data on investment could indicate which industries in which regions would give the best returns for a given level of investment.

However these advantages are only achieved at a cost, for regional accounts have heavy data requirements which raise a number of problems. Conceptually, regions are not micronations and perhaps need a different form of accounts to those used at the national level. In addition, the economic structure also varies greatly from region to region, yet for comparison between regions, standard accounts must be used which may mask important aspects of a particular region's economy. As compared with nations, regions are also 'open' economies with numerous cross-boundary transactions but no trade barriers and hence little information on such movements. (It is particularly difficult to balance the income and expenditure approaches at the regional level as a person may work in one area and live in another.)

Specific data problems include most of those already outlined in the previous section on regional statistics—infrequency of some series, time delay in publication and non-comparability in time and space. But there are also additional problems. The disaggregation of national data raises the problem of confidentiality, with a regional industry composed of perhaps only a handful of firms. Disaggregation also raises the question of the statistical accuracy at sub-national levels of national sample based surveys. With the growth of multi-product, multi-plant firms it may also be difficult to identify and obtain the relevant data for the specific plants in the region under study.

In spite of these problems there have been several attempts to construct regional accounts. Estimates of gross domestic product (GDP) for Wales,[3] Scotland[4] and Northern Ireland[5] have all been prepared. Statistically these 'national' areas present fewer problems than the English regions, and until the recent publication of regional accounts by Woodward arising from research done at the National Institute of Economic and Social Research,[6] accounts for English regions were limited to tentative calculations by Deane[7] and Stone,[8] both for 1948. Woodward, using dis-aggregated national accounts and a wide variety of regional sources such as Inland Revenue Reports and Family Expenditure Surveys, draws up comprehensive tables for GDP (including industrial subdivisions), domestic expenditure and personal income. The accounts provide a fascinating insight into regional variations, suggesting many of the underlying factors responsible for the variations. For example, the wide divergence in GDP per head of population at factor cost between South East England and Northern Ireland in 1961—£503 (SE) as compared with £289 (NI)—is clearly shown to be influenced by several factors such as the economic composition of the regional population, variations in regional productivity and the different industrial structures.

Notwithstanding that regions are not micro-nations, most attempts to draw up regional accounts have opted for the traditional national accounts approach. This approach as has been shown, does have many problems, especially income spillovers, and although recent works have met with some success it is arguable whether such accounts do provide the most useful framework of the regional economy. There is the general question of divergence between economic welfare and general welfare with only the former reflected in the accounting framework. There is also the point that regional accounts tend to focus on 'the wood and not the trees'. However changes in individual 'trees' some-times bring about substantial changes in the 'wood' as a whole. Concentrating on the production sector, an industrial breakdown of a region, showing inter-industry relationships in the form of an input-output matrix, may be more useful than income and expenditure components enabling us to see both the 'wood' and the 'trees'. This particular aspect of the wider regional accounts will now be examined in more depth.

3 Descriptive regional input-output tables

INPUT-OUTPUT TABLES

Since the pioneering work of W. W. Leontieff[9] in the 1930's, input-output has grown into one of the most widely accepted methods of not only describing the industrial structure of an economy but also, linked with other techniques, of predicting changes in that structure. This section will be limited to an examination of input-output as a descriptive framework. Discussion of input-output as a predictive technique and examples of its predictive use are discussed more fully in the next chapter.

The input-output table is a set of accounts, usually in monetary form, prepared for an economy. It pays explicit attention to inter-relationships between different sectors of the economy, concentrating in particular on inter-industry relationships. The format of the input-output table is outlined in Table 3.1. Usually the framework is a matrix of '$n \times n$' dimensions divided into four parts with each part describing a particular relationship. The overall system is a series of correlating rows (output) and columns (input).

Sector 1 is usually the largest sector and describes the inter-industry relationships as sales from one industry representing inputs to the production process of other linked industries. For example, in the hypothetical three-industry economy of Table 3.1, Industry 1 has sales of £50m to Industry 2 and £20m to Industry 3, and receives inputs of £20m from Industry 2 and £40m from Industry 3. Sector 1 is generally referred to as the intermediate or processing sector.

Sector 2 represents the sales from the industries to the external sectors of the economy. This sector, the final demand or household sector, consists of relationships more dependent on socio-political factors than economic criteria and includes commodities

51

for personal consumption, public expenditure, exports and the like. Thus Industry 1 has sales of £40m to final demand (including home consumption and exports), giving total sales or output of £110m.

The third part, Sector 3, refers to external inputs to industrial production, including factors such as wages for labour, taxes and subsidies, profits and imports. In our example, Industry 1 has household inputs (primarily wages for labour) of £40m and £10m of imports, giving total inputs of £110m.

Sector 1					Sector 2
Inputs From: / Output To:	1	Industry 2	3	Final Demand	Total Output
Industry 1	—	50	20	40	110
Industry 2	20	—	80	110	210
Industry 3	40	50	—	60	150
Household Inputs	40	100	50	—	190
Imports	10	10	—	20	40
Total Inputs	110	210	150	230	700
Sector 3					Sector 4

Table 3.1. *Simple Input-Output Flow Table for One Area.* (£ *million*).

Sector 4 represents the relationships between the external sectors. In Table 3.1 half of the total imports go straight to final demand. In practice this sector is not too important, mainly serving as a balancing factor in the total accounts. Finally, by summing the rows, total outputs are obtained. Likewise by summing the columns, total inputs are obtained. Obviously total inputs must equal total outputs, and the inputs and output of each industry and the external sectors must also balance out.

This combination of the four sectors presents a sophisticated method of describing an economy by input and output relationships, and has been enlarged to include a large number of industrial and external sectors in several national studies. However, the format of Table 3.1 limits relationships with other economies to simple import and export rows and columns. But regional economies are much more open than this with numerous cross-boundary transactions and consequently present more problems.

REGIONAL INPUT-OUTPUT TABLES

The problem of constructing regional tables can be approached in three ways. The first, and simplest, is to use a single region table identical in form to the national tables with all trade with the rest of the world relegated to a single row and column (as in Table 3.1).

Inputs

Region A to Region A (basically Table 3·1)	Region A to Region B (Exports)
Region B to Region A (Imports)	Region B to Region B

Outputs

Table 3.2 *Outline framework for a two-region input-output table*

The second method is more sophisticated using two regions, with both the region of primary interest and a second region (often the rest of the nation) treated in detail. A further three matrices are added to the original model of Table 3.1. The first matrix relates to the intra-regional system; the second and third to relationships between the primary region and the other region (regional exports and imports); and the fourth to the other region as a whole. Table 3.2 illustrates this approach.

The third and undoubtedly most difficult approach is the construction of a multi-region input-output table. This extends the second approach by treating three or more regions on an equal footing. Table 3.3 illustrates the approach, with each block representing an input-output system for a region, each consisting of the basic framework similar to that described in Table 3.1. Although the multi-region tables add greatly to the realism of

Inputs

	A/A	A/B	A/C	A/D
	B/A	B/B	B/C	B/D
Outputs	C/A	C/B	C/C	C/D
	D/A	D/B	D/C	D/D

Table 3.3 *Outline framework for a multi-regional input-output table*

the approach, implicitly or explicitly introducing distance as a factor affecting inter-regional flows, they also impose extra data problems.

INPUT-OUTPUT DATA PROBLEMS

Regional input-output tables require two broad types of information: firstly, regional accounting data and secondly, inter-regional and inter-industry flow estimates. The problems of regional accounting data have already been outlined, but with the recent NIESR[10] study there are signs of improvement. Data on the second area however is much thinner. The problem of disaggregating inter-industry inputs presents a major problem. The most accurate method would probably be to survey the industries within the region to identify their input composition. This however, is usually ruled out on cost grounds and tends to be replaced by a disaggregation of national input-output data. Thus if 10% of the inputs for the engineering industry nationally come from the manufacturing industry, then it is also assumed that 10% of the inputs for the regional engineering industry also come from the same industry. This use of national input coefficients rep-

54

resents a considerable economy in data collection and is probably not too misleading provided that the regional industry does not differ too markedly in technology from the same industry in other regions.

In addition, regional input-output tables also need to identify the regional source of the inputs. Data on regional trade in the UK is of limited availability. Even the 1962 MOT Road Goods Transport Survey[11] data and British Rail Wagon Movements Survey data are of dubious reliability for inter-industry flows. Direct surveys would again appear to be the panacea, although even here the presence of middlemen may distort the picture. Faced with these problems most input-output tables assume that regions are self-supporting wherever possible. If an industry requires an input which is produced within its own region, it will use the internal source, only drawing on other regions when the internal supply is insufficient. Similarly only when an industry can more than meet internal demands will there be any export of its commodities to other regions. This approach, implying no cross-hauling of the same commodity between regions is of doubtful validity.

A more interesting approach to inter-regional trade flows is the use of synthetic trade coefficients based on a gravity formulation. From their recent work on patterns of flow for Severnside, Edwards and Gordon[12] suggest the possibility of developing a synthetic model relating inter-regional trade flows in a particular commodity directly to the supply and demand for the commodity (using either gross output or proxy employment data) and inversely to the distance between the regions involved, with constants for relative accessibility and competitive factors. Such an approach not only provides a rational basis for trade coefficients, but may also introduce a more spatial element into this basically non-spatial input-output approach.

REGIONAL INPUT-OUTPUT IN PRACTICE*

In spite of the basic problems, a large number of regional input-output tables have been constructed. Table 3.4 summarises

* This section draws partly on Fletcher, R. J., *Regional Input-Output Analysis,* unpublished thesis, Department of Town Planning, Oxford Polytechnic.

Input-Output Studies		1	2	3	4	5	6	7	8	9	10	11	12	13	14	15	16	17
Characteristics		New England	New York – Philadelphia	Interregional USA Model	Utah Model	Pacific NW. Study	St. Louis Study	California Study	Los Angeles Study	Philadelphia	Washington State	Rio Grande Valley	Stockholm	Welsh Study	Dundee Study	W. Midlands	S.E. Kent	Peterborough
1	**Origin**																	
	Year of Completion (19)	53	53	55	57	59	59	63	64	66	68	69	59	67	67	67	70	71
	Sponsorship : Research Project	X	X	X	X	X	X	X	X	X	X	X	X	X	X	X	X	X
	Public Policy																	
2	**Scale and Size**																	
	Regional	X	X	X	X	X		X	X	X	X	X	X	X		X	X	X
	Urban						X								X			
	Single Region	X	X		X	X	X		X	X		X			X	X	X	X
	Two Regions						X							X	X			
	Multi-Regional			X				X			X		X					
3	**Table Composition**																	
	Number of Processing Sectors	45	45	11	26	45	27	28	41	496	54	12	31	31	12	45	45	38
	Number of Final Demand Sectors	4	–	–	7	–	–	7	–	86	6	–	15	–	6	–	–	5

4. Data

	47	47	47	47	55	60	60	59	63	64	50	64	65	54	63	68
Coefficients: National	X	X	X	X	X											
Modified National		X	X				X									
Direct Survey			X	X		X	X	X	X	X		X	X	X	X	X
Base Year of Table (19)	47	47	47	47	55	60	60	59	63	64	50	64	65	54	63	68
Units: Monetary	X	X	X	X	X	X		X	X	X	X	X	X	X	X	X
Labour						X	X	X								

5. Planning Functions

	47	47	47	47	55	60	60	59	63	64	50	64	65	54	63	68
Descriptive	X		X	X	X	X	X	X		X	X	X	X	X	X	X
Predictive		X		X		X	X	X	X	X			X			
Specific Uses: Structural Analysis	X	X	X	X	X	X		X			X	X	X			X
Trade Flow Analysis	X	X									X		X			
Production Output Forecast												X				
Impact Analysis		X			X		X	X	X	X		X		X		
Income Multipliers	X					X	X	X	X	X	X					
Employment Multipliers		X		X	X	X										X

Table 3.4 *Examples of regional input-output studies and their characteristics*

57

a sample of such tables. Although the sample is small and limited to a number of general criteria on primarily British and American studies, it does give some indication of the evolution of the approach over a period of 20 years or so.

The first section in the table contains information on the year of construction and form of sponsorship. It is interesting that all are research projects—although this is not true of every input-output study. The second section illustrates the predominance of regional scale studies, although the approach can also be used with effect at 'sub'-regional levels, and Artle's[13] famous Stockholm Study and recent British work on a table for Peterborough[14] provide interesting examples. The single region approach with all external trade relegated to a single row or column is the most common. However the Welsh Study by Nevin[15] provides an interesting example of a two-region approach, using Wales and the rest of the UK as the two regions.

The third section illustrates the range of size in processing and final demand sectors. The tables have tended to be limited to approximately 45 processing sectors and seven final demand sectors, partly due to the difficulties of dealing with large matrices on limited financial budgets. However, the recent study by Isard[16] for the Philadelphia Standard Metropolitan Statistical Area demonstrates the feasibility of a highly detailed (500–600 sector) regional input-output study, using the capacity of modern computers. In several of the studies some final demand sectors have been integrated into the processing sector to close the table for predictive purposes.

The fourth section shows that the majority of studies use national or modified national data. The time span between the base year for this data and the publication date of the study is seldom less than three years, those with the shorter periods being based on direct survey material. Most inputs are expressed in monetary terms which can be readily converted into approximate labour equivalents if required.

The final section shows that input-output has the valuable dual function of not merely describing the inter-industry relationships of a region but also predicting how they may change in the future. As a descriptive device, Isard sees input-output tables as extremely useful because:

'1   they record rather concisely, in an internally consistent manner, a large amount of information about a regional economy and the interrelations of its sectors

2   they impose a desirable statistical discipline on data collection agencies and empirical investigations

3   they reveal gaps in our data and may help in filling them

4   they present an economy in perspective and facilitate comparison of the magnitudes of its major sectors and bonds with other economies.'[17]

One particularly useful descriptive role is that of 'structural analysis'. This is concerned with the qualitative properties of an input-output table, especially the properties of the processing matrix. From this matrix, the extent of technical interdependence among sectors can be seen, and by comparing two tables covering different time periods, trends in inter-industry dependences become apparent. There are also a whole range of predictive roles, which will be outlined in the next chapter, and it is this wide practical flexibility of input-output which urges on development in face of all the constraining problems.

4 Summary

The quality of the regional data base is a major influence on the definition, analysis and planning of regions. With the increasing demand over the last ten to fifteen years, UK regional statistics are fairly comprehensive in some areas and are improving all the time. However, as has been shown, there are some major inadequacies, although these would not appear to constitute an unsurmountable obstacle to effective regional planning. This is not to suggest that there is not room for further improvement. One possible line of development could be through the construction of regional accounts, and in particular, regional input-output tables. Such tables provide a comprehensive and ordered picture of the regional economy, and it is interesting to speculate that if the resources were available, a nested hierarchy of such tables as in Figure 3.1, relating region and sub-region to their adjacent levels, would be of considerable value.

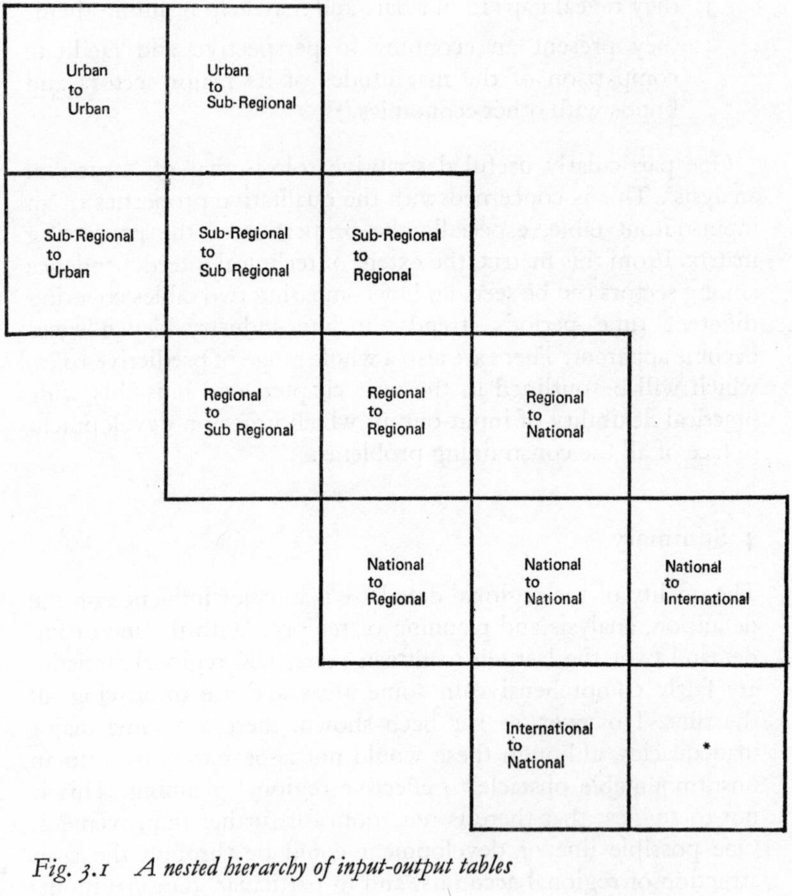

Urban to Urban	Urban to Sub-Regional			
Sub-Regional to Urban	Sub-Regional to Sub Regional	Sub-Regional to Regional		
	Regional to Sub Regional	Regional to Regional	Regional to National	
		National to Regional	National to National	National to International
			International to National	*

Fig. 3.1   A nested hierarchy of input-output tables

References

1 Chester, T. E., The Challenge of Regional Planning, *District Bank Review*, page 20, June 1964.
2 McCrone, G., The application of regional accounting in the UK, *Regional Studies*, pages 39–45, **1**, 1 (1967).
3 Nevin, E. T., *et alia*, *The Structure of the Welsh Economy*, Univ. of Wales, Welsh Economic Studies 4 (1966).
4 McCrone, G., *Scotland's Economic Progress 1951–60*, Allen and Unwin, (1965).
5 Carter, C. F., Estimates of the Gross Domestic Product of Northern Ireland 1950–56, *Journal of the Social and Statistical Inquiry Society of Ireland*, (1958–59).
6 Woodward, V., *Regional Social Accounts for the United Kingdom*, National Institute of Economic and Social Research (NIESR) (1970).
7 Deane, P., Regional Variations in UK Incomes from Employment, *Journal of the Royal Statistical Society*, (Series A), pages 123–35, **116**, 2 (1953).
8 Stone, R., Social Accounts at the Regional Level: A Survey, in *Regional Economic Planning*, O.E.E.C., pages 263–96 (1961).
9 Leontieff, W. W., *Input-Output Economics* (1966).
10 Woodward, V., NIESR, *op cit.*
11 Ministry of Transport, *Survey of Road Goods Transport 1962, Final Results*, Part IV (London, 1965).
12 Edwards, S. L., and Gordon, I. R., The application of input-output methods to regional forecasting: the British experience, *Proceedings of the Twenty-Second Symposium of the Colston Research Society*, Bristol, April (1970), 1971.
13 Artle, R., *Studies in the Structure of the Stockholm Economy*, Stockholm (1959).
14 See: Centre for Environmental Studies, *Seminar on the Construction and Use of Small Area Input–Output tables*, CES, CP1, June 1970.
15 Nevin, E. T., *et al, op cit.*
16 Isard, W., and Langford, T. W., *Regional Input-Output Study: Recollections, Reflections and Diverse Notes on the Philadelphia Experience*, MIT Press (1971).
17 Isard, W., *Methods of Regional Analysis*, p. 327, MIT Press (1960).

4 Regional change—short run

The fortunes of regions and sub-regions vary greatly. Some are relatively prosperous, others are not so fortunate. A basic factor in this variation is the economic structure of the region. The various sources of regional statistics and the development of regional accounts and input-output tables, outlined in the last chapter, can provide a descriptive framework of this structure. But this is essentially a static picture and of course regions are not static, with prosperity changing according to the ability of the region to produce goods and services that are in demand. The decline of a firm within a region, perhaps owing to the cancellation of a government contract or because of an unexpected loss of export trade, may result not only in a loss of jobs for workers in that firm but may also have a 'multiplier' impact on the wider regional economy. Auxiliary industries will be affected and service trades will also feel the pinch. On the other hand, if a firm expands, the process is reversed with a beneficial 'multiplier' effect.

There are a series of economic theories, known collectively as regional multiplier theories, which seek to explain these changes, stressing the interrelationships of sectors within the regional economy and the spread of impulses originating in any one sector to all other sectors either directly or indirectly. The economic base theory is the most simple and probably the most well known. More complex approaches include the development of inter-regional trade multipliers. Input-output analysis can also be utilised as a technique for analysing and predicting short-run change in the regional economy. Unfortunately these approaches tend to suffer from either over-simplicity or over-complexity, and more recent models suggest the emergence of a middle course between the economic base and other aggregate models and the input-output approach. All the approaches are similar however in that they are spatially aggregate, abstracting from space and looking at the region as a whole. They are also all basically attempts to explain short-run change rather than long-run trends of growth or decline which will be considered in the next chapter.

The various models are not only useful in explaining regional change and in predicting the implications of economic decisions, they are also useful in forward planning. It is obvious that many different industries, having different structures, will affect the regional economy in different ways. One may import most of its inputs, another may obtain them within the region. One may employ a large quantity of labour, another may be capital-intensive. Thus, although most regions, especially depressed regions, would welcome almost any type of industry, some industries may be better than others and, given the ability to plan and choose, it would be advantageous to know the relative contribution of each industry to an overall strategy and to concentrate encouragement on those which make the greatest contribution.

1 Economic base theory

ECONOMIC BASE CONCEPT[1]

Academically, the regional economy can be subdivided into two sectors: basic activities and non-basic activities. Basic activities are those which export goods and services to points outside the economic confines of the community, or which market their goods and services to persons who come from outside the community's economic boundaries. Non-basic activities are those which provide for the needs of persons resident within the community's economic limits. They do not export any finished goods or services, but are primarily local in their productive scope and market areas.

63

Implicit in this division of activities is the cause and effect relationship which constitutes the economic base theory. An increase in the amount of basic activity within a region will increase the flow of income into the region, increasing the demand for goods and services within it and effecting a corresponding increase in the volume of non-basic activity. Alternatively a decrease in basic activity would lead to a fall in income coming into the region, and a decline in demand for the products of the non-basic sector. Hence, basic activity as its name suggests has the prime mover rôle with any changes having a multiplier effect on the regional economy.

The economic base multiplier is usually calculated in terms of employment and can be expressed as:

$$\frac{\text{total employment in basic and non-basic activities}}{\text{total employment in basic activities}}$$

For example, a region with 500 000 persons in employment, 250 000 in basic activities and 250 000 in non-basic activities, that is a 1 : 1 basic : non-basic ratio, will have a multiplier of:

$$\frac{250\ 000 + 250\ 000}{250\ 000} = 2$$

Extensive use has been made of the employment multiplier for projection purposes. By evaluating the future prospects of the basic activities in the regional economy, and then applying the employment multiplier derived from the total : basic ratios relating to existing industrial composition, future employment totals have been forecast. This predictive rôle can be illustrated by considering the impact of an increase in employment of 20 000 in a basic industry in the above region. With an employment multiplier of 2, an extra 20 000 non-basic jobs will be created, and total employment will increase from 500 000 to 540 000. That is:

$$\triangle T = \triangle B\,(k)$$
$$40\ 000 = 20\ 000\,(2)$$

where $\triangle T$ = change in total employment

$\triangle B$ = change in basic employment

k = employment multiplier

There will also generally be a similar relationship between total employment and the regional population. If, in our study region, total employment of 500 000 supports a population of 1 500 000, there is a 1 : 3 ratio, and the extra 40 000 jobs would increase the population to 1 620 000.

Unfortunately, the attractive simplicity of the economic base theory can be deceptive and misleading, and there are several technical and conceptual problems which, although they do not disprove the theory, cast some doubt on the use of economic base studies in forecasting changes in the regional economy.

LIMITATIONS

The major technical problems involve the unit of measurement, the identification of basic and non-basic activities and the choice of study area. Taking the first problem, until now almost all economic base studies have used employment (number of jobs) as the unit of measurement. This partly reflects the fact that employment figures are relatively easy to obtain compared with other economic data. It may also reflect the political significance of employment totals. But employment as a unit of measurement has serious drawbacks. It does not consider the fact that equal changes in employment in two basic industries paying widely differing wage levels, such as farming and computer technology, may have significantly different multiplier effects, Not does it consider changes in productivity whereby a firm may increase output dramatically leading to higher wages and more spending without increasing its labour force. The use of total payroll data as a unit of measurement may overcome these difficulties, although the associated problems of allowance for inflation and non-consideration of numbers of jobs should not be discounted.

The identification of basic and non-basic activities is a particularly thorny problem. In most economic base studies the general practice with respect to industrial and commercial firms has been first to divide them into those that are wholly basic, then those that are wholly non-basic, and finally those that are 'mixed'. In one study by Mattila and Thompson,[2] aircraft firms were considered wholly basic, construction firms wholly non-basic, and wholesale and retail trading firms, mixed. It is in dealing with the 'mixed' class of firms that the serious allocation problems arise.

The basic/non-basic allocation of the 'mixed' firms can be done by either direct survey of the individual firms or by some indirect approach making use of information already available such as the levels and kinds of employment in individual industries. The direct empirical 'firm-by-firm' approach seeks information regarding each firm's proportion of export and local sales, usually by personal interview or questionnaire. These proportions are then applied to the firm's total employment or payroll to determine the basic and non-basic components. There are a number of limitations to this method. In addition to being tedious, time-consuming and expensive to carry out at the regional scale, it is also heavily dependent on the estimates of the firms which may be misleading with respect to the final destination of a firm's sales. An associated problem is that of intermediate sales—for example, the sale of coal mined locally as fuel for a local steel producer exporting finished steel—which may result in seemingly basic industries being classified as non-basic.

The indirect approach to the basic/non-basic split may use one or a combination of three methods, none of which is completely satisfactory.

1. The assumptions or arbitrary method simply assumes that all primary and manufacturing industry (SIC 1–16) is basic, and all service industry (SIC 17–24) is non-basic. No recognition is given to the fact that any one order can contain industries which are either export or local or both in some proportions.

2. The second method, that of location quotients (LQ) has greater academic respectability but very little if any more reliability than the first method. The location quotient for each industry in a region can be derived from the following ratio:

$$LQ = \frac{\text{percentage of regional employment in industry } A}{\text{percentage of national employment in industry } A}$$

Ratios greater than unity are taken to indicate an export or basic activity, and the number of workers surplus to those necessary to give an LQ of 1 (that is surplus to regional self-sufficiency) are assumed to serve the export market. Ratios of less than unity indicate a local or non-basic activity. This method has some advantages. It does take care of intermediate sales (thus the local coal industry selling to the local steel industry will appear as basic if the LQ is greater than unity) and it is inexpensive and easy to apply. However some of the underlying assumptions, such as the uniformity of regional and national demand patterns and the uniformity of regional productivity by industrial sector, do weaken its reliability.

3. The third method, minimum requirements,[3] is a modification of the LQ method, using the minimum distribution of employment necessary to support a regional industry rather than the average distribution. For each region, a computation is made of the percentage share which each industry claims of the region's labour force. The percentages are then compared and discounting atypical situations, the lowest percentage is taken as the minimum requirement for that particular industry. This minimum represents the benchmark and all employment in other regions above this percentage share is considered as basic employment. This process can be repeated for each industry in the region to give the total basic employment. This method would seem to be even more arbitrary than the LQ method, being highly dependent on the selection of the minimum percentage and the level of industrial disaggregation—a very fine disaggregation would in fact turn most sectors into basic, export activities.

The fact that all three methods can produce very different estimates of basic and non-basic activities for any one particular region underlines the difficulty of identifying the split. Table 4.1 illustrates the divergence of results when the three methods were applied to the South East of England.

The choice of study area constitutes the third technical problem. This obviously depends on a whole range of factors discussed in earlier chapters, such as the purpose of the study, administrative factors, regional consciousness and data availability. But whatever the choice of area, it must be remembered that the basic/non-basic split changes as the analyst proceeds from the one extreme of a small hamlet to the other of the entire nation. In the small hamlet, the country inn and petrol station are primarily export activities. At the urban level, these functions become service and non-basic; and at the national level, the majority of activities are non-basic with a relatively limited export sector.

Additional to these technical problems are a number of more conceptual problems. The theory assumes that basic industry is the prime mover behind regional change and that for any region there is a given basic/non-basic employment ratio which remains constant as changes in the economic structure of the region take place. Although basic industry probably is a major factor behind

Employment	Basic Employment		Non-Basic Employment	
Method	Numbers	% Total	Numbers	% Total
Assumption Method	2 561 180	32	5 445 250	68
Location Quotient Method	1 040 800	13	6 965 630	87
Min. Requirements Method	3 266 623	41	4 739 807	59

Table 4.1. *Basic/Non-Basic Employment in South East England (1966).*

SOURCE: *Strategic Plan for the South East,* 1 *Population and Employment* (Appendix 2D), HMSO, London (1970).

many changes in the regional economy, there can be little doubt that in certain situations well developed non-basic activities will themselves attract basic industries to a region and may therefore be amongst the determinants of that area's level of economic activity. It also appears more than likely that the basic/non-basic ratio will actually change with the very growth or decline it is supposed to estimate—with the non-basic element becoming relatively more important over time.

By concentrating on basic or export activity, the theory also unfortunately turns a blind eye to the importance of imports. An increase in basic employment and income may have a very limited multiplier effect on non-basic activity if much of the extra income flows out of the region in the form of expenditure on imports. Although it must be noted that the influence of the trade factor may not always be negative, for as the regional economy grows, there may come a point when it can produce a service or good for itself rather than importing it.[4] The resultant increase in non-basic activity may attract new basic industry, which again generates yet more non-basic activity. The fundamental point here of course is that an economy may grow not only by increasing exports from basic industries but also by replacing imports.

RELEVANCE OF THE THEORY

The outline of only some of the limitations of economic base theory would seem to suggest that it is of little practical relevance in regional analysis and planning. This is not the case. It has the undoubted advantages of simplicity and easy application and can shed useful light on a region's economic structure and the general impact of short-run changes. In certain situations, for example when dealing with small regions with a high level of dependence on specialised export activities, the limitations are least severe and it can provide a very useful basis for short-run forecasting. It can also serve as an important point of departure for more elaborate models. These include more sophisticated methods of analysing aggregate regional change and also the more recently developed spatially disaggregated land-use models, such as the Garin-Lowry Model.[5]

2 Inter-regional trade multipliers

Many of the criticisms levelled at economic base theory can be avoided by the use of a more sophisticated inter-regional trade multiplier. This is a rather more realistic but also rather more complicated approach, accepting that regions receive imports from other regions and are affected by national economic factors such as levels of direct and indirect taxation.

This multiplier, calculated in money terms as compared with employment in the base theory, is much more akin to the short-run Keynesian income type multiplier of macro-economics. It is based on the fact that an injection of a certain amount of money into the regional economy will increase regional income effecting an increase in consumer spending (although by an amount less than the original injection). The proportion of income spent becomes someone else's income, some of which they spend, and so the procedure is continued through several rounds. The question is what will be the impact of this injection of say £x million in Region A? Will it generate three times its own value through the multiplier effect or perhaps only one and a half times its own value? The difference is obviously of some importance to the planner.

DETERMINANTS OF THE MULTIPLIER

If the initial injection of money is passed on intact at each round, the multiplier effect would be infinite. The £x million initial injection would provide £x million extra income to workers in Region A which would all be spent on locally produced goods, which in turn would generate an extra income of £x million for local producers, who would then spend it and so on *ad infinitum*.

But the multiplier is not infinite because there are a number of fairly obvious leakages out of the stages of the multiplier process, which quickly bring about convergence. Three major leakages are savings, taxation and imports.

a Savings. People do not spend all of their extra income, generally preferring to save some proportion of the increase. The proportion of extra savings to extra income is known as the marginal propensity so save (s). The marginal propensity to consume (c) is of course ($1—s$).

b Taxation. Extra income is also reduced by taxation. This may be directly in the form of income tax or indirectly in the form of purchase tax.

c Imports. A substantial proportion of regional income is usually spent in goods produced outside the region, which represents an important leakage to other regions and countries.

Allowing for these leakages, the regional multiplier (k) can be expressed as:

$$k = \frac{\text{Initial Injection}}{\Sigma \text{ (Leakages)}}$$

For example, if a major regional industry injects an extra £1 000 000 into a regional economy through its expansion programme, it will generate an extra £1 000 000 of regional income. However, if £100 000 of this extra income is lost to the government via taxes, £200 000 is saved and £200 000 is spent on goods and services imported into the region, the resultant multiplier will be:

$$k = \frac{£1\ 000\ 000}{\Sigma\ (£100\ 000\ +\ £200\ 000\ +\ £200\ 000)}$$

$$= \frac{£1\ 000\ 000}{£\ 500\ 000}$$

$$= 2$$

Thus, because of the various leakages, the initial injection will only have limited multiplier effects. The basic problem is how to calculate the regional multiplier in a real-life situation with limited data resources.[6]

BRITISH REGIONAL MULTIPLIERS

Given a planned injection into a regional economy, it is of course impossible to observe and measure directly the round-by-round leakages. As such, the multiplier must be estimated by some indirect method. This involves the estimation of the regional marginal propensities to consume, save, import and the marginal rates of taxation, which can then be incorporated into a Keynesian type formula from which a general regional multiplier can be derived. Even this unfortunately presents problems, for several of the factors, especially the import relationship, are difficult to estimate. Nevertheless, there have recently been some interesting attempts to estimate British regional multipliers.

A very general and intuitive approach has been used by Archibald.[7] His multiplier is:

$$k = \frac{1}{1 - (c - m)(1 - t)}$$

where c = marginal propensity to consume,
m = marginal propensity to import,
and t = marginal rate of taxation.

Using approximate estimates of the factors involved, he placed UK regional multipliers within the range 1·2 to 1·7.

To be more precise than this requires more accurate and empirically based estimation of the various marginal propensities. Amongst British regional multiplier studies, some of the most empirically based estimates are those compiled by Steele.[8] He uses a modified Archibald multiplier, including both direct and indirect taxation. Estimates of the various factors are made primarily from regional Family Expenditure Survey consumption and income data, although estimates of the difficult regional import factors are derived largely from statistics for freight flows. Table 4.2 illustrates the multiplier estimates for

Table 4.2. *British Regional Multipliers*

Region	Multiplier	with Feedback
North	1·37	1·42
Yorkshire and Humberside	1·19	1·26
East Midlands	1·37	1·45
West Midlands	1·20	1·33
East Anglia	1·22	1·33
South East	1·41	1·57
South West	1·37	1·42
Wales	1·33	1·38
North West	1·27	1·39
Scotland [a]	1·70	1·77

SOURCE: Steele, D. B., *Oxford Economic Papers*, July 1969, by permission of The Clarendon Press, Oxford.

[a] Steele did derive two possible estimates for Scotland based on differing import factors. This is the lower multiplier estimate.

each of the British regions. It also includes Steele's estimates of the regional 'feedback effect'. This is the effect of the import leakage from a particular region stimulating, via increased income in other regions, an increased demand for the exports of the original region.

Although too much should not be read into Steele's results,

they do illustrate several important features of regional multipliers which are of some relevance to an understanding of short run regional change and the guidance of that change. Firstly, the multiplier is low. This of course makes the resolution of regional problems more difficult, for pouring aid into a region may be like pouring water into a bath with the plug out. This can also be embarrassing for the rest of the country, for if Scotland, by way of example, has a regional multiplier of 1·7, then approximately 60% of any extra investment into the region will inevitably leak into other regions, much of it into pressured areas such as the South East. The results also suggest a considerable regional variation in multipliers ranging from 1·7 in Scotland to 1·19 in Yorkshire. The high Scottish figure is not explained by a high marginal propensity to save (contrary to expectations!), but is more influenced by a much lower import ratio than any other region. This no doubt reflects the relative geographical isolation of the region. The low multipliers for Yorkshire, the West Midlands and East Anglia are mainly explained by high savings and high import ratios. These variations indicate that in some regions investment in the short run may be more effective than in others. Steele's detailed results also emphasise the relative importance of the import factor. Whereas the combined marginal savings and direct tax ratios are low and vary only from 0·14 to 0·22, the ratio of imports to final demand is much higher and varies more widely from 0·41 to ·074.*

However, the regional multiplier is not without problems. It suffers from severe data problems, with the most vital factor, that of imports, the most difficult to estimate. In addition, the problem of integrating the 'feedback effect' is only partially solved. Like the economic base theory, it is also an excessively aggregated approach, abstracting from specific industries and inter-industry linkages. This is an important consideration for although a region may overall have a low multiplier, specific industries within that region may have much higher multipliers with their individual actions exerting a substantial influence on the wider regional economy.

* More recent estimates by Steele indicate a range of 0·44 to 0·82. See Steele, D. B., A Numbers Game (or The Return of Regional Multipliers), *Regional Studies*, pages 115–130, 6 (1972).

The input-output matrix previously presented as a descriptive framework can also be used in the analysis and prediction of short-run changes in the regional economy. To some, this is indeed its most valuable use and it has several advantages over the approaches already outlined, providing an industry-by-industry breakdown of the regional economy and placing particular emphasis on inter-industry relationships. This use of input-output for predictive purposes involves a number of additional procedures and basic assumptions extra to its descriptive rôle. The procedure will first be outlined and then the vital assumptions will be examined.

PROCEDURE

The procedure for using input-output for analysing and predicting short-run changes can be illustrated by using the hypothetical situation outlined in Table 4.3. This table is a simple two-region

Inputs From: \ Output To:	Region A Industry			Region B Industry			Final Demand		Total Output
	1	2	3	1	2	3	A	B	
Region A Industry 1			10	50	10		30		100
Region A Industry 2									
Region A Industry 3	20						30		50
Region B Industry 1									
Region B Industry 2	20	20				60	20	80	200
Region B Industry 3	20			50				30	100
Households A	40	20		20					80
Households B				80	30				110
Total Inputs	100	50		200	100		80	110	640

Table 4.3 *Input-output inter-regional flow table for two regions, A and B (£ million).*

input-output matrix, based on a subdivision of Table 3.1, but with foreign trade (imports and exports) omitted for simplicity in exposition. Region A is dependent on Industries 1 and 3 with a combined output of £150m. Region B on the other hand is dependent on Industries 2 and 3, which have a combined output of £300m. twice that of Region A. This difference is to some extent reflected in the differences in household output, with the payments for labour being £110m in Region B as compared with only £80m in Region A (although relative population figures would be necessary for an estimate of relative prosperity between the two regions). Although the regions do specialise, they are also very much interdependent. For example, Industry 1 in Region A sells over half its output to Industries 2 and 3 in Region B, the rest going to its own Industry 3 and internal final demand. Similarly, it also derives much of its inputs from Region B, although it is, as would be expected, dependent on labour inputs from its own household sector.

But this is a simple descriptive picture of inter-regional relationships. Prediction requires the calculation of Table 4.4.

Inputs From:	Output To:	Region A Industry			Region B Industry			Final Demand	
		1	2	3	1	2	3	A	B
Region A Industry	1			0·20	0·25	0·10		0·37	
	2								
	3	0·20						0·38	
Region B Industry	1								
	2	0·20	0·40				0·60	0·25	0·73
	3	0·20				0·25			0·27
Households	A	0·40	0·40		0·10				
Households	B				0·40	0·30			
TOTAL		1·00	1·00		1·00	1·00		1·00	1·00

Table 4.4 *Input and supply coefficients for Table 4.3 (direct inputs per £ of output)*
(Rounded to the nearest penny)

This table shows the direct inputs per £ of output for the various industries in both regions. Thus, to produce £1 of output, Industry 1 in Region A requires 20p of inputs from its own Industry 3, 20p of inputs from both Industries 2 and 3 in Region B, and 40p of inputs from the household sector in Region A. Hence, this table of coefficients shows not only the input coefficients but also the regional origins of the inputs in percentage terms, the supply coefficients.

The table of coefficients is the key to the predictive rôle, for by assuming constant coefficients (an assumption that will be examined later) the impact of any change in either of the regional economies on the rest of the inter-regional economic structure can be traced. Suppose that population projections indicate a rapid increase in the population of Region B over the next five years, leading to a doubling of its final demand for the output of its own Industries 2 and 3. At the same time there will be no change in final demand in Region A. What will be the impact on the inter-regional economies?

The projected change, the doubling in final demand in Region B, will mean an increase in output of £80m for Industry 2 and £30m for Industry 3 in Region B. But both industries rely on inputs from elsewhere. The size and incidence of these inputs can be found by multiplying down the column for Industry 2 (Region B) in the coefficient table (Table 4.4) by the £80m, and likewise down the column for Industry 3 by £30m.* The results of this first multiplication are an increase in demand for Industry 1 of £23m (£20m and £3m), for Industry 2 of £18m, and for Industry 3 (Region B) of £20m. These are the first round of input requirements. But of course they must be produced too, and they will also need extra inputs. For example, the £23m increase in Industry 1 will necessitate extra inputs of approximately £5m from each of three other industries. This is the second round of the process, which will generate a demand for further inputs, and so the iterations continue.

After about seven iterations, however, the extra input require-

* The household sector (both column and row) however, is eliminated from this procedure, because projected household expenditure (final demand) has already been stated. It was the starting point and its inclusion would lead to double counting.

ments are minimal and the process converges. The use of an 'inverse matrix' and a computer facilitates this process for more complex situations.[9] The original increase plus the summed round-by-round input requirements can then be added to the original table, providing a full picture of the predicted inter-regional economies in five years' time. In our example, the net result of the doubling of final demand in Region B is a two-thirds increase in the total industrial output of Region B from £300m to approximately £500m, but also an increase, although more limited, in the industrial output of Region A from £150m to £200m, thus reflecting the economic interrelationships of the two regions.

THE COEFFICIENT PROBLEM

Unfortunately, the benefits of the regional input-output approach have their price. There are the numerous data problems outlined in Chapter 3, especially the problems of disaggregating inter-industry inputs and identifying their regional source; but for prediction, there is also the problem of the validity of the assumption of constant coefficients. The assumption that an industry will constantly use the same composition of inputs is undoubtedly dubious for many industrial sectors over anything but a very short time period. Changing technology, relative movements in price level, the development of economies of scale and a wide variety of social, psychological and political factors can all radically alter an industry's input pattern. Trends in technology are particularly difficult to forecast although change does appear to be occurring at an increasing rate. (Servan Shreiber[10] has pointed out that the time lag between invention and manufacture was 112 years for photography (1727–1839), twelve for television (1922–34) and only three years for the integrated circuit (1958–61).) When, as in regional input-output analysis, the assumption of constant supply coefficients is also added, the whole approach looks rather problematic.

But this is too pessimistic a view. All projections guess at some factors, and less factors are overlooked in the disaggregated input-output approach than in the more aggregated methods already discussed. Further, it may also be possible to build rather more flexibility into the determination of the input-output coefficients, by anticipating future changes. If it is argued that under a given technology there is only one best input combination for a specific industry, and that once adopted it will be retained for some time, then the incorporation of this combination into the analysis may ensure some consistency in the short run. This depends on 'the assumption . . . that the average input pattern of the most efficient establishments at time t will approximate the average input patterns of all establishments at $t + k$, where k is a time period to be determined'.[11] In time, it is also hoped that the more frequent production of input-output tables based on more up to date survey data will, besides producing a more accurate static picture, also allow the measurement of trend changes in average regional input coefficients. Since these trends would include both technological input and supply pattern influences, they could also be used for forecasting.

THE USE OF PREDICTIVE INPUT-OUTPUT ANALYSIS

There have been several regional applications of input-output models in predictive rôles, mainly in the USA but also more recently in Britain. Some of these were outlined in Table 3.4, where the various predictive rôles were noted. Of particular importance is the rôle of impact analysis assessing, for example, the impact of a sudden population influx into a region, the impact of the abandonment of the Concorde project on the Bristol sub-region, or the impact of changes in the US space programme or American involvement in the Vietnam War on certain areas of the USA[12]. An early and well known impact study is that by Isard and Kuenne[13] on the impact of the establishing of three-million-ton-capacity iron and steel mills at Trenton, New Jersey, in the Greater New York–Philadelphia industrial region. After estimating the size of new steel fabricating and other activities linked directly to the basic iron and steel activity, the impact of the investment was forecast using an incremental input-output model—providing a round-by-round insight into the impact on 45 sectors of the regional economy.

Input-output can also be used for estimating income and employment multipliers for each industrial sector within the region. Thus, given some target such as the maximisation of regional income or, more usually, regional employment, the analysis can be used to isolate the industrial sectors in which expansion induced by an investment injection would have the greatest effect. Recent work at the University of North Wales provides interesting examples of such applications. In a study, *Regional Income Multipliers*,[14] developed from an attempt to assess the impact of a new aluminium smelter on the economy of the county of Anglesey, an input-output matrix was constructed for thirty-three sectors of the economy, and a series of multipliers were derived. Interestingly some of the highest multipliers were found in the agriculture sector. Of course this is not to say that Anglesey's future should necessarily be tied to agriculture, for local authorities may wish to encourage balanced employment opportunities. Nevertheless the varying multipliers should not be ignored in policy decisions. Other interesting results cast doubt on the usual assumption that no matter how small a region any extra expenditure which takes place has positive multiplier effects, for they show that the increase in income of some consumers can change consumption patterns in such a way that the net multiplier effect is negative. A second study, *The Impact of Domestic Tourism*,[15] showed that an increase of £10 000 in tourist spending would on average generate an additional £3000 of income in the Anglesey study area. It also showed, however, that the multiplier effect varied between different categories of tourist, with the £10 000 increase in the 'hotel' and 'tent' categories generating the average figure of £3000; 'farmhouse and bed and breakfast' accommodation (with a lower income leakage)—an extra £7 600; and 'caravans' (with a higher income leakage)—only a little more than £2 000.

Future developments suggest even more potentially useful rôles in regional planning. In addition to the development of dynamic coefficients, the whole input-output process could be made more dynamic.[16] The approach to date has been primarily of a comparative static form, with the emphasis on the new equilibrium level of output following a change, rather than on the processes in production and especially the time required in reaching that new equilibrium. The time factor is crucial. Some inputs to supply increasing output demand may meet capacity constraints and demand may divert elsewhere. There has been some interesting research into ways and means of incorporating these wider dynamic aspects into the approach. Other interesting general developments are the widening of the input-output approach to include spatial land use implications[17] and, as at the national level, a growing interest in the inclusion of the wider environmental impacts of growth and change, 'the effluence of affluence', into the accounting framework.[18]

It would therefore seem that this wide range of rôles would make input-output a very valuable approach for understanding and predicting short-run regional change—that is change in the regional economy over a period of possibly five to ten years when the assumption of constant coefficients is less dubious. The situation is neatly summed up by Stone: 'we buy the possibility of answering complicated questions at the price of building in certain rigidities.'[19]

4 A compromise approach

Although the various approaches outlined so far have many advantages, they also have many problems; and more recent models do suggest the emergence of a middle course, a compromise approach, between the oversimplicity of the highly aggregated economic base and inter-regional trade multipliers and the complexities and heavy data requirements of input-output.

Moving from one end of the spectrum, Weiss and Gooding[20] have outlined a method of disaggregating the export base of a region into a small number of significant sectors and calculating multipliers for each sector. In a case study of the small regional economy centred around Portsmouth, New Hampshire, USA, they have calculated employment multipliers for three major export employment categories. Private export employment is shown to have the highest multiplier of 1·8, civilian employment at the local naval shipyard has a multiplier of 1·6, and employment at a local air force base has the lowest multiplier of 1·4. The low nature of all the multipliers reflects the 'open' nature of the small regional economy, with numerous import leakages out of the area. They also suggest however that in a small region such as the study area the loss of private export jobs will have a greater impact on the regional economy than a loss of the same number of jobs from a government defence installation.

Moving from the other end of the spectrum, the Regional Economic Development Institute of Pittsburgh have developed Technique for Area Planning (TAP).[21] This is a technique which simplifies input-output relations and restricts the expensive data collection process. It is a cross between economic base and input-output and divides the economy into a limited number of major sectors and minor sectors. The major sectors would be made up of large, predominrntly basic firms, experiencing considerable change and hence exerting considerable influence on the regional economy. A full inter-industry analysis is computed only for these major sectors, with the minor sectors being consolidated within the household sector. Examples of the application of the approach in impact analysis show it to give results deviating by at the most ± 5% from those produced for full input-output analysis. As with the other compromise approaches, TAP is most effective in small specialised regions.

5 Summary

Over the years there has developed a considerable armoury of economic models concerned with analysing short-run changes in the regional economy as a whole. Such models are of considerable value to the regional planner, providing an understanding of regional change, predicting the implications of economic decisions and thus aiding forward planning. However, as with all models, they have their limitations.

The attractiveness of the simple economic base theory relating changes in total regional employment to changes in basic employment, must be balanced against the numerous conceptual and technical problems, especially the thorny and perpetual problem of identifying the basic/non-basic split. The highly aggregated inter-regional trade multiplier introduces relevant import, savings and taxation factors and throws interesting light on to large-scale regional multiplier variations, but it is severely limited by the assessment of the regional import leakages. Data problems, plus the assumptions of constant coefficients, also constrain the more technical input-output approach, which is nevertheless potentially a most valuable method of regional analysis. The recent developments also have their problems, but they do suggest that the modification and integration of some of the other approaches may offer useful rule-of-thumb methods of analysing short-run regional change which will be of considerable practical value in regional planning.

References

1 Useful source references on the economic base concept include:
Pfouts, R. W., *The Techniques of Urban Economic Analysis,*
Chandler-Davis (1960);
Andrews, R. B., series of articles in *Land Economics,* 29–31 (1953–6);
Blumenfeld, H., The Economic Base of the Metropolis, *Journal of the American Institute of Planners,* 21 (1955);
Thomas, M. D., The Economic Base and a Region's Economy, *Journal of the American Institute of Planners,* 23 (1957).
2 Mattila, J. M., and Thompson, W. R., Measurement of the Economic Base of the Metropolitan Area, *Land Economics,* 31 (1955).
3 See: Ullman, E., and Dacey, M. F., The Minimum Requirements Approach to the Urban Economic Base, *Papers and Proceedings of the Regional Science Association,* 6 (1960);
Ullman, E., Minimum Requirements after a decade, *Economic Geography,* 44 (1968).
4 See for example: Jacobs, J., *The Economy of Cities,* Jonathan Cape (1969).
5 For a recent survey of land-use modelling in Britain, see:
Batty, M., Recent Developments in Land-Use Modelling: A Review of British Research, *Urban Studies,* 9, 2 (1972).
6 See for example: Allen, K. J., *The Regional Multiplier: Some Problems in Estimation,* Chapter 4 in Cullingworth, J. B., and Orr, S. C., *Regional and Urban Studies,* Allen and Unwin (1969).
7 Archibald, G. C., Regional multiplier effects in the UK, *Oxford Economic Papers,* 19 (1967).
8 Steele, D. B., Regional Multipliers in Great Britain, *Oxford Economic Papers,* 21 (1969).
9 See: Isard, W., *Methods of Regional Analysis,* pages 363–71, MIT Press (1960);
also: Yan, C. S., *Introduction to Input-Output Economics,* Holt, Rinehart and Winston, New York (1969).
10 Servan-Schreiber, J. J., *The American Challenge,* page 59, Penguin (1969).

11 Miernyk, W. H., Long-Range Forecasting with a Regional Input-Output Model, *Western Economic Journal,* pages 165–76, **VI** (1968).

12 See: Isard, W., and Langford, T. W., *Regional Input-Output Study: Recollections, Reflections and Diverse Notes on the Philadelphia Experience,* MIT Press (1971).

13 Isard, W., *Methods of Regional Analysis, op cit,* pages 349–62.

14 Sadler, P. G., Archer, B. H., and Owen, C. B., *Regional Income Multipliers,* Bangor Occasional Papers in Economics: 1, University of Wales Press (1973).

15 Archer, B. H., *The Impact of Domestic Tourism,* Bangor Occasional Papers in Economics: 2, University of Wales Press (1973).

16 See: Yan, C. S., *op cit.*

17 Hirsch, W. Z., Input-Output Techniques for Urban Government Decisions, *American Economic Review: Papers and Proceedings,* **58** (1968).

18 Isard, W., and Langford, T. W., *op cit.*

19 Stone, J. R., Social Accounts at the Regional Level: A Survey, in *Regional Economic Planning,* page 289, OEEC, Paris (1961).

20 Weiss, S. J., and Gooding, E. C., Estimation of Differential Employment Multipliers in a small Regional Economy, *Land Economics,* **44** (1968).

21 Regional Economic Development Institute of Pittsburgh, *Technique for Area Planning: A Manual for the Construction and Application of a Simplified Input-Output Table* (1967).

5 Regional growth—long run

All regions and sub-regions experience the short-run ups and downs outlined in the previous chapter. But the long-run rate of growth of regions, usually measured in terms of otuput and/or income varies widely, and some regions may actually experience long-run decline. At the regional level in the United Kingdom the South East has been more prosperous than the North East over a long period of time. Similarly, within regions, certain sub-regions are considerably more prosperous than others. But what factors account for these variations?

Theories of long-run regional growth must obviously consider those factors held constant in short-run analysis—that is factors such as population, wages, prices, resources, technology and the distribution of income. The mobility of factors, especially labour and capital is a particularly important consideration. However, as yet, there is no one generally accepted theory of regional growth (or development). Indeed it is doubtful whether a single comprehensive theory is possible, although recent attempts at synthesis by Hilhorst[1] and Siebert[2] are interesting. There are, however, a number of partial theories and concepts which between them focus on the major determinants of regional growth.

It is generally accepted that regional growth may result from either endogenous or exogenous determinants, that is from factors inside the region or outside the region, or more usually from some combination of both. Major internal determinants include the distribution of factors of production such as land, labour, capital,

84

while a major external determinant is the level of demand for the region's commodities from other areas. This endogenous/exogenous split is similarly reflected in the theories; some such as the sector theory suggest that regional development is essentially an internal evolutionary process, others such as the export base theory emphasise demand for the region's exports.

As with short-run analysis, the theories can be subdivided into those which are highly aggregated and those that are more disaggregated. The aggregate models include those already mentioned plus several more sophisticated but spatially abstract models derived from national economic growth theory. An example of the disaggregated approach is industrial structure analysis which, although perhaps more a technique than a theory, provides a useful insight into both the internal and external elements of regional growth.

In addition to gaining an understanding of the process and determinants of regional growth which explain regional variations it is also useful to know whether the various regional imbalances are self-righting. The question of whether regional growth is convergent or divergent is debatable, and an outline and discussion of certain relevant concepts, such as 'cumulative causation' and the centre-periphery concept conclude the chapter.

1 Aggregate growth models

GROWTH FROM INSIDE

One of the simplest theories of regional growth is the so-called *sector theory*. The theory arises from empirical observations by Clark and Fisher[3] that a rise in per capita income in different areas at different times is generally accompanied by a resource reallocation, with a decline in the proportion of labour force employed in primary (agriculture) activities, and a rise first in secondary (manufacturing) and then in tertiary (service) activities. The rate of occurrence of such sector shifts, and the resultant internal evolution of specialisation and division of labour, is seen as providing the main dynamic of regional growth.

The rate of shift in the relative importance of different sectors is explained by the income elasticity of demand for their products and by the different rates of change in labour productivity. As incomes rise, the demand for commodities supplied by the secondary and tertiary sectors rises faster than the demand for primary products, and thus these sectors grow faster. But it is also argued that the secondary and tertiary sectors benefit more from productivity advances and are therefore able to offer higher earnings to factors of production, thus causing a shift from sectors in which rewards are low to those in which they are high.

An extension of the basic theory is the *stages theory*[4] which suggests that regional development is primarily an internal evolutionary process with the following stages:

a The first stage is that of the self-sufficient subsistence economy, with little investment or trade. The basic agricultural population stratum is distributed according to the localisation of natural resources.

b With the improvements in transport, the region develops trade and specialisation. A second stratum develops carrying on simple villages industries for the farmers. Since the materials, market and labour are all furnished originally by the agricultural population, this new stratum is located in relation to the basic stratum.

c With increasing inter-regional trade, the region progresses through a succession of agricultural crops from extensive grazing to cereals to intensive dairying and fruit growing.

d With increasing population and diminishing agricultural returns, the region is forced to industrialise. Secondary industry develops, at first processing primary products but then becoming more specialised. (A failure to industrialise would lead to population pressure, a fall in living standards and general stagnation and decay.)

e The final stage is the development of tertiary industry producing for export. Such a developed region exports capital, skills and specialised services to less advanced regions.

Implicit in this process of growth to maturity are fundamental changes in the organisational structure of industry. The major change is the decrease in the number of establishments within a particular industry, with the closure of small establishments and the concentration into a limited number of bigger and stronger firms. This organisational rationalisation plus the original internal reallocation between sectors also causes major changes in the locational and settlement patterns within regions, favouring migratory movements from small to bigger centres, from rural to urban areas. (Such locational changes are discussed in more detail in later chapters.)

But does the sector theory and its extension into the stages theory constitute a useful and adequate explanation of regional growth? There are several objections to the approach. In particular, the rigid 'primary–secondary–tertiary sequence', or the five stages with their heavy emphasis on the necessity of industrialisation, invariably bear little resemblance to the actual development of regions. This is especially true of regions which were developed primarily to serve external markets. This of course introduces a second criticism—the lack of insight provided into the external relationships of a region. Although the theory does not rule out external shifts in demand, it is much more useful the greater the degree of self-sufficiency in the regional economy. However, regional economies are open economies and the one-sided nature of the approach is a fundamental weakness. A third criticism which can be applied to all the aggregate theories, is the grossness of the factors. Primary, secondary and tertiary categories can hide a multitude of industrial variations. A final criticism questions whether the approach does in fact constitute a 'theory' of regional growth. Such a theory would clearly focus on the critical factors that aid or impede growth. The sector approach merely outlines a process of growth, on the assumption of a rise in per capita income, failing to provide any insight into the causes of growth and change. However, the approach is not without merits. It does provide a general picture of the stages of regional development and throws light on the conditions for moving from one stage to another. It focusses on the major factors of industrial and occupational structure, and changes in the pattern of demand and sector productivity, and as such provides a useful starting point for the disaggregated analysis of regional growth which will be outlined in a later section.

A more recent approach to an explanation of the internal determinants of regional growth is via the use of *macro-economic models*[5] used in national economic growth theory. These models are supply oriented and seek to explain regional output in terms of certain regional factors, each of which can be analysed individually. Thus:

$$O_n = f_n (K, L, Q, Tr, T, So)$$

where O = Potential Output of Region n
$\quad K$ = Capital
$\quad L$ = Labour
$\quad Q$ = Land (Natural Resources)
$\quad Tr$ = Transport Resources
$\quad T$ = Technology
$\quad So$ = Socio-Political System.

Taking the more important, and more easily quantifiable factors, a growth equation can be produced, for example:

$$o_n = a_n k_n + (1 - a_n) l_n + t_n$$

where o, k, l and t = growth rates of output, capital, labour and technology
$\quad a$ = capital's share of income (the marginal product of capital).

This simple neoclassical growth model can be adjusted to provide a model of steady regional growth, and tests with US data show a high degree of correlation between the results of such a model and reality.[6]

Although this macro-economic approach does isolate some of the major determinants of regional growth and can be adapted to describe growth in a system of regions, it still possesses certain basic weaknesses—in particular its highly aggregate nature and its concentration on the supply side.

GROWTH FROM OUTSIDE

The emphasis of the last section was on the internal productive capacity of a region and on the supply of factors such as capital, labour, natural resources and technical progress which determine that capacity. These internal supply factors are undoubtedly major determinants of regional growth, but their narrow emphasis on 'closed' regions can be misleading. In the highly interdependent economies of today, regions are not vacuum sealed against all external impulses, but are 'open' to the flows of trade and information from the outside world. The degree of 'openness' does vary according to factors such as topography, the stage of economic development and the size of the region, but external factors must be considered in any explanation of regional growth.

The *export base theory* provides one possible explanation of the external demand factor in regional growth. The theory is simply an application of the short-run comparative static economic base model to long-run dynamic growth situations. It states that a region's growth is determined by the exploitation of natural advantages and the growth of the regional export base which are in turn largely influenced by the level of external demand from other regions and countries. The income from export sales will lead to the development of residentiary activities, capital and labour movements, the development of external economies, and further regional growth. Thus, the level of external demand for the products of a region's export industries is set up as a critical determinant of regional growth. (One of the main exponents of the theory, North,[7] uses some 'colonial' examples—the decline in demand for beaver hats and the growth in demand for wheat from England in the late nineteenth century, with the resultant impacts on certain US export industries and regions—to illustrate the relationship.)

Unfortunately, this attractively simple concept is not without problems. In addition to the various technical and conceptual limitations outlined in the previous discussion of the economic base concept in short-run analysis, there are several other problems when the theory is adapted for long-run dynamic analysis, many of which are outlined in the published discussion between North and Tiebout.[8] The highly aggregate nature of the theory can be particularly misleading. The simple split into the region and the rest of the world hides the interrelationships between regions which are of considerable importance in regional growth. Aggregation also masks the fact that an increase in some export base industries may have much greater regional growth effects than others in particular regions.

But there are also other fundamental questions. Will export growth always lead to regional growth? Is export growth solely determined by external demand? What of the other internal and external influences that are relegated into insignificance in the

89

theory? Taking the first question, the successful translation of the export sector growth into residentiary growth and large-scale regional growth depends on several variables—variables such as the income and expenditure patterns of the export sector, the initiative of local business and the rôle of the government. If export income goes mainly on imported luxury goods, or local businessmen fail to invest in the region, or the government fails to provide the necessary infrastructure, the region may remain in a state of colonial dependence on external areas, and will experience only limited growth.

Secondly, even if the export base is a major determinant of regional growth, its fortunes may not be solely determined by the level of external demand. Internal factors may be of considerable importance. Such factors were in fact recognised by supporters of the theory although the emphasis of the theory was still on the level of external demand as the major determinant. North, for example, recognised that the reasons for the decline of an existing exportable commodity might include the exhaustion of natural resources (e.g. coal seams), the increasing cost of land and labour within the region relative to those of competing regions (e.g. the decline of the Lancashire cotton textile industry), and technical progress changing the relative composition of inputs. Further, the growth of new exports may be influenced by factors such as major transport developments (canals and railways) allowing a region to compete in commodities from which it was previously barred by high transfer costs.

Thirdly, there are other influences on regional growth besides the fortunes of the export base. The internal growth influences may be vital factors in their own right. The growth of local (residentiary) activities by replacing imports may stimulate regional development. Other exogenous influences, such as the level of government spending, shifts in investment and consumption patterns, may also have a greater impact on regional growth than changes in the export base.

But the theory does stress the important fact that the growth of any sub-national unit is directly tied to developments within the national economy and international trade as well, suggesting that regional growth cannot be studied in isolation from changing patterns of national demand and investment. It clearly introduces the Keynesian concept of aggregate demand as a growth determinant, although highlighting exports as the primary component in that demand.

A more comprehensive and equally familiar method of incorporating the external factors in regional growth is through the application of the theory of international trade to regions. The *inter-regional resource allocation models*, first developed by Ohlin,[9] assume that factors of production, especially labour and capital will flow from regions in which the rewards are low to those in which the rewards are high. For example, if the wages for labour were lower in one region than all the others, there would either be an outflow to other regions or an inflow of capital to take advantage of the low labour costs, or some combination of both. This inter-regional resource allocation provides the major growth factor.

As might be expected, *national economic growth models* have also been adopted in an explanation of the external determinants of regional growth. Richardson[10] provides an example of the use of the Harrod-Domar group of models in regional analysis. This formulation is a demand-dominated theory which explains rates of growth in terms of exogenous demand factors such as investment and exports. It is wider in scope than the export base theory, but is similarly limited by its one-sided approach and high level of aggregation.

2 A disaggregated approach

INDUSTRIAL STRUCTURE ANALYSIS—ORIGINS

Although the general growth theories recognise the importance of industrial structure in the process of regional growth, their aggregate nature often hides important industrial variations. Industry is not homogeneous and some industries grow much faster than others. Similarly, some regions grow faster than others. As industrial structure varies from region to region, it is tempting to draw the obvious conclusion that there is a causal relationship between industrial structure and regional growth. Industrial structure analysis examines this relationship.

The approach was pioneered by Jones[11] and Leser[12] in the UK and was later rediscovered and further developed by Dunn and Perloff[13] in the USA. An early UK application was by Hemming,[14] and more recently under the new title of 'shift-share analysis', the approach has enjoyed great popularity. Recent applications to British regional problems include studies by Brown,[15] Stilwell,[16] the Hunt Report on Intermediate Areas[17] and the South East Economic Planning Council.[18]

INDUSTRIAL STRUCTURE ANALYSIS—SHIFT-SHARE COMPONENTS

The approach requires an isolation of the effects of a region's industrial structure on its growth over a particular period of time. This involves the breaking down of a region's growth performance, as indicated by some representative variable (such as employment, population or income) into a number of components. The usual variable is employment, and total regional employment growth (G) can be separated out into 'shift' and 'share' components.

The 'national share' component (N) represents the amount by which regional employment would have grown if it had grown at the national rate over the study period. This is the norm for the region from which deviations can be measured.

The 'shift' component represents any deviations in regional employment growth from the national share. It is positive in prosperous growth areas and negative in relatively depressed areas. Net shift for any region can be subdivided into two components:
   the 'proportionality shift component' (P), sometimes known as the 'structural' or 'industrial mix' component, measures the amount of net regional shift attributable to the composition of industrial sectors in the region. This component would be positive in areas specialising in nationally fast-growing sectors and negative in areas specialising in nationally slow-growing or even declining sectors.
   the 'differential shift component' (D), sometimes known as the 'locational' or 'regional' component, is the remainder. It measures the amount of net regional shift resulting from specific industrial sectors growing faster or slower in the region than

nationally owing to internal locational factors. Thus, a region with locational advantages, such as good resources, would have a positive differential shift component, whereas a region with locational disadvantages would have a negative component.

These two shift components separate out the external and internal elements of regional growth, with the proportionality shift resulting from the influence of 'outside' influences operating nationally and the differential shift resulting from the influence of factors operating 'inside' the region.

In algebraic notation, the various components can be expressed as follows:

$$G_j = E_{j_t} - E_{j_o} \dots\dots\dots\dots\dots\dots\dots\dots\dots\dots\dots 1$$
$$= (N_j + P_j + D_j)$$
$$N_j = E_{jo}(E_t/E_o) - E_{j_o} \dots\dots\dots\dots\dots\dots\dots 2$$
$$(P+D)_j = E_{j_t} - (E_t/E_o)E_{j_o} \dots\dots\dots\dots\dots\dots 3$$
$$= (G_j - N_j)$$
$$P_j = \Sigma_i[(E_{i_t}/E_{io}) - (E_t/E_o)]E_{ij_o} \dots\dots\dots\dots\dots 4$$
$$D_j = \Sigma_i[E_{ij_t} - (E_{i_t}/E_{i_o})E_{ij_o}] \dots\dots\dots\dots\dots\dots 5$$
$$= (P + D)_j - (P_j)$$

where G_j, N_j, $(P + D)_j$, P_j, D_j are the total regional employment growth, national share component, net shift component and proportionality and differential shift components respectively for region 'j'.

and E_j = total employment in region 'j'
   E = total national employment
   o, t = initial and terminal time periods
   i = industry subscript.

BRITISH REGIONAL GROWTH—SHIFT-SHARE COMPONENTS

Stilwell[19] has isolated the shift and share components of regional employment growth in Britain between 1959 and 1967, using Department of Employment and Productivity statistics, and the results are presented in Table 5.1. The results show four areas of substantial absolute and percentage employment growth, with the remaining regions lagging far behind. An insight into these

Table 5.1.   *Analysis of the regional pattern of employment growth (1959–67)*

Region [a]	*Absolute increase in employment* (*in thousands and as percentage of employment in region*) *G*	*National Share* *N*	*Total Shift* *P + D*	*Proportionality Shift* *P*	*Differential Shift* *D*
South East	+ 691 (8·9)	+ 460 (5·9)	+230 (+2·9)	+251 (+3·2)	− 21 (−0·3)
South West	+ 114 (9·5)	+ 71 (5·9)	+ 44 (+3·6)	+ 3 (+0·2)	+ 41 (+3·4)
West Midlands	+ 175 (8·2)	+ 126 (5·9)	+ 49 (+2·3)	+ 29 (+1·4)	+ 20 (+0·9)
East Midlands	+ 133 (10·3)	+ 76 (5·9)	+ 57 (+4·4)	− 60 (−4·7)	+117 (+9·1)
Yorkshire and Humberside	+ 64 (3·2)	+ 116 (5·9)	− 52 (−2·6)	− 64 (−3·2)	+ 11 (+0·6)
North West	+ 25 (0·9)	+ 171 (5·9)	−146 (−5·0)	− 24 (−0·8)	−122 (−4·2)
North	+ 15 (1·2)	+ 75 (5·9)	− 60 (−4·7)	− 64 (−5·0)	+ 4 (+0·3)
Scotland	+ 28 (1·3)	+ 122 (5·9)	− 95 (−4·6)	− 40 (−1·9)	− 55 (−2·7)
Wales	+ 28 (3·0)	+ 55 (5·9)	− 27 (−2·9)	− 32 (−3·5)	+ 5 (+0·6)
Great Britain	+1272 (5·9)	+1272 (5·9)	—	—	—

a The regions used are the current Economic Planning Regions with the exception that East Anglia is included in the South-East Region for statistical comparability over the study period.

SOURCE: Stilwell, F. J. B., Regional Growth and Structural Adaptation, *Urban Studies*, June 1969.

growth variations is provided by the identification of the shift and share components using the approach outlined in the previous section.

For example, in the prosperous South East, only two-thirds of the regional employment growth (G) is explained by the national share component (N). The remaining positive deviation of 230 000 must be explained by the shift components $(P + D)$. Indeed it is more than explained by the proportionality shift component (P) only, which suggests that the main reason for the growth in the South East is its industrial mix with the specialisation in nationally growing industries,* such as services and electronics. The negative differential shift component (230 000–251 000) suggests in fact that certain locational factors in the South East, perhaps congestion, are actually inhibiting the growth potential reflected in the industrial mix.

Another region with a negative differential shift component is the North West, but unlike the South East it is not offset by a favourable industrial structure, and this is reflected in the poor growth performance of the region between 1959–67. The only other region experiencing a negative differential shift component is Scotland—no doubt influenced by its relative isolation. In contrast, six of the nine regions have negative proportionality shift components, reflecting the overwhelming dominance of the South East with regard to possession of growth industries.

AN APPRAISAL OF THE APPROACH

There has recently been much discussion on the relative merits of the approach (see: Stilwell, Buck[20]). It is now generally accepted that industrial structure analysis is not in itself a theory of regional growth. This would require a fuller explanation of the underlying factors influencing the two shifts—why do some

* By way of example, if the South-East economy was dependent on two industries only: A, employing 5 million people at the beginning of the period, and B, employing 3 million, and both were growing faster than the national rate of approximately 6%, A at 8% and B at 11%, then from Equation (4), the proportionality shift component would be:

$$= \Sigma\,[\,(8\% - 6\%)5\mathrm{m} + (11\% - 6\%)3\mathrm{m}\,]$$
$$= (100\ 000 + 150\ 000)$$
$$= 250\ 000$$

industries grow faster than others nationally and what are the location factors encouraging an industry to grow faster in one region than another? It is indeed doubtful whether such a dis-aggregated approach, considering a wide variety of regions and industrial sectors, could in fact be easily handled in the form of a theory.

There is also some scepticism about its value in other rôles, such as the description, analysis and prediction of regional growth and its general use as a guide to regional policy. This results from fundamental criticisms of some of the basic concepts of the approach. Mackay[21] and Buck[22] question whether the proportionality and differential shifts truly reflect the relative influences of industrial-mix and locational factors in a region. Because of industry interdependence in the regional economy, the proportionality shift may be underestimated. For example, a depressed region with a below average representation of national growth industries will also have less of the auxiliary industries supplying the growth industries, and consequently part of the negative differential shift may be traced back to industrial structure. The proportionality shift may also be underestimated owing to the non-homogeneity of industry groups. Thus, demand for particular models of cars made on Merseyside may be growing faster than the demand for cars nationally, and hence the application of national car industry growth rates to the Merseyside sub-region may underestimate the proportionality shift. In addition, differential shift may also be distorted by the impact of factors such as the positive induce-ments and the negative controls of regional policy.

Industrial structure analysis is also highly sensitive to the level of aggregation of data input. Analysis of employment growth by the finer Minimum List Headings (MLH) will usually reveal a larger proportionality shift than analysis at the SIC order level, and Buck presents empirical evidence to illustrate this in the North West Region.[23] The analysis is also sensitive to the base year of the data input. The proportionality shift reflects the relative industrial specialisation of the region at the beginning of the study period. It takes no account of the change in the industry mix of the region over the study period.

A final criticism concerns the policy implications to be drawn from the analysis. It has sometimes been assumed that a region with poor differential effects would benefit from improved locational advantages, such as better infrastructure, and that a region with poor proportionality effects requires an injection of new growth industry. But this mechanical relationship to policy is an over-simplification, for a region with poor differential effects could also benefit from new industry, as could the region with poor proportionality effects benefit from improved infrastructure.

Despite this barrage of problems, the approach still has much to commend it. Although not a growth theory, it does complement the other more formal theories emphasising the relationship between industrial structure and regional growth, and separating out the internal and external elements of that growth. Its industrial emphasis suggests a particular affinity to the sector theory and export base theory approaches. Certain modifications and assumptions can also maintain the approach as a useful method of analysis. The assumption that the proportionality shift represents only a minimum estimate of the influence of industrial structure; the recognition that the level of data aggregation is to some extent dependent on the scale of region to be investigated; and the inclusion of a 'proportionality modification shift'[24] to accommodate the impact of time on the industrial structure counter some of the major problems.

3 Regional Growth—convergence or divergence?

A question of some importance to the regional planner is whether regional growth is convergent or divergent. Will the gaps between the prosperous and the depressed regions widen or narrow over time? Some of the regional growth theories outlined suggest that regional imbalance may be self-righting, thus reducing the need for intervention. The sector theory suggests that the scope for internal resource reallocation is greater in the poorer agrarian regions than in the more developed regions, eventually leading to a convergence of regional prosperity. Similarly, the factor flows of the inter-regional trade models also suggest convergence of regional per capita income. The development of diseconomies of scale may also limit the growth of the prosperous areas. In practice however, convergence trends may be limited by the immobility of factor movements between sectors and regions, and the failure of diseconomies to have impact on the growth of the prosperous regions. Thus, if regional balance is an objective, policies to improve factor mobility would be necessary.

One final hybrid group of regional growth theories which clearly recognise that regional growth may be divergent rather than convergent are the *centre–periphery* theories of Hirschman,[25] Friedman[26] and Myrdal.[27] The general argument of such theories can be simply illustrated by comparing the relative fortune of two regions, *A* and *B*. Region *A* initially develops faster than Region *B* because it possesses a variety of natural and/or man-made advantages. However, contrary to many growth theories, this divergence may not be self-righting and indeed the process may be cumulative with the 'rich getting richer and the poor getting poorer', or using Myrdal's biblical quotation:

'for unto everyone that hath shall be given, and he shall have abundance, but from him that hath not shall be taken away even, that which he hath.' (St. Matthew xxv. v 29).

Myrdal explains this process of *cumulative causation* in terms of the relative strength of *spread* and *backwash* effects. The spread effects are those forces favouring convergence between the rich and poor regions. As the rich region grows it may demand more products from the poor region thus stimulating its growth. Similarly, outmigration of factors from the poor region may induce a more efficient use of resources, with the internal reallocation from low wage to high wage/high productivity sectors generating growth. Diseconomies of scale may also set in in the prosperous region. However, Myrdal believed that such spread effects will invariably be more than offset by backwash effects. The increased demand for peripheral goods resulting from an increase in the prosperity of the centre may not materialise if the peripheral goods are primarily agricultural goods with a low income elasticity of demand. In addition, the selective outmigration of capital and skilled labour from the poor region to the rich may do more harm than good, reducing the ability of the poor region to compete, Finally, as already mentioned, the diseconomies of the rich region have also little impact being offset by other economic and socio-psychological benefits ('better the devil we know . . .'!).

The centre–periphery theories with their emphasis on cumulative causation and divergent regional growth provide a valuable insight into the growth process, bringing together many of the elements of the other theories. They also have important policy implications for if the economic growth process is not self-equilibrating there may be need for government intervention to help the poorer regions. The initiative may come from within the problem region. In Britain, the strength of the Northern Region lobby has had some impact on government intervention in the region. Similarly, at the sub-regional level, the political opposition of North East Lancashire to Central Lancashire New Town, has brought Intermediate Area status and large-scale public investment in the infrastructure of the area in an attempt to break out of the 'vicious circle' of stagnation. However, a history of economic backwardness may so debilitate the poor region that there is a failure to perceive economic opportunities and the whole socio-political structure becomes incompatible with rapid regional growth. In such a situation, the initiative may have to come directly from the central government.

4 Summary

Regional growth is a product of many factors, some internal to the region, others external. The complexity of this variety of economic and socio-political factors, makes the formulation of a single, generally accepted and comprehensive regional growth theory very difficult. The simple aggregate models, such as the sector theory and export base theory are only partial attempts. The new generation of macro-economic models offer an interesting development but as yet have limitations as explanatory tools of the process of regional growth. In this situation, there does seem to be a case for considering approaches, which although of limited theoretical pedigree, do attempt to identify some of the underlying internal and external determinants of inter-regional differences in regional growth in a simple but comprehensive framework. Industrial structure analysis is such an approach which, in spite of its weaknesses, is of considerable practical value in examining variations in regional growth. Finally, the concept of cumulative causation suggests that the inter-regional differences may not be self-righting, at least in the short run. Even if they do eventually converge over a longer period, the hardship in the poorer regions in the intervening period may necessitate some form of intervention.

References

1 Hilhorst, J., *Regional Development Theory: An Attempt to Synthesize,* Institute of Social Studies, The Hague (1967).
2 Siebert, H., *Regional Economic Growth: Theory and Policy,* International Textbook Co., Pennsylvania (1969).
3 Clark, C., *The Conditions of Economic Progress,* London Macmillan (1940); Fisher, G. B., Production, Primary, Secondary and Tertiary, *Economic Record,* **15,** June 1939.
4 Hoover, E. M., and Fisher, J., Research in Regional Economic Growth, Universities—National Bureau Committee for Economic Research, *Problems in the Study of Economic Growth,* N.Y., Chapter V (1949).
5 See: Richardson, H. W., *Regional Economics,* Chapter 13, Weidenfeld and Nicolson (1969).
6 Romans, J. T., *Capital Exports and Growth among U.S. Regions,* Wesleyan University Press (1969).
7 North, D. C., Location theory and regional economic growth, *Journal of Political Economy,* **63,** pages 243–58 (1955).
8 Tiebout, C. M., Exports and Regional Economic Growth, *Journal of Political Economy,* **64** (1956). Reply by North, D.C. and Rejoinder by Tiebout, C. M., **64.**
9 Ohlin, B., *Inter-regional and International Trade,* Cambridge, Mass. (1933).
10 Richardson, H. W., *op cit.*
11 *Report of the Royal Commission on the Distribution of the Industrial Population* (Cmnd. 6153), Appendix II, London (1940).
12 Leser, C. E. V., *Some Aspects of the Industrial Structure of Scotland,* Univ. of Glasgow, Dept. of Social and Econ. Research, Occ. Paper V (University of Glasgow) (1951).
13 Perloff, H. S., Dunn, E. S., Lampard, E. E., and Muth, R. F., *Regions, Resources and Economic Growth,* Resources for the Future Inc., Johns Hopkins Press, Baltimore (1960).
14 Hemming, F. W., The Regional Problem, *Nat. Inst. Econ. Review,* August 1963.

15 Brown, A. J., Regional problems and regional policy, *Nat. Inst. Econ. Review,* November 1968.
16 Stilwell, F. J. B., Regional Growth and Structural Adaptation, *Urban Studies,* June 1969.
17 *Report of the Committee on the Intermediate Areas* (The Hunt Report), Cmnd. 3998, London, HMSO (1969).
18 South-East Economic Planning Council, *South-East Kent Study,* Economic Planning Council, London (1969).
19 Stilwell, F. J. B., *op cit.*
20 See: Buck, T. W., Shift and Share Analysis—A Guide to Regional Policy?, *Regional Studies,* 4, 4, pages 445–8 (1970); also Stilwell, F. J. B., Further Thoughts on the Shift and Share Approach, *Regional Studies,* 4, 4, pages 451–8.
21 Mackay, D. I., Industrial Structure and Regional Growth: A Methodological Problem, *Scottish Journal of Political Economy,* XV, June 1968.
22 Buck, T. W., *op cit.*
23 Buck, T. W., *op cit.*
24 Stilwell, F. J. B., Regional Growth and Structural Adaptation, *op cit.*
25 Hirschman, A. O., *The Strategy of Economic Development,* Yale (1958).
26 Friedmann, J., *Regional Development Policy: A Case Study of Venezuela,* MIT Press (1967).
27 Myrdal, G., *Economic Theory and Underdeveloped Regions,* Duckworths (1957).

B. Intra-regional Analysis

6 The location of industry

A knowledge of the 'laws' underlying regional structure is essential if the regional planner is to predict the reaction of particular areas to particular pressures and policies. Interference in the existing patterns of activity within a region is of fundamental importance in structuring economic opportunities, and regional development strategies are invariably expressed in terms of patterns of relative locations. The location of industry is of particular importance and provides a useful starting point for an explanation of the internal structure of regions.

1 Location of industry: theory and practice

Production involves the use of inputs—factors of production—to produce output—goods and services—as efficiently as possible. The location of the unit of production, the firm, will obviously be determined in relation to the source of the inputs and the market for the output. The various factors of production—land, labour, capital and enterprise—plus the market factor, thus constitute primary determinants of location. These factors can of course be refined into more specific determinants such as the quality and quantity of labour, the geographical location of a site and the availability of the necessary infrastructure. Other determinants, such as central and local govenment policy and behavioural factors can also be added. There have been two main approaches to the study of these factors of industrial location—one theoretical and the other empirical. This divergence reflects the difference of approach between the economist with his love of abstract theories and the geographer with his concern for empirical study and generalisation from real world situations.

The theoretical approach attempts to abstract from reality, constructing an all-embracing system of 'pure' rules. The search is for a general theory of industrial location, which can explain the existing structure of industrial location and changes in that structure.

The empirical approach involves the listing of factors which might be important, together with examples of situations where they have in fact been important, in the location of particular industries. There is usually little or no attempt to formulate such factors into a general theory, and hence this approach is generally limited to the provision of a descriptive picture. Unfortunately the two approaches have developed independently with little attempt at reconciliation. This chapter will first consider the theoretical approach, and then attempt to marry it into the general complexities of the real world.

2 Industrial location theory

The major work on industrial location theory has been carried out by economists attempting to integrate location into the main body of economic theory—in particular, into the 'theory of the firm'. However, location is concerned with spatial relationships, and this has over time also attracted the attention of numerous geographers. The resulting contributions have aimed at providing an all-embracing system of 'pure rules' of location, attempting to derive the 'optimum location' for the individual firm. But such a goal is very difficult to achieve when one considers:

a the wide range of industry—including the primary sector, such as mining and quarrying; the secondary sector with a multitude of manufacturing industries, the tertiary sector with rapidly growing service trades, and the so-called 'quaternary sector'— composed of high expertise information based industries;

b the wide variety of firms, each with its own input combination and market characteristics, within each industry.

Forerunners of the theoretical approach include Adam Smith, Ricardo, Von Thünen and Mill, but here the outline will be limited to post-1900 developments. Even within this context, space restricts analysis to a very limited number of the numerous contributions on the subject. The analysis is structured around three approaches to industrial location theory:

a the *least cost approach*, which attempts to explain location in terms of the minimisation of factor costs;

b *market area analysis*, where there is more emphasis on the demand, or market factors;

c *the profit maximisation approach*—the logical outcome of the other two.

These three 'umbrella' approaches provide a useful framework for the analysis of the theoretical approach to industrial location, although they are by no means mutually exclusive.

The differences in approaches can be clearly illustrated by using the recent work of Smith,[1] who seeks to synthesise the various theoretical statements to produce an approach of more practical relevance. Smith's diagrams (Figure 6.1) present cost-price situations in a simplified and very useful way. Assuming a profit maximisation objective, the most profitable location for a firm will be where total revenue exceeds total cost by the greatest amount. Figure 6.1 shows three examples of how cost and revenue curves for the individual firm might vary according to location. Profitable locations lie between points *A* and *B*, and *O* is the optimum point. The historical evolution of the three approaches will now be considered in a little more detail.

THE LEAST COST APPROACH

Alfred Weber[2] (1909) was the first person to work up a comprehensive theory of industrial location—although many of his ideas had been partially formulated by another German, Launhardt, some 20 years earlier. Weber's basic principle was that a businessman would choose a location where his costs were least. For the purposes of his model, he made the following simplifying assumptions:

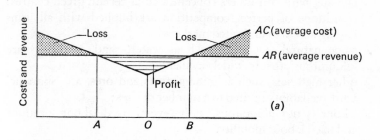

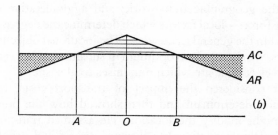

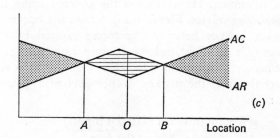

Fig. 6.1 Optimum locations (re profitability to firm) in different cost-price situations—assuming constant output

SOURCE   D. M. Smith, 'A theoretical framework for geographical studies of industrial location', *Economic Geography*, **42** (2), (1966).

a the unit of study is a single isolated country, homogeneous in climate, with consumers concentrated at certain given centres; conditions of perfect competition are implied with all firms having access to unlimited markets;

b some natural resources, such as water, sand, and clays are 'ubiquitous', that is, widely available;

c other materials, such as mineral fuels and ores, are 'sporadic' with availability limited to a number of sites;

d labour is not ubiquitous, with several fixed labour locations and fixed labour mobility.

Within these assumptions, Weber believed three factors influenced industrial location. These are transport costs and labour costs—general regional factors which determine the fundamental location pattern and the geographic framework; and agglomerative or deglomerative forces—local factors which determine the degree of dispersion within the general framework. The locational objective for the businessman involves an optimum in substitution between these factors, selecting a site which minimises total costs.

Weber first considered the impact of transport costs, the primary location determinant and then showed how the other two factors might modify the location. He assumed transport costs to be directly proportional to distance moved and weight carried. Thus the point of least transport costs is that at which the total weight movement of assembling inputs and distributing output is at a minimum. He illustrated the concept using his famous *locational triangle*, (see Figure 6.2*a*), where the optimum location (T) is a balance between the forces exerted by the material sources (M_1 and M_2) and the consumption point (C). To indicate whether the optimum location was closer to the source of materials or to the market, Weber devised a *material index*, which is:

$$\frac{\text{(Weight of Local Material Inputs)}}{\text{(Weight of Final Products)}}$$

If the index was greater than one, the firm was material oriented; if the index was less than one, it was market oriented.

Labour costs, the second location factor, can attract a firm to a location other than the least transport cost if the savings in labour costs per unit of output are greater than the extra transport

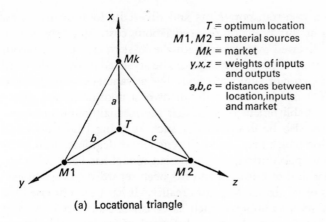

T = optimum location
M1, M2 = material sources
Mk = market
y,x,z = weights of inputs and outputs
a,b,c = distances between location,inputs and market

(a) Locational triangle

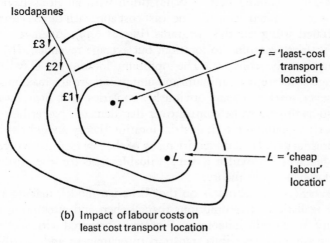

Isodapanes

T = 'least-cost transport location'

L = 'cheap labour locatior'

(b) Impact of labour costs on least cost transport location

Fig. 6.2 The Weber 'least-cost' approach

costs per unit involved. This is illustrated in Figure 6.2*b*, where T is the point of least transport costs and the contour lines, *isodapanes*, show the increase in unit transport costs away from this point. L is a labour market where labour costs are £2 per unit less than that at T. As L is within the critical £2 isodapane, the firm would, other things being equal, substitute between transport costs and non-transport costs and divert its location to a new location at this point of reduced labour cost. Similarly, a firm may be diverted away from both the least transport and labour cost locations if cost economies can be achieved through the third location factor of agglomeration. The advantages of agglomeration might include the development of a pool of skilled labour and the establishment of specialist services, although of course there may also be diseconomies such as rising land prices and congestion which may eventually encourage deglomeration.

Since its publication, the Weberian model has been subjected to a great deal of criticism and has been regarded as very 'noisy' in terms of its abstraction from reality.[3] It has been criticised for some of its assumptions, such as constant transport costs and production costs, and for its disregard of institutional factors, such as government policy. But in particular, the model is very one-sided, assuming perfect competition with all firms having access to unlimited demand. The least cost approach can be clearly illustrated using Smith's diagrams (Figure 6.1a). Average cost (AC) varies according to location, but average revenue (AR) is assumed to be constant. The optimum location is O where average costs are at a minimum and unit profits are at a maximum. However, market demand obviously also varies, with firms locating so as to gain some control over that demand. Nevertheless, Weber's contribution to industrial location theory should not be underestimated. He did identify many of the key factors involved and his work provides a very valuable base for the further development of the theory.

Hoover[4] (1948) elaborates on the Weberian model, making far more realistic cost assumptions than Weber, and attempting to modify some of the inherent weaknesses. Compared with Weber, Hoover divides costs into transport (procurement and distribution) and production, each of which is analysed in a more detailed and realistic way. For example, transport costs are not directly proportional to distance and weight as Weber assumed, but may vary according to the length and direction of haul and the composition of the goods involved. Hoover also gives more emphasis to institutional factors, such as local taxes, which may have a considerable impact on locational decisions. He also mentions market areas, but only from an assumed location, and his concern is much more with cost than with demand. Thus, although Hoover's approach is more one of location within a capitalist economy compared with Weber's general theory, it still remains firmly within the least cost approach.

MARKET AREA ANALYSIS

One of the fundamental weaknesses of the least cost approach is the overemphasis of the input side (cost minimisation), and the underemphasis of the output or demand side, simply assuming that the firm can sell all it produces wherever it locates. But the market is a variable. Buyers are scattered over a wide area and the intensity of demand varies from place to place. Firms will seek to gain access to the market and serve the greatest demand. The market may therefore be a major location determinant, perhaps overriding the least-cost location, and its rôle in industrial location has been analysed by serveral scholars.

Lösch[5] realised that the optimum location is the place of maximum profits, where revenue exceeds costs by the largest amount. However, a theoretical formulation of this optimum is very complex. As such Lösch to some extent compromises, and in *The Economics of Location* (1954) attempts to incorporate demand into the theory by considering the optimum size of the market. On the basis of the following assumptions:

a no spatial variations in the distribution of factor inputs—raw materials, labour and capital—over a homogeneous plain;

b uniform population densities and constant tastes;

c no locational interdependence between firms;

he considered a fixed individual producer, a farmer, producing beer, and attempted to determine his market area and market revenue.

For the analysis, Lösch uses and adapts a simple demand curve. (Figure 6.3). At the centre of the market area near to the farm (*P*), the unit price of beer is *OP*, with demand *PQ*. Further from the centre (*R*), extra distribution costs result in a higher price, *OR*, and demand falls to *RS*. At the far extremities of the market area, extra distribution costs are prohibitive, pushing up the price to *OF*, and demand is nil. If the shaded quadrant, *FPQ*, is now rotated around the axis, *PQ*—*P* being the farm at the centre of the market, a 'demand cone' is produced (Figure 6.3). The base of the cone represents the market area, the height represents the quantity sold at any one point, and the volume represents the total revenue from the market demand. In time, if beer production is profitable, other farmers will develop their own circular market areas, which, according to Lösch, will finally adjust into a series of hexagonal market areas covering the entire plain.

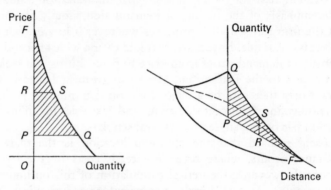

Figure 6.3. Löschian Demand Curve and Cone

But this is the other side of the coin to the Weberian approach and equally one-sided. For by assuming no spatial variations in the distribution of factor inputs, Lösch eliminates spatial cost variations. Thus, where Weber neglects demand in his attempt to find the least cost location, Lösch neglects input supply, and the optimum location is primarily a function of market demand. The overall approach can be seen in Figure 6.1*b* where average revenue (AR) varies according to location, but average cost (AC) is assumed to be constant. Optimum location is at O, where average revenue is at a maximum.

There have been several attempts to modify some of Lösch's assumptions in an attempt to create a more realistic model. Richardson[6] is particularly concerned with the limiting assumption of a uniform population density. Densities do of course vary, being high in urban areas and low in rural areas. Demand and potential sales revenue will therefore vary markedly from place to place. Harris[7] shows the variation in market demand between different locations in the USA, using a simple index of gravitational potential, as outlined in Chapter 2.

THE PROFIT MAXIMISING APPROACH

The *least cost* and *market area* approaches are both one-sided, although in different ways—holding either the input supply or market demand constant. In practice, both costs and revenue vary with location and the optimum location is the one which yields the greatest profit. Figure 6.1*c* conceptualises the approach, showing both cost and revenue varying with location. In such a situation, the optimum, profit-maximising location may be neither the least cost nor the maximum revenue location. Recent theorists, Isard[8] and Greenhut[9] in particular, have attempted to remould the Löschian approach into a more profit-maximising approach. (However, the idea is not at all new. Loria, an Italian, suggested that industrialists seek locations that will give them maximum profits, considering both markets and costs, in 1884. But, owing to Weber's influence, the least cost approach dominated early twentieth-century thinking.) However, as Lösch concluded, there are problems in deriving the profit-maximising location.

There is firstly the question of *locational interdependence*. In the typical modern oligopoly structure, a major location determinant for an individual firm is the location and markets of like firms. Firms manoeuvre to control or share competitors' markets ('follow the crowd'). This is very difficult to incorporate into a theory as it involves a consideration of not only what rivals have done, but what they might do in the future. Nevertheless, several theorists, such as Hotelling[10] and Greenhut[11] have suggested certain general rules. Perhaps a possible approach in this area of uncertainty lies in the use of game theory[12].

A second problem is the difficulty of evaluating the relevant variables. In practice, the determination of the profit-maximising location is difficult and involved. Major areas of difficulty are the evaluation of differing costs in differing locations, differing market conditions and the policy of rival firms. Hence most locations may be sub-optimal, and the Weber least cost location may be more common in reality than it should rationally be if profit maximisation was the locational criterion.

The impact of large modern corporations[13] constitutes a third problem. It is difficult to incorporate large concerns such as ICI and Unilever into location theory as they contain a wide variety of plants which may originally have located for reasons independent of the present concern. They may also produce a wide variety of products, not all of which can be produced at one optimum location.

The fourth problem raises the evergreen question of whether firms actually do 'maximise' profits. For a state concern, an 'adequate' return on public money with some consideration of social costs and benefits may be more important than maximum returns. Alternative aims have also been suggested for non-state concerns. Firms may have philanthropic motives (but with profit maximising undertones?). They may only maximise in the long run or concentrate more on maximising turnover (equating revenue with the ego of the management?). Simon[14] suggests that firms are 'satisficers' seeking locations giving a satisfactory level or profits and growth, and that the difference between optimising and 'satisficing' is similar to 'the difference between searching a haystack to find the sharpest needle in it and searching the haystack to find a needle sharp enough to sew with'.

The fifth and final problem introduces the long neglected subject of behavioural factors. To consider only the simple mechanical factors so far discussed is to deny that man is human. Behavioural factors, such as the businessman's attitude to the troubled labour conditions of certain areas, or his attitude to the 'social life' of 'the North' compared with that of 'the South', may play an important rôle in industrial location. Certainly if, as Figure 6.1c shows, profit may vary little over quite a large area (A to B), then a firm may locate within fairly wide limits without too much concern. Within these limits, other factors, especially behavioural factors, may become relatively more important. There is certainly a growing awareness of the importance of these factors and Pred has attempted to structure them presenting 'a verbal formalisation of the fairly obvious'.[15]

In summary, there have been several theoretical approaches to the complex problem of industrial location. Each has something to contribute to the general body of theory, providing a valuable insight into the relevant locational factors. But there are also several problems. In particular, there are the problems of formulating a general theory for a wide variety of industries and firms, the problem of searching for an 'optimum' rather than a 'satisfactory' location, and the various problems of the profit-maximising approach outlined above.

3 Industrial location in practice

To accept that a businessman will fall in with a plan based solely on the concepts of location theory may be very misleading. More subjective criteria may be important. Hence, if bad location decisions are to be avoided, it is necessary to examine location determinants in practice. Clark[16] illustrates the importance of location decisions quoting an American researcher in Chicago who found that 20 location decisions by major retailers would control the location of 20 000 other retailers for the next twenty-five years.

THE CONTEXT OF LOCATION/THE LOCATION PROBLEM

The location problem must be faced not only by new firms seeking their first site, but also by established firms relocating. That new firms face a location decision is self-evident. That established firms must also face locations decisions is perhaps less obvious. The relocation of an established firm can result from pressures both internal and external to the firm. Several studies[17] have shown that the main *internal* pressure comes from growth in output, which itself imposes pressure on the existing location, in particular on the limited floorspace. However a decline in output with a subsequent rise in unit fixed costs may also sometimes encourage a reduction in floorspace and a move to smaller premises. *External* pressures may come from a variety of sources: from other firms bidding up the price of labour, or perhaps from the government with its local planning controls and national taxation policies.

Faced with these pressures, most firms would first investigate whether or not their existing site could be used more efficiently, perhaps by an increase in shift working. If the pressures are too great, there are several options open to the firm. It may do nothing, forgoing the increase in output, or it may possibly increase the amount of sub-contract work put out. It may also choose to relocate. If the decision is taken to move, involving either the entire firm, or as is more common, merely a branch of the parent concern, a new site must be chosen, and this choice involves a consideration of several general location factors.

THE CHOICE OF A NEW LOCATION/GENERAL FACTORS AFFECTING INDUSTRIAL LOCATION

Location factors are difficult to quantify, varying from firm to firm, and are difficult to rank in any order of importance. For many large-scale capital intensive projects, such as steelworks or oil refineries, physical location factors may be of overriding importance. For many others—particularly those involving factory processes—physical considerations are less important, and the analysis here is mainly concerned with these. There have been several surveys[18] of mobile firms seeking to identify the major location factors, and they seem to suggest the following as major categories:

a Labour—quality and quantity;
b Transport and communications;
c Site and premises;
d Government aid;
e Environmental factors—in the widest sense.

The first two factors influence variable costs, whereas the third factor is concerned with capital costs. Government policy may affect both cost categories. The final factor may also affect costs, but is more concerned with attitudes.

Labour—quality and quantity. Most research indicates that labour availability is the most important single factor. This does not necessarily equate with high levels of unemployment. Indeed long dole queues, with their degrading effect on labour morale, may be more of a deterrent than an attraction. Firms however, are particularly concerned with local competition for the labour supply and the quality of that supply. Many firms show a preference for small localities where there is sufficient labour for their immediate requirements and anticipated build-up, but not enough to attract other firms into the area. Such firms, by becoming the principal employer in a locality, hope to keep labour turnover to a minimum. Other firms on the contrary, for advantages of linkage, prefer to be close to other establishments. The quality of labour is particularly important. This does not necessarily mean a large supply of trained labour, for inbred skills may often be more of a hindrance than a help. However, a large supply of adaptable, trainable labour is particularly attractive, especially if complemented by the existence of local training facilities. With the rapid growth in light industry, a large supply of female labour is at a special premium.

Contrary to expectations wage rates tend to be of only marginal importance as a location factor in Britain. This is partly because collective national union agreements tend to standardise rates and make any wage advantage only short term, and also because lower wage rates often equate with lower productivity. The history of labour relations on the other hand, is a factor of increasing importance. Once an area has established a bad reputation for labour relations it is very difficult to shake off, and this can have a deterrent effect on new industry.

Transport and Communications. Transport factors are usually regarded as major locational determinants. Yet certain studies tend to query this. The Toothill Report on the Scottish Economy,[19] from a survey of firms operating on industrial estates in Scotland, showed that more than half of the firms had total transport costs not above 2% of turnover. But despite this evidence (and it may be somewhat biassed relating to firms that have actually moved to distant locations and which could therefore be assumed to have low transport costs) it remains true that many firms are still strongly influenced by communications. One only needs to witness the pressure on industrial sites close to the motorway network to illustrate the point, at a local level.

A location giving good access to the main markets is still important. A remote location may involve two drivers and an overnight stop for a distribution journey—hence increasing costs. In addition, and perhaps more important, rush orders may be more difficult to meet on time, which may encourage consumers to buy elsewhere, hence revenue also suffers. A location giving good access to linked producers is also important. If the firm is a branch concern, this would allow the minimisation of transport costs between the parent factory and the branch and easier executive control by main plant management. Good access by road, rail and air also reduces the feeling of geographical isolation of a relocated plant.

Site and premises. Although land cost may be a major cost item in the initial setting up of a firm, it becomes much less important when costed over a long period and may be relatively insignificant in determining choice between comparable sites, although of course it may rule out certain very expensive locations. The provision of a wide variety of ready-built factories on fully serviced sites, facilitating immediate production and minimum 'teething' problems, can be a more important factor. Factory rents for similar properties in similar locations do not vary too markedly; although certain areas with a supply of old, but sound, industrial accommodation (such as Lancashire with its legacy of cotton mills 'built to last') may be able to offer 'cut price' rentals. However even such premises may constitute a 'mixed blessing' in that they hinder the efficiency and constrain the innovative spirit of the occupant firms.

Government aid. Many countries now seek to actively divert industry to particular problem regions using a wide variety of measures. These measures emanating from a variety of sources at national, regional and local levels can have a major impact on a firm's location and will be briefly outlined here prior to a more detailed discussion in Chapter 9. The UK has a long history of 'carrot and stick' incentives administered by central government. The positive incentives, including capital cost grants, subsidies to variable costs via measures such as the Regional Employment Premium, and numerous tax and depreciation allowances, appear quite generous bait. But a recent costing by Professor Wilson[20] suggests that they may represent no more than 5% of a firm's total costs. In Eire, the Shannon Free Airport Scheme provides a rather different example of government aid.

Under this scheme, firms operating for export markets can import and export without customs restrictions, and also benefit from investment grants and tax exemptions on export profits. Such measures have obviously played a major rôle in the rapid development of this area of South West Eire in recent years.

Aid at the local level is more organisational than financial. Local help, with regard to matters such as housing requirements and planning permission, can be a real factor in the choice between alternative locations. In addition many local authorities band together to sponsor regional scale industrial development associations, each seeking to lure the limited supply of mobile industry to its own constituent authorities through a combination of publicity campaigns, industrial promotion and political pressure. Some development associations, such as those for North East and North West England have had considerable success, despite the inherent difficulties of selling their regions. An official of the North West Industrial Development Association summed up the problem and the rôle of the association as follows:

'To sell a region is a very difficult task. The main functions of an association like the North West Industrial Development Association in the field of industrial development are to smooth the path of expanding firms by having the right information available, and the right contracts, to advise on locations where the firms have not already made up their minds and to emphasise the advantages of the region to those people from outside whose impressions of Lancashire are still dominated by Coronation Street and the paintings of L. S. Lowry.'[21]

Environmental factors. If economic criteria suggest a limited number of satisfactory locations, environmental factors may come into play in deciding the final choice. The factors considered may be simply the climate and landscape or perhaps the wider concept of the total environment. Climate and landscape appear to be of growing importance as location determinants. This is particularly true for the new lighter industries—such as computers, electronics and research establishments—which are less constrained by raw materials and transport factors. Such industries are prospering in the Californian sun; in Britain, locations in the South West, South Hampshire and perhaps the periphery of the Lake District may be equally attractive.

But climate and landscape are only part of the total environment which help to determine the 'quality of life'. Other major determinants include the quality of the social infrastructure—housing, schools, roads and town centres—and also various social and psychological factors. The latter have been entertainingly discussed by Eversley,[22] who suggests that businessmen prefer the 'good life' of the South, with its good schools, clubs, shops, theatres and common accent, fearing that many of these social attributes may not exist in other areas. As the divorce between business ownership and management grows, and the maximisation of profits perhaps diminishes in importance in management priorities it would appear likely that these environmental factors will become of increasing importance.

Finally, it should be noted that many of the locational determinants discussed here depend on 'agglomeration economies' derived not from a specific geographical position but from the stimulus given by a concentration of firms. Advantages of such a concentration might include the provision of a skilled labour pool, the greater availability of local ancillary industry and improved social infrastructure—such as educational and entertainment facilities.

EMPIRICAL STUDIES

The location factors outlined are those commonly listed in surveys of mobile firms. For example, in a survey by Cameron and Reid,[23] 18 firms, which considered a Scottish location but then decided to locate elsewhere, were given a list of location factors and asked to rank them in order of importance and to compare them with the facilities of their chosen site. The results in Table 6.1 clearly emphasise the factors already discussed.

Of course, the relative importance of location factors varies from industry to industry and firm to firm and there have been numerous specific studies. Cameron and Clark[24] have attempted a classification of industry and location factors into a limited number of categories. From a sample survey of mobile firms, they identified several location types varying from small market

Table 6.1. *Location Factors: An Empirical Study*—factors effecting the rejection of Scotland as a production location by 18 firms. The factors are ranked in order of importance to the industrialists and are compared with the facilities at the chosen site.

| Main location category | Location factor | Ranking | Compared with selected site | | | $\dfrac{(A+B)}{(B+C)}$ |
			Better A	Same B	Worse C	
Labour	1 Supply of trained labour	8	3	6	2	9/8
	2 Supply of trainable labour	1	2	9	2	11/11
	3 Low labour rates	—	1	6	4	7/10
	4 High productivity of local labour	16	2	5	4	7/9
	5 Good local management relations	5	1	3	7	4/11
Geographical location	6 Access to main markets	2	2	—	14	2/14
	7 Access to main suppliers	12	—	2	15	2/17
	8 Access to linked producers	8	—	3	11	3/14
Factory/Site	9 Ready built factories	5	—	2	6	2/8
	10 Factory rents	8	2	5	1	7/6
	11 Fully serviced site	5	1	4	2	5/6
Local Services	12 Transport facilities for goods	4	—	5	8	5/13
	13 Transport facilities for personnel	12	1	7	4	8/11
	14 Local technical education facilities	12	2	6	1	8/7
Environment	15 Attractiveness of local environment for transferred key workers and executives	8	2	2	5	4/7
Agency	16 Local authority co-operation	2	1	9	—	10/9
co-operation	17 Local agency co-operation	12	1	9	—	10/9

NB: Government inducements ignored as they are generally in a standard form in each development area.

SOURCE: Adapted from Cameron, G. C., and Reid, G. L. *Scottish Economic Planning and the Attraction of Industry*, University of Glasgow Social and Economic Studies, Occ. Paper number 6, Oliver and Boyd, Edinburgh (1966), pages 15–17.

oriented firms, often retail or wholesale concerns, which were mainly attracted by ready-built factories and access to the parent concern, to companies establishing divisions or large branches, which were more concerned with labour, transport and government aid factors.

LOCATION FACTORS IN THE FUTURE

As with most things, location factors change over time. The growth of light industry may result in a decline in the importance of proximity to markets and supplies. Similarly, improvements in transport and communications are also likely to make movement over larger distances more acceptable, with the emphasis changing from 'how far' to 'how long'. The capital intensive nature of new industry may also diminish the power of attraction of the labour factor. On the other hand, with increased automation and rationalisation and more space intensive processes, sites and premises are likely to become of increasing importance. Further, for the new quaternary industry and office employment freed by new developments in telecommunications and data transmission, the environmental advantages of new locations may outweigh the environmental consequences of congested conurbations.

4 Summary

This analysis of industrial location factors in theory and practice illustrates the divergence between the two approaches but also isolates certain factors of fundamental importance. The key elements in location theory—transport, labour, agglomeration and market factors—are all seen to be of importance in practice, setting the basic parameters to any location decision. But practice suggests that there are also behavioural and institutional factors, difficult to quantify in a simple model, which may also influence location decisions within the framework provided by the other factors. Hamilton combines these various influences in diagrammatic form, as illustrated in Figure 6.4

All this is of considerable importance to the regional planner. It provides him with a valuable insight into the economic structure of regions. It also provides him with basic information for future planning, and a starting point for the identification of suitable industrial locations and the formulation of inducements to attract firms to them. Thus, the industrial revitalisation of an area may require a restructuring of certain factors—an improvement of communications, labour retraining, improved sites and financial aid to new industry—but also some interference in more

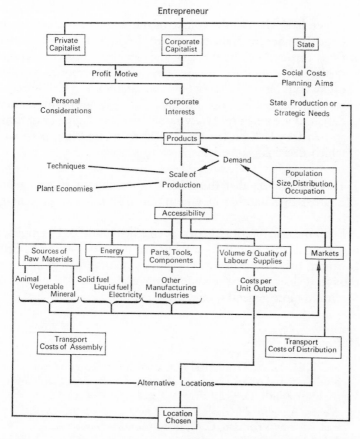

Fig. 6.4   A basic model of the factors influencing industrial location decisions

SOURCE   F. E. I. Hamilton, 'Models of industrial location' in R. J. Chorley and P. Haggett (eds.), *Models in Geography*. Methuen (1968).

behavioural type factors. As such, attempts to improve the 'image' of an area through improvement to both the physical and social environment, via campaigns like the North West's 'Operation Springclean', may be of considerable importance.

Overall however, the study of industrial location is an inexact science and it would not be surprising if most firms did not consider, specifically, all relevant factors. The Hunt Committee came to a similar conclusion:

> 'We have also, in the course of our enquiries, talked with a large number of industrialists in large, medium and small firms throughout the country and we are concerned that the quality of many firms' investment decisions is not as sophisticated and thorough as would be desirable. This reflects a number of factors—notably the fact that major investment decisions are taken relatively rarely by a large number of firms, so that they lack experience and expertise; and the speed with which decisions sometimes have to be taken.'[25]

It may also reflect that the costs and benefits of choosing one site rather than another may be minimal in terms of percentage profit.

But industrial location theory, even when modified by empirical evidence, is still essentially a theory of the location of the firm. It cannot properly explain the spatial structure of regions, even though it does isolate the major industrial factor. We now need to turn to more general spatial theories.

References

1 Smith, D. M., A Theoretical Framework for Geographical Studies of Industrial Location, *Economic Geography*, **42,** 2 (1966); see also: Smith, D. M., *Industrial Location,* Wiley (1971).

2 Weber, A., *Alfred Weber's Theory of the Location of Industries,* translated by Friedrich, C. J., from *Über den Standort der Industrien* (1909), Chicago (1929).

3 Hamilton, F. E. I., *Models of Industrial Location,* in Chorley, R. J., and Haggett, P., *Socio-Economic Models in Geography,* page 373, Methuen (1968).

4 Hoover, E. M., *The Location of Economic Activity,* McGraw-Hill, New York (1948).

5 Lösch, A., *The Economics of Location;* translated by Woglom, W. H., from *Die räumliche Ordnung der Wirtschaft* (1940), Yale (1954).

6 Richardson, H. W., *Regional Economics,* Weidenfeld and Nicolson, Part A (1969).

7 Harris, C. D., The Market as a Factor in the localisation of Industry in the U.S., *Annals of Association of American Geographers,* **44** (1954).

8 Isard, W., *Location and Space Economy,* Wiley (1956).

9 Greenhut, M. L., *Plant Location in Theory and Practice,* University of North Carolina Press (1956).

10 Hotelling, H., Stability in Competition, *Economic Journal,* **39,** pages 41–57 (1929).

11 Greenhut, M. L., *op cit.*

12 Isard, W., Game Theory, Location Theory and Industrial Agglomeration, *Papers and Proceedings of the Regional Science Association,* pages 1–11, **18** (1967).

13 See: Galbraith, J. K., *The New Industrial State,* London, Pelican (1969).

14 March, J. G., and Simon, M. A., *Organisations,* pages 140–1, NY, (1958).

15 Pred, A., *Behaviour and Location: Foundations for a Geographic and Dynamic Location Theory,* Part 1, Lund Series in Geography, Series B, **27** (1967).

16 Clark, C., *Population Growth and Land Use,* pages 281–2, Macmillan (1967).

17 See: Cameron, G. C., and Clark, B. D., *Industrial Movement and the Regional Problem,* Univ. of Glasgow Social and Economic Studies, Occ. Paper 5, Oliver and Boyd, Edinburgh (1966); Luttrell, W. F., *Factory Location and Industrial Movement,* 2 vols., NIESR, London (1962); McGovern, P. D., Industrial dispersal, *Planning* **31,** No. 485 (1965); Townroe, P. M., Locational Choice and the Individual Firm, *Regional Studies,* pages 15–24, **3,** 1 (1969); Townroe, P. M., *Industrial Location Decisions: A Study in Management Behaviour,* Centre for Urban and Regional Studies (University of Birmingham), Occ. Paper 15 (1971).

18 *Ibid.*

19 Scottish Council, *Report on the Scottish Economy,* pages 72–5, (1962);
See also: Luttrell, *op cit*

20 Wilson, T., Finance for Regional Industrial Development, *Three Banks Review,* September 1967.

21 Nuttall, T., The Work of an Industrial Development Association, *Regional Planning Seminar: Paper 5,* Dept. of Town Planning, Lanchester Polytechnic (1971).

22 Eversley, D. E. C., Social and Psychological Factors in the Determination of Industrial Location, *Papers on Regional Development* (supplement to the *Journal of Industrial Economics*), page 105 (1965).

23 Cameron, G. C., and Reid, G. L., *Scottish Economic Planning and the Attraction of Industry,* University of Glasgow Social and Economic Studies, Occ. Paper 6, Oliver and Boyd, Edinburgh (1966).

24 Cameron, G. C., and Clark, B. D., *op cit.*

25 *Report of the Committee on the Intermediate Areas* (The Hunt Report), Cmnd. 3998, paragraph 358, London, HMSO (1969).

7 The spatial structure of regions

The spatial structure of most regions can theoretically be sub-divided into three basic elements:

a a backcloth of service or tertiary industry locations, including administration, finance, retail and wholesale trades and other similar services, which tend to group into systems of central places uniformly distributed over the landscape giving access to the largest market population;

b a scattering of locations with specialised industry such as manu-facturing, mining and recreation, which tend to group into clusters or agglomerations according to the localisation of physical resources such as coal, and physical features such as river valleys and beaches;

c a pattern of transport links, for example roads and railways, which may give rise to a linear pattern of settlement.

These basic elements, *a* and *b* in particular, have been investi-gated within a number of conceptual frameworks, but as yet no one framework has satisfactorily taken into account all three elements. However, the various frameworks or models have one thing in common in that they all assume a measurable degree of order in spatial behaviour—although in certain cases possible chance factors seem to have played some part in deciding specific locations within the regional framework (for example, William Morris (Lord Nuffield) and the development of the motor industry at Cowley, Oxford). Garner[1] believes the assumption of order rests on the following six premises, which form the basis of most models of regional spatial structure:

a the spatial distribution of human activity rests on ordered adjustment to the factor of distance, which may be measured using linear or non-linear criteria

b location decisions are taken in general so as to minimise the frictional effects of distance, this concept is generally known as 'the principle of least effort'

c all locations are endowed with a degree of accessibility but some locations are more accessible than others

d there is a tendency for human activities to agglomerate to take advantage of scale economies, that is—advantages of specialisation made possible by concentration at common locations

e the organisation of human activity is essentially hierarchical in character, the hierarchy resulting from the interrelationship between agglomeration and accessibility

f human occupance is focal in character.

Of all the models of spatial structure, *central place theory* is probably the most researched and well known. The theory seeks to relate central places to their hinterlands and defines a central place as a settlement providing services for the population of its hinterland. However, although of considerable importance in an explanation of the size and spacing of settlements within a region, it should be noted at the outset that the theory is only concerned with the intensity and location of service industry—only one of the basic elements—and as such can only provide a *partial* explanation of regional structure.

1 Central place theory

The notion of central place theory is linked with the name of Walter Christaller and his pioneering work on *The Central Places of Southern Germany*.[2] However, several of the concepts of the theory were anticipated by others such as Dickinson,[3] and there have been numerous developments since, in particular by Lösch,[4] Berry and Garrison.[5] From the voluminous literature on the subject, certain basic concepts can be abstracted.

Service activities can be classified in a variety of different ways. A recent EFTA study[6] classifies them into four homogeneous trade groups on the basis of functional qualities:

a repair work and other services carried out directly on physical objects

b distribution and transport of goods

c processing and distribution of information including organisation, administration and education

d attendance to various personal and collective needs, such as security and health.

Within these groups activities may vary greatly in scale. Thus postal services may vary from a rural post box to a General Post Office, retail trades may vary from a small corner shop to a large departmental store. In other words, there is a *hierarchy* of service activities, ranging from 'low order' services found in every centre—city, town or village—to 'high order' services found only in the major centres. Thus major towns and cities are likely to have most services, with smaller towns and villages having a more limited number. Each service activity has a threshold population and market range.

The *threshold population* is the minimum population necessary to support the service activity. It may be as low as 250 for a corner shop or as high as 150 000 for a theatre. If the population falls below the threshold level, the activity will run at a loss and will face closure in the long run. If the population increases above the minimum, the activity will increase its profits, which may also lead to increased competition through increased provision of service activities. The frequency of use of the service is of course a vital influence on the threshold population. A theatre needing 500 visitors per night will need a threshold population of approximately 150 000 if the average number of visits per head of population is only one per year. But if the average number of visits is three per year the theatre could exist on a threshold population of only 50 000.

The *market range* of a service activity is that distance which people are willing to travel to reach the service. It is the outer limit of the market area for the service activity beyond which people will look to another centre. For example, people may be willing to travel to the nearest large town for jewellery and good clothing but only to the local corner shop for sweets and tobacco. The market range may be a simple function of linear distance but will more likely be influenced by time and cost factors. Nor is it a constant factor for a particular service activity, for range may vary between centres according to such factors as the size and importance of the centre and the income level of the hinterland. Figure 7.1 summarises the relationship between threshold and range for three levels of centre.

The Lösch analysis of Chapter 6 is also relevant to the demand

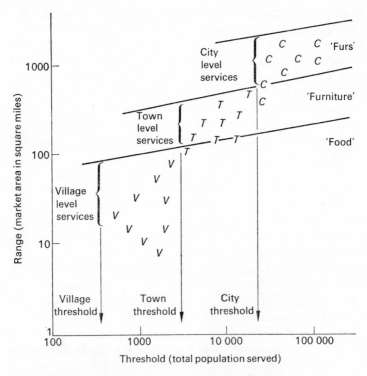

Fig. 7.1   Service activities: hierarchy, threshold and range

SOURCE Adapted from B. J. L. Berry, *Geography of Market Centres and Retail Distribution*, page 28. Prentice-Hall Inc. (1967). (Reproduced by permission of Prentice-Hall, Inc., Englewood Cliffs.)

situation for any service activity. Lösch's demand cone, in his example for a farmer selling beer, produces a circular market area for a good or service with market demand greatest at the centre and tailing off to the periphery—the market range.

SPATIAL COMPETITION BETWEEN PROVIDERS OF AN INDIVIDUAL SERVICE

The various service activities are distributed over the landscape and to explain this distribution, central place theory makes the usual simplifying assumptions. The landscape is assumed to be an even plain with an even distribution of natural resources and an even spread of population—invariably assumed to be farmers! In this landscape, the individual farmer retailing beer or his wife taking in laundry or running a small store may service a circular market area as illustrated in Figure 7.2a. Other farmers are willing to travel up to a distance a to purchase from the farmer. But beyond a, the benefits of purchase are out-weighed by the travel costs involved. In time, if retailing is profitable, other enterprising farmers may develop their own circular market areas, as in Figure 7.2b and spatial competition will develop between providers of the service activity. But at this stage not all the market area is being served.

If it is assumed that with improved transport and communications, consumers are willing to travel further, and that with improved production methods, producers can lower their prices, market areas will expand, with radius b as in Figure 7.2c, to cover most of the landscape. But although the market areas are now touching, certain consumers are still left out. Figure 7.2d illustrates the next stage where the market areas with radius c overlap. The white area is that in which consumers make exclusive use of one centre, but in the shaded areas consumers may actually use more than one centre. However, if those in the shaded areas are assumed to be rational beings seeking to minimise transport costs they will choose the nearest centre. This results in a division of the shaded area and the development of hexagonal market areas (Figure 7.2e) around a system of central places. This hexagonal packing of trade areas, each tangential to the other, is mathematically the most efficient system.

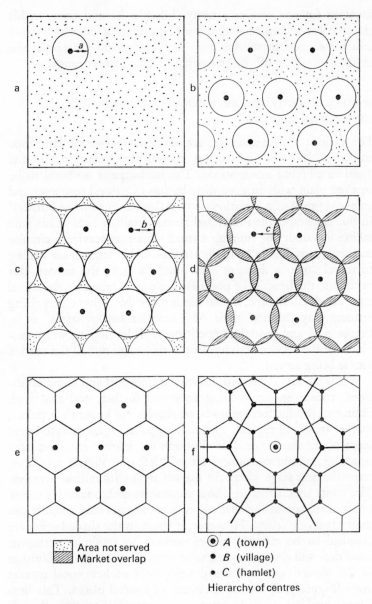

Area not served
Market overlap

A (town)
B (village)
C (hamlet)
Hierarchy of centres

Fig. 7.2   Evolution of hierarchy of central places

With the consideration of more than one service activity the situation can develop in several ways. The original central places may attract additional services such as doctors and banks, with threshold populations and market areas similar to the original service activity. Smaller central places may also develop at the points where the hexagonal service areas meet, perhaps providing more 'low order' service activities. As these service activities require smaller threshold populations and market areas, the resultant central places will be more numerous than the original centres.

In addition, certain of the original central places may attract more 'high order' service activities such as a cinema or a supermarket, requiring a larger threshold population and market range. There will only be a limited number of these higher order central places. Already three levels in a hierarchy of central places are apparent, with a 'nesting' pattern of lower order trade areas within the trade areas of higher order centres. Figure 7.2f illustrates this hierarchy. A centres might possess service activities 1 to n, with 1 being the local store and n a large supermarket. B centres would possess a more limited range of activities, perhaps from 1 to $(n - 10)$, while the smaller C centres would only possess a small number of service activities, perhaps from 1 to $(n-20)$.

In his study of Southern Germany, Christaller identified seven levels of central place ranging from the small hamlet to the metropolitan city. The initial distance of 7 km between the smallest centres is based on the assumption that half that distance, approximately 4 km, roughly represents the distance one man can walk in an hour and appears to be the normal range for the smallest centre. Table 7.1 outlines the Christaller hierarchy and offers a comparative classification of English central places, based mainly on the work of Smailes.

ALTERNATIVE FORMS OF HIERARCHY

Christaller believed that the hierarchy of central places could be organised according to one or other of the following principles (see Figure 7.3).

a The marketing or supply principle gives maximum choice of central places to individual sub-centres. In this heirarchy, the central place has the allegiance of one third of each of six sub-centres plus the original centre, giving a total equivalent of three dominated centres. Christaller termed this three the *k*-value, which is the total number of settlements of a certain order served by a central place of the next higher order.

General Hierarchy	Christaller Hierarchy					English Equivalent
	Central Place	Towns		Hinterland		
		Distance Apart (km)	Popn. (000's)	Size (km^2)	Popn. (000's)	
1st (lowest)						Roadside hamlet
2nd	Marktort	7	0·8	45	2·7	Village
	Amtsort	12	1·5	135	8·1	
3rd	Kreisstadt	21	3·5	400	24·0	Sub-town
	Bezirkstadt	36	9·0	1200	75·0	
4th	Gaustadt	62	27·0	3600	225·0	Town
5th	Provinz-haupstadt	108	90·0	10 800	675·0	Major Town City
6th	Landstadt	186	300·0	32 400	2 025·0	Major City
7th	Reichstadt					World City

Table 7.1. *Christaller's hierarchy*

b The transporting principle leads to a hierarchy which minimises the distance between the sub-centres and the main centre, with as many important places as possible lying on one traffic route between main centres. As the sub-centres lie along the routes between main centres they have only dual loyalty. Thus, under the transporting principle the *k*-value is four.

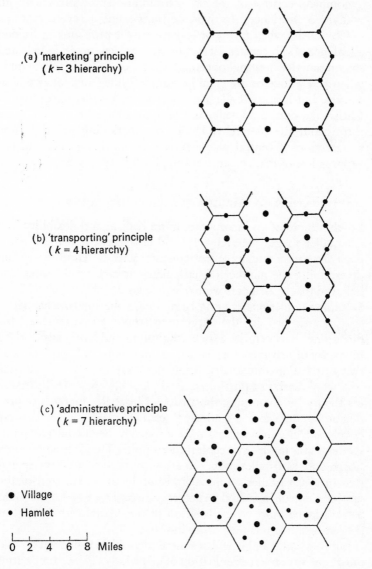

(a) 'marketing' principle
(k = 3 hierarchy)

(b) 'transporting' principle
(k = 4 hierarchy)

(c) 'administrative principle
(k = 7 hierarchy)

● Village
• Hamlet

0   2   4   6   8   Miles

Fig. 7.3   Alternative hierarchies

c The administrative principle requires that each centre has complete control of the six surrounding sub-centres with no divided allegiances. In this case the *k*-value is seven.

Obviously, when *k* = 3 or 4, there are the problems of divided allegiance of sub-centres. Christaller recognised this and suggested that in practice 'nesting' of centres would occur with, for example when *k* = 3, one centre gaining complete allegiance of two sub-centres, but losing all allegiance to the remainder. According to Christaller, once the *k*-value has been determined it remains fixed throughout the hierarchy. Under the marketing principle, the progression of central places runs 1, 2, 6, 18, 54 . . . , and the progression of market areas at each level is 1, 3, 9, 27, 81 . . .

MODIFICATION TO THE CHRISTALLER HIERARCHY

Lösch attempted to incorporate more realism and flexibility into Christaller's rigid hierarchy. He did not accept that there was a *discontinuous* hierarchy of settlements with a rigid *k* system determining the number of settlements at each level. Instead he believed that settlements were of a *continuous* distribution, with for example populations ranging from 100 in the smallest hamlet to over 10 000 000 in the largest metropolitan complex. This dichotomy between the Lösch continuum and Christaller's rigid hierarchy of urban centres has led to much debate. Lösch believed that Christaller's hierarchial principles were merely special cases of a whole series of possible central place systems. He illustrated his theory by combining the various Christaller hierarchies producing an 'economic landscape' characterised by six densely developed 'city rich' sectors and six sparsely developed 'city poor' sectors radiating from a central metropolis. Thus, although both Lösch and Christaller agree on many basic principles of spatial structure, Christaller's approach is purely an explanation of the service element in spatial structure, whereas that of Lösch could be said to be more an explanation of the spatial distribution of market-oriented manufacturing industry.

But how valid and useful are these theoretical frameworks? We must now turn to an examination of empirical evidence for central place theory and an assessment of its relevance in regional planning.

134

2 The validity of central place theory

There has been a considerable amount of work in various countries in the search for empirical regularities to support the theoretical systems. The various studies can be classified into inter-urban and intra-urban. *Inter-urban studies* which will be briefly outlined, involve the classification of towns into a hierarchical framework. This may be on a national basis, such as the early pioneering work by Smailes[7] and its recent updating by Smith,[8] or on a regional basis, such as the studies of Brush and Bracey,[9] Carter,[10] and Berry and Garrison.[11] *Intra-urban studies* involve the classification of centres within an urban area into a hierarchical framework. The works of Carruthers,[12] Smailes and Hartley,[13] and Thorpe and Rhodes[14] provide examples of this scale of study. Admittedly, the distinction between the two approaches may not be all that clear when the urban areas considered are conurbations such as Greater London, Tyneside and Manchester.

To Smailes[15] goes the credit for the first hierarchical classification of central places on a national scale. His hierarchy for England and Wales was formulated on the basis of certain selected activities, which he considered to be the retail and service attributes of a 'fully-fledged' town. These activities were:

a banks
b branches of major chain stores (Woolworths)
c secondary schools
d hospitals
e cinemas
f weekly newspapers.

In order to qualify as a 'fully-fledged' town a centre had to possess all these functions, with the exception of hospitals and secondary schools which Smailes treated with some flexibility. Above this 'town' level, Smailes identified three higher levels of central place. At the top came 16 'major cities', with London as the world city and provincial centres such as Manchester and Glasgow. Next came 21 'cities' such as Carlisle and Exeter, and almost 100 'major towns' such as Barrow and Burnley. Below the 'town' level, itself with approximately 300 centres, were two further levels of 'sub-towns', lacking from two to four of the basic activities, and 'urban villages' possessing at the most two of the activities. The Smailes approach has been criticised on many counts, in particular for its interpretation of what constitutes a central function, and has been recently updated by Smith. Nevertheless, it does provide a hierarchical ordering of centres based on service activities—although it should be noted that the clustering of some of the major centres, such as Liverpool and Manchester or Leeds and Bradford, suggests evidence of some distortion of the regular hierarchy.

At the regional scale, Dickinson[16] in his early work in East Anglia, established a definite hierarchy of towns. Using bus route data and information obtained from auctioneers, he established a regular pattern of small market towns, such as Stowmarket and Debenham, approximately eight miles apart. On top of this basic tier, were two further levels—a top level of large centres such as Norwich, Cambridge and Ipswich and a lower level of smaller centres such as King's Lynn and Bury St Edmunds. In another regional example, Brush and Bracey[17] compared the central places of South West Wisconsin and South West England —two areas differing markedly in economy, history and population density. Different methods of identifying centrality were used. Brush in Wisconsin used the Smailes method of identifying centres on the basis of the possession of certain service activities, whereas Bracey ranked centres by assessing their hinterlands for four representative services (chemist, ordinary shopping facilities, local bank and cinema). Yet despite these differences in setting and method, both studies showed two distinct tiers of central places, with high order centres, such as Oxford, Reading, Banbury and Swindon, at approximately 21 miles apart, and lower order centres, such as Witney, Woodstock and Chipping Norton at 8–10 mile distances.

Such empirical evidence, plus other studies such as Carter's[18] study of the towns of Wales, lends support to the existence of central place hierarchies. They may vary from the rigid theoretical system, but they appear to exist nonetheless.

SPATIAL HIERARCHIES AND THE RANK SIZE RULE

Central Place Theory of course considers not only the spacing of settlements but also their size. It has already been shown that there are many small centres with small market areas but only a limited number of large centres with large market areas. The vertical relationship between the number and population size of these settlements has been formalised as the *rank size rule*. This rule, which originated from the work of Auerbach and Singer,[19] but which has been most popularised by Zipf,[20] says that if urban settlements in an area are ranked in descending order of population size (from 1 to *n*), the population of the '*n*th' settlement will be 1/*n* the size of the largest settlement. That is:

$$P_n = \frac{P_1}{n^q}$$

where P_n = population of the *n*th settlement,
P_1 = population of the largest settlement,
n = settlement rank,
q = an exponent which usually approximates to unity.

Although several theorists are sceptical of the rule, there has been a considerable body of empirical support.[21] However, there has been much disagreement as to whether the ranking of settlements forms a continuum or a tiered hierarchy, conforming more to the Christaller theory. The problem appears to be mainly one of scale. When all the centres of a country are considered, industrial centres are inevitably included and the rank-size relationship approximates to a continuum. However, with a more limited area, at the regional or sub-regional level, the ranking tends to be more tiered and discontinuous providing empirical support for the central place hierarchy. As an example, Batty[22] tested the distribution of zonal populations in three sub-regions (Central Lancashire, Notts–Derby and Bedfordshire) for rank-size regularity. Although the results are probably somewhat biassed by the arbitrary definition of population zones, they do provide strong evidence of rank-size regularity at the sub-regional scale and indicate a definite hierarchy of centres.

PROBLEMS OF CENTRAL PLACE THEORY

Yet in spite of the empirical evidence, central place theory, as a model of regional spatial structure, has been subject to numerous criticisms. In particular, many areas seem to contradict the basic hierarchial rules. This is partly because the theory relates only to the service element. But of course settlements may develop due to the localisation of natural resources—for example a tourist centre may develop in an area with a good coastline and fine climate, while a coalfield may give rise to a manufacturing centre. The Christaller model holds such factors constant assuming an even plain and a uniform distribution of natural resources. In rural areas where the conditions are comparable with this ideal Christaller landscape, as in many of the empirical studies, the theory may provide a good explanation of reality; but in other areas, such as industrial Northern England, resource localisation distorts the regular hierarchy. As such, central place theory cannot provide an all inclusive general theory and there is a need to introduce other theories to explain the agglomerations of many areas—although even in these areas the service hierarchy invariably provides the backcloth.

The theory also assumes a uniform distribution of population. But this is unlikely to occur in practice since the factors upon which population density depends, such as soil fertility and climate, vary markedly from place to place and thus distort the picture. Another implicit assumption is that consumers will act rationally and patronise the nearest centre for the relevant service activity, giving rise to mutually exclusive hexagonal hinterlands. Several factors, especially the impact of multi-purpose trips to a centre, may undermine this assumption leading to overlapping market areas.

Central place theory has also been criticised from time to time for its apparently static and descriptive approach. It identifies the relationship between centres and their hinterlands at one point in time but fails to take into account the evolutionary process of spatial structure. A central place system indeed is not fixed and is in a constant state of change. Thus an increase in the service activity of one centre, perhaps with the development of a new multiple store, will have an impact on the service activity of other competing centres. The theory does not provide a thorough dynamic explanation of these changes, although some authors believe it is possible to place a limited dynamic interpretation on the theory in the explanation of changes in relative location.

Other more detailed criticisms include the possible distortion of the hierarchy by the domination of large centres which may create a 'shadow effect' discouraging the growth of appropriately sized smaller settlements. An alternative distortion could be caused by the development of a dispersed city—a group of cities which although physically separated function together as one unit. Interdependence between them is reflected in patterns of retailing and functional specialisation. Burton[23] believes the Derby–Chesterfield–Nottingham area of the East Midlands may develop into, or already be, an example of such a city. With the development of private transport the area would develop into a cohesive unit, truncating the hierarchical system.

One final technical criticism of the theory is the problem of actually ranking central places. This involves the dual problem of the actual identification of central places (which may be confused by the problem of sprawl) and the choice of criteria to rank the centres. Christaller realised that population alone was an insufficient measure of centrality—a mining or manufacturing centre may have a large population but exercise few central functions. Therefore, in addition, he used an index based on the number of telephone installations. This, in brief, involved the subtracting from the actual number of telephones in a centre, the number that it should have in proportion to its population, according to the average of the area. More recent approaches to the measurement problem have used mainly retailing information including simple numerical counts of the number of retail shops in a centre; the identification of key facilities and the ranking of centres according to the number they possessed (such as the Haydock method);[24] and more sophisticated quantitative approaches (such as Davies's[25] 'functional index' based on location coefficients). Unfortunately, as a recent study by McEvoy[26] demonstrates, different ranking methods may result in different rankings of central places within a particular area.

3 Central place theory and regional planning

In the face of encouraging empirical studies and discouraging criticisms, does the theory have any relevance for regional planning? It would seem to have two potential rôles—firstly as a framework for understanding the regional spatial structure and secondly as a model for future planning. There is little doubt that central place theory does provide a very valuable partial framework for the understanding of regional structure, but what of its rôle for future planning?

A basic argument supporting the use of central places in regional planning is that a hierarchical system of centres avoids duplication and waste. It is a relatively efficient way of administering and allocating resources within a region, facilitating the realisation of social benefits accruing from economies of scale. In addition, the network of interrelated centres means that the planning of any centre within an area must take into account the implications for other centres within the area (the lack of recognition of this principle has led to much wasteful duplication of shopping facilities in certain areas of the country). Hilhorst,[27] in an interesting approach at a synthesis of regional theory, also suggests that a region's economic shock resistance is much greater where the region's spatial structure is 'closely knit'. An area with such a structure is one in which the distribution of settlements approximates to the rank size rule. It is an area which has reached a stage in its development in which certain sub-systems focussing on subsidiary centres are clearly discernible and there is no undue reliance on one primate city.

Yet, although the basic principles have been used in various shopping studies (such as those for the North West and West Midlands) and may be implicit in several regional strategies, there has been only a limited number of comprehensive practical applications of the theory in regional planning. Of these, recent schemes in Holland, Ghana and Israel are of particular interest providing examples of application in both developed and developing countries. The Dutch Physical Plan,[28] to be discussed in more detail in Chapter 12, recognises a four-tier hierarchy of settlements ranging from the smallest unit of 5000 people to major cities with populations in excess of 250 000. Within this framework, probably the most renowned applications of central place theory was that carried out when the North East Polder was reclaimed from the Ijsselmeer and a two-level hierarchy of market centres was established around the centre of Lelystad.

The application of the theory in the regional planning of a developing country, Ghana, has been examined by Grove and Huszar.[29] Like many developing countries, Ghana has initiated comprehensive economic planning in an attempt to achieve 'take-off' economically. Such planning involves the location of vast investments; but some locations may involve a better use of resources than others. In an attempt to identify such locations, Grove and Huszar drew up a hierarchy of central places. The ranking or centrality of towns was defined as a function of the quality (variety and level) of the services offered, rather than of the quantity of services (such as the number of shops). Services were weighted, with for example a specialised hospital ranking three times more important than a health centre, and a total service weight was established for each centre. When these weights were plotted in the form of a frequency distribution a definite five-tier hierarchy of centres was evident. When the centres were plotted on a map according to grade, the first tier centres were approximately 50 miles apart with service areas of 25 miles' radius. However, the hierarchy revealed certain first-tier 'gaps' with minor settlements in their place. These settlements represented potential first-tier centres, and twelve of them were identified for future population increase and economic development. The development of such centres would fit into the hierarchy, avoiding the waste of developing competing first-tier centres.

The development of a three-tier hierarchy of central places around the centre of Qiryat-Gat in the Lakhish Plains of Israel,[30] represents another application of the theory in a developing country. Here the development of a settlement structure is basically starting from scratch, for this previously barren area, 40 miles South of Jerusalem, was only opened up in 1955 with the advent of irrigation.

4 Summary

Central place theory is probably the most researched and well known model of regional spatial structure, it is also the most criticised. It is a purely deductive theory of a highly simplified and abstract nature developed on the basis of very idealised assumptions. It relates only to the service element of regional structure, failing to explain distortions in that hierarchy caused by the location of primary and manufacturing industry which tends to group into clusters or agglomerations due to resource localisation. The theory is also essentially static, explaining the existence of regional spatial structure but failing to explain how that structure has evolved and how it might change in the future.

Yet to admit that the model has problems is not to discount it out of hand. Its value as an explanatory model of regional spatial structure is borne out by empirical studies, and even where other locational elements are dominant, the service hierarchy of central places invariably provides the backcloth—the theoretical norm from which deviations can be measured. Similarly, although its direct application in regional planning practice may be less readily apparent, especially in developed areas with complex settlement structures, it still serves a very useful rôle identifying concepts of vital importance to the regional planner such as the interdependence of city and region, a hierarchy of functions and centres, and market range and threshold populations.

References

1 Garner, B. J., *Models of Urban Geography and Settlement Location,* in Chorley, R. J., and Haggett, P., *Socio-Economic Models in Geography,* pages 304–5 Methuen (1967).

2 Christaller, W., *Central Places in Southern Germany* (Trans. C. W. Baskin), Englewood Cliffs, New Jersey (1966).

3 Dickinson, R. E., The Metropolitan Cities of the United States, *Geographical Reviews,* 24 (1934).

4 Lösch, A., *The Economics of Location,* translated by Woglom, Yale (1954).

5 Berry, B. J. L., and Garrison, W., Recent developments of central place theory, *Papers and Proceedings of the Regional Science Association,* pages 107–20, 4 (1958);
Berry, B. J. L., and Pred, A., Central place studies: a bibliography of theory and applications; *Regional Science Research Institute, Bibliography Series,* 1 (1961);
Berry, B. J. L., *Geography of Market Centres and Retail Distribution,* Prentice-Hall (1967).

6 Allen, K. J., and Hermansen, T., *Regional Policy in EFTA,* page 147, EFTA Secretariat, Geneva (1968).

7 Smailes, A. E., The urban hierarchy in England and Wales, *Geography*, pages 41–51, **29** (1944).

8 Smith, R. D. P., The changing urban hierarchy, *Regional Studies*, pages 1–19, **2**, 1 (1968).

9 Brush, J. E. and H. E. Bracey, Rural Service Centres in South Western Wisconsin and Southern England, *Geographical Review*, pages 550–69, **45** (1955).

10 Carter, H., *The Towns of Wales: A Study in Urban Geography*, Cardiff (1965).

11 Berry, B. J. L., and Garrison, W. L., The Functional Bases of the Central Place Hierarchy, *Economic Geography*, pages 145–54, **34** (1958).

12 Carruthers, W. I., Service centres in Greater London, *Town Planning Review*, pages 5–31, **33** (1962).

13 Smailes, A. E., and Hartley, G., Shopping centres in the Greater London area, *Institute of British Geographers, Transactions and Papers*, pages 201–13, **29** (1961).

14 Thorpe, D., and Rhodes, T. C., The shopping centres of the Tyneside urban region and large-scale grocery retailing, *Economic Geography*, pages 52–73, **42** (1966).

15 Smailes, A. E. (1944), *op cit.*

16 Dickinson, R. E., The distribution and functions of the smaller urban settlements of East Anglia, *Geography*, pages 19–31, **17** (1932).

17 Brush, J. E., and Bracey, H. E. *op cit*

18 Carter, H., *op cit*

19 Singer, H. W., The Courbe des Populations: A Parallel to Pareto's Law, *Economic Journal*, **46** (1936).

20 Zipf, G. K., *Human Behaviour and the Principle of Least Effort*, Addison-Wesley, Cambridge, Mass. (1949).

21 See: Haggett, P., *Locational analysis in human geography*, Arnold (1965).

22 Batty, M., *Spatial Theory and Information Systems*, W.P. 3/0, Urban Systems Research Unit, University of Reading, pages 31–3 (1970).

23 Burton, I., A restatement of the dispersed city hypothesis, *Annals of the Association of American Geographers*, **53**, 3 (1963).

24 Univ. of Manchester, *Regional Shopping Centres: A Planning Report on North West England, Parts 1 and 2*, Department of Planning, (1965).

25 Davies, W. K. D., Centrality and the Central Place Hierarchy, *Urban Studies*, **4**, 1 (1967).

26 McEvoy, D., Alternative methods of ranking shopping centres, *Tijdschrift voor Economische en Sociale Geografie* (1968).

27 Hilhorst, J. G. M., *Spatial Structure and Decision Making*, in Hilhorst, J. G. M. and D. M. Dunham, *Issues in Regional Planning*, Institute of Social Studies (The Hague), page 71, Mouton (1971).

28 *Second Report on Physical Planning in the Netherlands*, Government Printing Office of the Netherlands, The Hague (1966).

29 Grove, D., and Huszar, L., The Application of Central Place Theory in the Regional Planning of a Developing Country, *Town and Country Planning School*, Exeter (1964).

30 *Operation Lakhish: Stage 2*, a publication of the United Israel Appeal;
Jackson, G., Regional Policy and Planning in Israel, *Oxford Polytechnic O.P.* (1970).

8 Growth pole theory

Many of the criticisms levelled at central place theory as a model of regional spatial structure can be answered by the theory of growth poles. Although the concept can be traced back to the agglomeration factors of early location theories, outlined in Chapter 6, its modern development owes much to French economists, especially Perroux, who believed that the basic fact of spatial, as well as industrial development is that 'growth does not appear everywhere and all at once; it appears in points or development poles, with variable intensities; it spreads along diverse channels and with varying terminal effects to the whole of the economy'.[1] More specifically, Boudeville defines a regional growth pole as a 'set of expanding industries located in an urban area and inducing further development of economic activity throughout its zone of influence'.[2] Owing to its versatility, the theory has been adapted not only for understanding regional structure, but also as a method for predicting changes in that structure and prescribing solutions to certain regional problems. It has enjoyed great popularity in recent years becoming 'an idea in good currency', and if only for this reason merits further investigation.

Unfortunately though, application tends to have progressed further than the theoretical underpinnings. Because of some minor inconsistencies in Perroux's original works, there has been much confusion in subsequent literature. This can be clearly seen in the vast confusion of terminology with not only growth poles and growth points, but also growth centres, development poles, development axes, growth zones and growth areas. Indeed there seems to be as many definitions as authors writing about them. Darwent, who has written the most recent review of the growth pole concept states that 'it has become associated with an enormous variety of indistinct and ill-defined concepts and notions.'[3] Hansen believes that the whole of 'growth pole' literature is badly in need of a thorough semantic reworking. It is thus necessary to identify the basic concepts of this much used theory, first in outline and then in more detail.

1 Basic concepts of growth pole theory

The basic concepts and subsequent refinements and developments are to be found in the 'core' literature[4] of Perroux, Boudeville, Hansen, Hermansen, Hirschman and Myrdal. There is a definite French domination of this field of regional theory providing an interesting complement to the earlier German work on central place theory. In contrast to the deductive nature of the latter, the theory of growth poles is inductively derived from observations of the process of economic development.

Perroux's original work focusses on the development of growth poles in *economic space*. This was a deliberate attempt to break away from the limiting geographical dimensions adopted by Christaller and Lösch. He developed a typology of economic spaces, the most important being that of economic space as a field of forces, from which he derived the notion of a pole as a vector of economic forces '... as a field of forces, economic space consists of centres (or poles or foci) from which centrifugal forces emanate and to which centripetal forces are attracted'. Perroux did acknowledge that growth poles would also exist in geographical space, but it was Boudeville who extended the original theory to include more comprehensively the geographical dimension. To keep the distinctions clear and in perspective, the term *growth pole* can be taken to refer to the original concept of Perroux without any specific geographical dimension, while the term *growth centre* or *growth point* refers to a spatial location.*

* Some writers see a scale distinction between growth poles and growth centres, with growth poles relating to the national scale and growth centres to the regional scale. See: Kucklinski, A. R., Regional Development, Regional Policies and Regional Planning, *Regional studies,* 4, 3 (1970).

From the various writings on growth poles (*pôle de crois-sance*) and growth centres, the following basic economic concepts and their geographical developments can be identified:

a The concept of leading industries (*industrie motrice*) and propulsive firms, states that at the centre of growth poles are large propulsive firms belonging to leading industries which dominate other economic units. There may be just one single dominant propulsive firm or a core of them forming an industrial complex.

The original geographical location of such industries in certain focal points in a region may be due to several factors—the localisation of natural resources (water/shelter/fuel), the localisation of more man-made advantages (communications or existing service-based central places with advantages of infrastructure and labour supply), or possibly just chance. In reality, the growth points are often grafted on to the existing framework of central places.

b The concept of polarisation states that the rapid growth of the leading industries ('propulsive growth') induces the polarisation of other economic units into the pole of growth. Implicit in this process of polarisation are the various agglomeration economies (internal and external economies of scale.)

This economic polarisation will inevitably lead to geographical polarisation with the flow of resources to and the concentration of economic activity at a limited number of centres within a region. Even when the original *raison d'être* of such locations disappears, they will often continue to prosper due to the presence of the agglomeration economies.

c The concept of spread effects states that in time the dynamic propulsive qualities of the growth pole radiate outwards into the surrounding space. These 'trickling down' or 'spread' effects are particularly attractive to the regional planner and have contributed much to the recent popularity of the theory as a policy tool.

However, although these basic concepts might intuitively provide a reasonable and dynamic explanation of the industrial clusters or agglomerations in regional spatial structure, some regional theorists have cast doubt on their validity. Do growth poles grow indefinitely? What about the diseconomies of scale? Do the spread effects ever materialise? Before any attempt is

147

made to draw out the relevance of growth pole theory for regional planning, it is first necessary to examine each of the basic concepts of the theory in rather more detail.

LEADING INDUSTRIES AND PROPULSIVE FIRMS

These concepts can be clarified by outlining their major characteristics. A leading industry has the following characteristics:

a it is a relatively new and 'dynamic' industry with an advanced level of technology injecting an atmosphere of 'growthmindedness' into a region;

b it has a high income elasticity of demand for its products which are usually sold to national markets;

c it has strong inter-industry linkages with other sectors, (these linkages may be 'forward' linkages where an industry has a high ratio of intermediary industry sales to total sales, or 'backward' linkages, where an industry has a high ratio of intermediary inputs from other industries to total inputs).

Similarly, a propulsive firm has the following characteristics:

a it is relatively large;

b it generates significant growth impulses into its environment;

c it has a high ability to innovate;

d it belongs to a fast growing industry.

By analysing some of these characteristics it is possible to identify leading industries and propulsive firms in the UK context. For example, a very approximate guide to leading industries can be found by identifying the income elasticity of demand and the inter-industry linkages of the main Standard Industrial Classification categories. The use of such broad categories does of course mask variations within subdivisions of the broad classification, but nevertheless provides a rough guideline. Income elasticity of demand measures the change in demand for a good resulting from a change in income. In general, industries with elasticities less than unity will be expanding less rapidly than the norm, whereas industries with elasticities greater than unity will be expanding faster than the norm. By comparing increases in total sales for the industrial groups with the increases in national income, elasticities can be deduced. Similarly, by analysing inter-industry input-output tables, the forward and

148

backward linkages of each industrial group can be deduced. On the basis of such analysis, and applying the subjective criteria of 'newness', the following can be identified as leading manufacturing industries in Britain: chemicals (SIC IV), engineering (SIC VI and VII), vehicles (SIC VIII), metal goods (SIC IX), paper and printing (SIC XV) and other manufacturing industries (SIC XVI).

However, although most growth poles involve leading industries, not all leading industries necessarily generate growth poles. A much quoted example is the case of Lacq in South West France where it was anticipated that the discovery of large natural gas deposits would provide the growth pole focus for an industrial revitalisation of the whole of the South West Region. In reality, because of the presence of vastly greater external economies elsewhere, the Lacq complex has been essentially a local phenomenon, doing little to help the wider region and having little effect on the existing spatial structure. A further problem of leading industries is the inherent danger in relying on one particular industry. Many of the problem areas of today are the over-specialised growth points of yesterday. The development of an industrial complex with a variety of smaller firms is one solution to this problem.

POLARISATION EFFECTS AND AGGLOMERATION ECONOMIES

Once localised, the propulsive firm or complex of propulsive firms within the leading industry tend to grow rapidly reaping the advantages of agglomeration economies and effecting the polarisation of other economic activities around the original location. Three types of agglomeration economies can be identified.

a Economies internal to the firm. These are the lower average production costs resulting from an increased rate of output. Such large-scale production allows technical economies, such as job specialisation and the use of 'flow-line' processes instead of 'batch' processes, and various management, marketing and financial economies.

b Economies external to the firm but internal to the industry. These are the reductions in cost per unit of output to the firm as the industry expands at a particular location. Such 'localisation economies'[5] arise from the close locational proximity of linked firms, and include the development of a large and skilled labour pool, the easy interchange of materials and products ('the road is the conveyor belt'), the possibility of firms existing to process waste materials, and the development of specialised services available to all firms, such as access to R and D facilities and repair services.

c Economies external to the industry but internal to the urban area. These are the downward shifts in the average costs of each firm as many industries grow in one place. Known as 'urbanisation economies',[6] they include the development of urban labour markets, access to a larger market and the provision of a wide range of services by both the private and public sector for both people and industry. Such services might for instance include the availability of improved transport, commercial and financial facilities, and the development of a wide range of social, cultural and leisure facilities—hospitals, schools, museums, theatres and cinemas. In effecting polarisation, a highly developed infrastructure providing facilities at the centre for the wider region may be as important as the presence of a complex of leading industries.

History provides us with numerous examples of polarisation due to agglomeration economies—for example, the localisation of the textile industry in North East Lancashire and the development of the associated textile machinery industry. It is also possible to identify relatively recent examples of the localisation of economic units about propulsive firms. After the First World War, large firms of two leading industries (vehicles and aerospace) located in the town of Coventry. Associated metal and engineering firms have developed about these propulsive firms resulting in the development of a strong growth pole where approximately 90% of manufacturing employment is in the engineering and metal manufacturing industries. The growth pole has become localised in geographical space so that Coventry can be identified as a growth centre. The development of this growth centre has resulted in considerable increases in Coventry's population. Two more recent examples of polarisation are the development of an incipient electronics industry complex around 80 or so firms in the central valley of Scotland, and the growth of a scientific R and D complex West of London.[7]

However, there may be limitations on polarisation. As already indicated, the leading industry itself may decline, as in North East Lancashire. In addition, at some stage in the development of the growth point, diseconomies of scale may begin to outweigh the agglomeration benefits. Some diseconomies such as the rising costs of public services, rising factor prices such as wages and site rents, and congestion costs, may directly affect industrial growth. Other more general social costs—noise and air pollution and longer journeys to work—may initially have a more limited effect, but in the long run may also limit polarisation.

An interesting and much discussed offshoot of this question of diseconomies is that of optimum town size. This involves an analysis of how the agglomeration economies (the benefits), and the diseconomies (the costs), vary with population size. The benefits to industry and people, such as the advantages of good communication, theatres and a technical college, are very difficult to measure but would probably follow a form similar to Figure 8.1a. Here small centres have few advantages, but these generally increase with size, although they will probably level off as diminishing returns set in. However, whether they will actually fall or not is debatable. The other side of the equation, the cost side, is a little more manageable although still rather vague. Considering the costs involved, that is the specific costs such as infrastructure—costs of sewerage, roads and hospitals, plus the general social costs, it would seem that the cost curve is of a flat-bottomed U-shape (see Figure 8.1b). Average costs are very high for small centres, but then fall quite rapidly levelling off over a wide range of population, before rising again. Figure 8.1c shows the net (benefit-cost) to population and industry as a whole over the population range. Such crude figures are of course largely conceptual and in practice would differ widely between countries and regions within countries. However, they do suggest that 'optimum' town size may vary over a wide range.

Finally, another possible limitation on polarisation has been raised by Lasuen.[8] He questions whether the polarisation concept is as strong today as it used to be. Comparing the modern Litton Corporation of the USA with the Krupp Company of Germany, he argues that firms are becoming more multi-product, multi-plant and spread-oriented with the external economies of con-

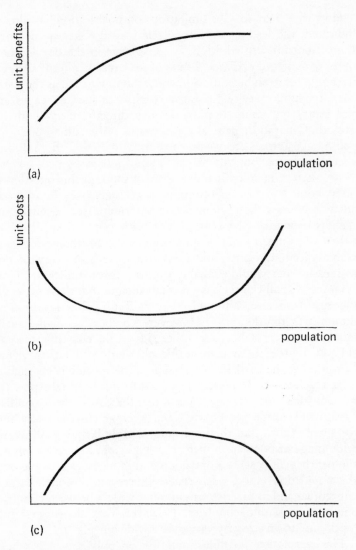

Fig. 8.1   The general relationships between agglomeration costs, benefits and population size

a   Gross benefits of agglomeration
b   Gross costs of agglomeration
c   Net (benefits—costs)

centration becoming of decreasing importance. Such an argument, if valid, does not reduce the value of growth pole theory as an explanation of existing regional structure, but it may have some relevance to future structures.

SPREAD EFFECTS

This is the most difficult aspect of the theory to examine, and although there has been some general discussion of the question of whether growth will diffuse outwards from a growth pole there is little empirical evidence that this does in fact take place. Myrdal and Hirschman[9] have talked of the 'spread' or 'trickling down' effects of growth poles in contrast with the 'backwash' or 'polarisation' effects. However, as noted in the discussion of macro 'cumulative-causation' growth theory in Chapter 5, there is scope for considerable doubt over the relative strength of spread in comparison with backwash.

One of the few empirical studies which actually tries to assess the spread effects is that by Vida Nichols[10] who seeks to measure the spread effects from the growth pole of Atlanta into the rest of the relatively depressed state of Georgia, USA. She observed that the change in median income distribution over a 10-year period (1950–60) included a region-wide increase associated with a general shift in employment, but also a residual element which was highest in the suburban ring around Atlanta and in other large towns in the area. She concluded that the residual element to some extent reflected the influence of the Atlanta growth pole. The locations of the spread effects, with the propulsive influence of growth pole felt first in other major towns in the region and in the rural area immediately surrounding the growth pole, and then spreading to other interstitial rural areas are interesting in themselves. They tend to concur with the results of other diffusion studies by Hägerstrand[11] and suggest, from a policy viewpoint, the advantage of injecting growth into intermediate areas as well as into the focal pole.*

*For a study which tends to cast doubts on the efficacy of the 'trickling down' development processes from growth centres, see: Moseley, M. J.; The impact of growth centres in rural regions—I Brittany; II East Anglia, *Regional Studies*, 7, 1 (1973).

Drawing this more detailed outline of the concepts together, it can be seen that although the various concepts of growth poles can be identified and clarified and may appear intuitively attractive, their theoretical basis and empirical validity are still rather thin, relying heavily on support from associated concepts of location and agglomeration. In addition, there are numerous problems— the dangers of over-reliance on large leading industries, the limitations on polarisation from diseconomies of scale and 'footloose' firms, and the problem of imbalance between spread and backwash effects. Yet, as a framework for understanding the regional anatomy it provides a valuable dynamic complement to central place theory and, despite its limitations, is of considerable value for regional planning. It introduces numerous planning-oriented concepts, stressing the advantages of industrial complexes, leading industries, polarised growth and agglomeration economies and the resultant spread effects, all of which are certainly robust if not rigorous.

2 Growth pole theory and regional planning[12]

The value of the growth pole theory as a policy tool in regional planning has been realised for some time. In Britain, it was first adopted in 1963 in plans for North East England and Central Scotland. The idea was later taken up in Northern Ireland and Mid-Wales. However, its relevance was not confined to declining areas, for as early as 1964 a policy of concentrating all industrial growth in a few large centres was proposed for the prosperous South East. 'Growth centre' policies have subsequently been proposed for the North West, South Wales, the Scottish Highlands and Eire, and modifications have been undertaken to the earlier applications.

Abroad, 'growth point' policies have been favoured in both advanced and under-developed countries. Well known examples are the Bari–Taranto–Brindisi industrial complex for the Mezzogiorno Region of Southern Italy, the national policy of growth points or *métropoles d'équilibrium* in France, and the development of new centres at Brasilia and Cuidad Guyana as attempts to generate growth into the backward areas of Brazil and Venezuela. The idea has also been recently accepted in the

USA to aid its depressed regions, and in the Soviet Union and India.

The theory is particularly attractive as a policy tool for several reasons:

a owing to the various agglomeration economies it tends to be a very efficient way of generating development

b the concentration of investment in specific growth points costs less in terms of public expenditure than wholesale grants to large areas

c the spread effects out of the growth point will help to solve the problems of depressed regions.

But the various and more and more frequent uses suggest some confusion over the rôle of the theory in regional policy, and there is a need for some clarification. Hermansen[13] originally introduced the idea of formulating distinctions in order to clarify this rôle, and building on his original ideas, a typology can be identified. This typology seeks to provide a comprehensive guide to the practical use of the theory, and consists of four categories, each with its own variations.

1. *Function* Policy of Development
              Policy of Relief
              Policy of Development and Relief
2. *Level*   Primary
              Secondary
              Tertiary
3. *Strategy* Active
              Passive
4. *Form*   Growth Pole Policy
              Growth Centre Policy

The first distinction is between the functions of the policy. This will be influenced by the particular problems of the region. The choice may be a pole of development which aims at generating growth in an area with no real industrial characteristics or where the economy is in a state of depression. In contrast, a pole of relief could be chosen which attempts to reduce the problems of a large industrial complex by establishing itself as a counter magnet. It is also possible for the pole to embody both functions. A second distinction is between poles belonging to different levels of the hierarchial system of settlements. The level of pole may vary from primary to tertiary depending on its function and the scale of the problem.

Another distinction is between an *active* and *initiating* growth policy or a *passive* and *reinforcing* approach. The former is more ambitious, involving a rejection of the existing settlement structure and the creation of new centres in an attempt to create development. The passive approach accepts the rationality of the existing system of centres and seeks to aid development by concentrating on the most promising of these centres.

The final distinction, but a most important one in the use of the theory, is between the use of a *growth pole policy* or a *growth centre policy*. The major difference between the two is that the pole policy necessitates the development of a selected industrial focus composed of propulsive firms from leading industries, the intention being to foster localisation economies. In contrast, the centre policy does not involve the selection of related industries, but rather entails the concentration of investment in the provision in a chosen location of those facilities which will create urbanisation economies that are attractive to industry. As industry must be localised, a growth pole policy will inevitably result in a growth centre and the resultant urbanisation economies. However this is not necessarily true in reverse for a growth centre policy may not lead to the development of a growth pole of linked industries.

Implicit in the growth pole explanation of regional structure and growth centre policy is intra-regional imbalance, at least in the short run. This imbalance however may be socially and politically unacceptable to certain areas of the region, and social and political factors can be of considerable importance in determining spatial structure. Such factors have been recognised by several theorists[14] although they are even more difficult to analyse than the predominantly economic concepts discussed so far.

3 Models of spatial interaction

Taken together, growth pole theory and central place theory provide a partial explanation of the spatial structure of regions. However neither theory satisfactorily explains the elements of spatial interaction—the movement between activities in space—although such elements are implicit in both models. In recent years there has been much research into this important area of spatial interaction, with major developments in mathematical land-use modelling arising out of the systems approach to urban and regional planning. Therefore to conclude the section on intra-regional analysis we now turn to examine some of the more important models of spatial interaction. Unfortunately the survey must be brief, only scratching the surface of the rapidly growing and highly technical literature on the subject. There are however several useful reviews of modelling by Harris,[15] Lowry,[16] Wilson[17] and most recently by Batty[18] which fill most of the gaps.

The starting point for many of the models is the gravity model of human interaction outlined in Chapter 2 . . . 'the force of interaction between two centres is directly proportional to the mass of the centre and inversely proportional to the distance between them'. There have been many developments and varia-tions of this model (potential models, models of intervening opportunities); there have also been many criticisms particularly of the lack of theoretical underpinnings. This concern has recently led to a completely new approach—a general theoretical derivation of the gravity model based on the concept of entropy as used in statistical mechanics. Advocated by Wilson,[19] this approach is 'quickly becoming the basis of a general framework for spatial interaction modelling'.[20]

Spatial interaction models can serve basically two rôles. Firstly they can be seen as an integral part of the development of the theory of spatial structure of towns and regions; secondly, they can be used in predictive rôles—forecasting into the future. Although recent developments have been primarily oriented towards the second rôle, they also provide a valuable insight into spatial structure. Two main types of models can be identified on the criteria of comprehensiveness—partial models relating to only one aspect of the urban or regional system and general models relating to two or more aspects.

Partial models have been extensively developed in the study of retail behaviour. In the retail context the models seek to explain the interaction between the consumer and the retail sources (shopping centres) in terms of the attraction of the source and its distance from the consumer. The attraction factor could be total retail sales at the source and the distance could be in terms of driving time. One of the most well known and popular of shopping models is that derived by Lakshmanan and Hansen.[21] This model, which can take the form of an economic model or a traffic model, can be used in forecasting—for example predicting the effect of a new shopping centre. As an economic model it can be used to predict the values of the transfers of money from origin zones (residential areas) to destination zones (shopping centres); as a traffic model the aim is to predict the numbers of shopping journeys from the origin zones to the destination zones. The economic model uses the formula:

$$T_{ij} = \frac{A_i C_i F_j{}^b}{d_{ij}{}^a}$$

where T_{ij} = money transfer from zone i to zone j
        C_i = total expenditure by consumers from zone i
        F_j = mass of the shopping centre j
        d_{ij} = distance from zone i to zone j
        A_i = scaling factor
        a and b are parameters.

A well known application of this model is in the Manchester University study of shopping centres in the North West.[22] In addition to shopping, partial models are also well developed in transport and are slowly being introduced into other areas.

Yet despite advances in partial modelling, *general* or *holistic* models are likely to prove the long-term goal of location land-use modelling, allowing the planner to take account of the effects of change in a single activity pattern on other activities in the urban/regional system. Batty subdivides general models into optimising and non-optimising classes. As the specification and measurement of optimality in systems involving human values is very difficult, the majority of general models are of a non-optimising nature. Of these, the Garin Lowry Model is the most popular.

Lowry's original model of a metropolis involved, in his own words, the following sequence of operations:

'We start with the given distribution of 'basic' workplaces by mile square tract, and with certain specifications as to the land available for residential settlement in each tract. The computer distributes around each cluster of workplaces a residential population which can supply an appropriate labour force . . . This spatially distributed residential population is then available as a base for the location of population serving activities, from department stores to elementary schools. The market potential of each location (in terms of accessible customers) is evaluated; and retail employment is spatially distributed in proportion to these potentials.

In a new round of calculations, the residences of retail and service employees are located. This event changes the distribution of residential population so that market potentials must be recalculated.'[23]

Iterations proceed until constrained by available land, efficiency scales of operation for enterprises and density ceilings for residential population. In short, the model is constructed around two structures: firstly population and service employment are derived from basic employment (this assumes a basic/non-basic split of economic activity) and secondly, service employment and population are allocated to zones of the system using sub-models based on potential models.

The original model has since been much modified. Of particular note are the improvements by Garin[24] who amended the model principally by simplifying the allocation process. Versions of the Garin-Lowry Model have been applied in Britain at both sub-regional and town scales. The sub-regional applications illustrate some of the uses. In Central Lancashire[25] and Bedfordshire[26] the model was used mainly for impact analysis—the impact of Central Lancashire New Town and Milton Keynes; in the Nottinghamshire–Derbyshire Study,[27] the model was used more to forecast the implications of alternative sub-regional strategies, and in Merseyside[28] a model was developed primarily for educational purposes.

The Garin-Lowry Model typifies many of the attractions and problems of contemporary spatial interaction models. It provides a relatively comprehensive coverage of urban and regional systems in that it is concerned with population and employment and the interactions between them; its sub-models can be developed and refined in themselves; it is simple to understand

and capable of practical application. However such sophistication has its price. In addition to the problems of application, the inevitable data problems, problems of measurement and estimation of variables and parameters, there are fundamental conceptual problems. It is a comparative static model describing the system in equilibrium at specific points in time and giving no explicit account of the dynamics of urban and regional systems. It also assumes that population and service employment are dependent on basic employment, and that basic employment is not dependent on other activities, which, as discussed in Chapter 4, is clearly unrealistic.

4 Summary

In many regions the regular central place spatial structure tends to be rather distorted by agglomerations. Growth pole theory has been adapted not only to explain such distortions but also as a policy tool in regional planning. Unfortunately its value in both explanatory and planning rôles suffers from much semantic confusion over the theory and its underlying concepts. This chapter has sought to clear some of the haze—making a distinction between growth poles and growth centres, outlining and examining the underlying concepts and suggesting a typology of applications. The basic concepts of leading industries, polarisation and spread effects appear intuitively attractive, yet their theoretical basis and empirical validity are rather thin. Nevertheless, when taken together they provide a valuable complement to central place theory in an explanation of the regional anatomy and provide several concepts of immediate value and relevance to the regional planner. However if we wish to examine the movement between activities within the region, a different form of model, a model of spatial interaction, is required. The last few years have witnessed considerable developments in mathematical land use modelling, and a range of partial and general models now provide an increasingly comprehensive picture of both regional and urban systems.

References

1 Perroux, F., *La notion de pôle de croissance, l'économie de xxème siècle,* 2nd edition page 143, Paris, (1964).

2 Boudeville, J., *Problems of Regional Economic Planning,* Edinburgh U.P. (1966).

3 Darwent, D. F., Growth Poles and Growth Centres in Regional Planning, *Environment and Planning,* 1, 1 (1969).

4 Perroux, F., and Boudeville, J., *op cit;*
Hansen, N. M., Development Pole Theory in a Regional Context, *Kyklos,* XX, pages 709–25 (1967);
Allen, K., and Hermansen, T., *Regional Policy in EFTA: An Examination of the Growth Centre Idea,* EFTA Secretariat, Geneva (1968);
Hirschman, A. O., *The Strategy of Economic Development,* Yale (1958);
Myrdal, G., *Economic Theory and Underdeveloped Regions,* Duckworth (1957);
UNRISD, *Concept and Theories of Growth Poles and Growth Centres,* Geneva (1970).

5 See: Hoover, E. M., *The Location of Economic Activity,* McGraw Hill (1948); and Isard, W., *Location and Space Economy,* MIT Press (1956).

6 Hoover, E. M., and Isard, W., *ibid.*

7 Buswell, D., and Lewis, E., Geographical Distribution of Industrial Research Activity in the United Kingdom, *Regiona Studies,* 4, 3 (1970).

8 Lasuen, J. R., On growth poles, *Urban Studies,* pages 137–61, 6 (1969).

9 Myrdal, G., and Hirschmann, A. O., *op cit.*

10 Nichols, V., Growth Poles: an evaluation of their propulsive effect, *Environment and Planning,* 1, 2 (1969).

11 Hägerstrand, T., *Innovation Diffusion as a Spatial Process,* Chicago (1967).

12 UNRISD, *Growth Poles and Growth Centres in Regional Policies and Planning,* Geneva (1971);
Allen, K., and Hermansen, T. *op cit.*

13 Hermansen, T., Development poles and development centres in national and regional development—elements of a theoretical framework, in UNRISD, *Concepts and Theories of Growth Poles and Growth Centres, op cit.*

14 See for example; Friedman, J., *Regional Development Policy: A Case Study of Venezuela,* MIT Press (1967);
Hilhorst, J. G. M., Spatial Structure and Decision Making, in Dunham, D. M., and Hilhorst J. G. M. (eds), *Issues in Regional Planning,* Mouton, The Hague (1971).

161

15 See: Urban Development Models—New Tools for Planning, *Journal of the American Institute of Planners,* May 1965.

16 Lowry, I. S., *Seven Models of Urban Development: A Structural Comparison,* P—3673, Santa Monica, California, RAND Corporation (1967).

17 Wilson, A. G., Models in Urban Planning: A Synoptic View of the Literature, *Urban Studies,* **5,** 3 (1968).

18 Batty, M., Recent Developments in Land Use Modelling: A Review of British Research, *Urban Studies,* **9,** 2 (1972).

19 Wilson, A. G., *Entropy in Urban and Regional Modelling,* Pion Ltd (1970).

20 Batty, M., *op cit.*

21 Lakshmanan, T. R., and Hansen, W. G., A Retail Market Potential Model, *Journal of American Institute of Planners,* **31** (1965).

22 Univ. of Manchester, *Regional Shopping Centres: A Planning Report on North West England, Part 2: A Retail Shopping Model,* Department of Planning (1965).

23 Lowry, I. S., *A Model of Metropolis,* RM—4035—RC, Santa Monica, California, RAND Corporation (1964).

24 Garin, R. A., A Matrix Formulation of the Lowry Model for Intra-Metropolitan Activity Location, *Journal of American Institute of Planners,* **32** (1966).

25 Batty, M., The Impact of a New Town, *Journal of Town Planning Institute,* pages 428–35, **55** (1969).

26 Cripps, E. L., and Foot, D. H. S., A Land Use Model for Sub-Regional Planning, *Regional Studies,* **3** (1969).

27 Steeley, G., Analysis by the Garin-Lowry Model, in *CES—IP— 11 Papers from the Seminar on the Notts–Derbys. Sub-regional Study,* London: CES (1970).

28 Masser, I., Notes on the Application of the Lowry Model to Merseyside, *Department of Civic Design, University of Liverpool* (1970).

PART THREE

The Practice of Regional Planning

9   Inter-regional planning in the United Kingdom

Inter-regional planning is primarily concerned with the centrally directed allocation of resources between aggregate regions to achieve certain regional and national objectives. This form of planning, often under the title of regional industrial development planning or regional policy, has been pursued in several countries for some years although its relative importance varies according to the stage of development of the country. Friedman[1] suggests that there are four stages of development: pre-industrial, transitional, industrial and post-industrial. In pre-industrial societies, such as Bolivia and Afghanistan, the policy emphasis is on the creation of preconditions for economic 'take-off' and regional policy is inappropriate. In transitional societies, such as Venezuela and Brazil, there is a need to create a spatial framework suitable for sustaining economic growth, and here regional policy becomes critical. The third stage, the industrial society, typical of much of Western Europe, including the UK, often reaps the costs of industrialisation, especially in the form of depressed regions resulting from overspecialisation. In the final stage, the post-industrial society, typified by the USA, there is a shift to a new focus with the emphasis on urban and metropolitan problems. Here the emphasis will be on the regional problems of industrial societies, concentrating on the UK situation. In the UK, the origins of inter-regional planning stem back to the depression years of the 1920's and 1930's, when there was government intervention to aid a few particularly depressed areas. Since that time the scope and content has widened and there are now a whole range of financial, infrastructural and control policies directed at a variety of problem regions.

An examination of the practice of inter-regional planning in the UK requires a consideration of several aspects. Firstly the broad problem regions must be identified. Conventionally, the problem regions in a country are those that as a whole are materially worse off, reflected by indicators such as unemployment, low activity rates, low growth rates and a high level of outmigration. There are however also those regions which because they are growing so fast are also suffering from certain problems such as congestion and rising factor prices.

But the identification of problem regions does not in itself constitute a case for intervention. Indeed, regional variations are universal and there is, therefore, secondly a need to investigate the case for intervention, outlining goals and specific objectives against which the effectiveness of any policy can be appraised. The ends of inter-regional planning, the goals and objectives, usually have a strong economic flavour such as the achievement of high growth rates and the efficient utilisation of resources. But what of the means to these ends?

Inter-regional planning can adopt a variety of broad strategies, but the two main approaches have usually been a Labour Migration Policy (workers to the work) or an Industrial Location Policy (work to the workers) or some combination of both. In Britain, a policy of encouraging the migration of labour out of the depressed industrial areas was adopted for some time in the depression years, but the emphasis quickly switched to a policy of industrial location which has been dominant ever since.

The actual tactics of inter-regional planning, the instruments for carrying out the broad strategies, provide a fourth area for investigation, and raise a multitude of questions. Should industry be encouraged to move to parts of problem regions rather than regions as a whole, concentrating aid on growth points with potential rather than spreading it thinly over a wider area? What type of industry should be encouraged to move—service or manufacturing, public or private? How should industry be encouraged to move, by controls over location, financial incentives or infrastructural investment?

A final and important factor in an examination of the practice of inter-regional planning, especially in the UK where there is a history of some 40 years of intervention, is a general appraisal of its effectiveness with regard to its intended goals and objectives. This general appraisal plus specific assessments of particular strategies and tactics may suggest possible new directions for future inter-regional planning in the UK.

1 The identification of UK problem regions—how many nations?

Every country has its regional variations, but it is probably true to say that Britain is more varied than most. The recent book by Rawstron and Coates[2] provides an interesting picture of some of these differences. These variations can be a source of strength, stability and progress to a country, but they can also indicate the presence of certain regions with deep-seated problems. These problems place the regions at a relative disadvantage to the rest of the country. The problem regions are usually identified by certain standard indicators or symptoms, such as income levels, activity rates, growth rates, unemployment levels and migration flows. Although such indicators are no more than the tip of the iceberg of the fundamental underlying economic problems, their variations do provide a useful picture of relative regional prosperity. The indicators tend to be largely interdependent and self-reinforcing. For example, low income levels, low activity rates and high levels of unemployment in themselves reflect slow economic growth and usually lead to a high level of outmigration.

Table 9.1 illustrates the application of these indicators to the UK Economic Planning Regions. At a first glance at the table it might seem that the UK subdivides simply into a prosperous South and East ('the centre') with generally higher than average income levels, activity rates and rates of employment growth, and lower than average unemployment levels plus net migration gains; and a relatively less prosperous North and West ('the periphery') with lower income levels, activity rates rates and of employment growth but higher levels of unemployment and outmigration. Such a broad division, however, hides many variations, for

Table 9.1. Standard indicators of UK problem regions

Region	Average total weekly household income (67–68) as % of UK	Activity rates (male and female) (June 1968)	Percentage change in employment (61–66)		Unemployment average annual percentage (65–71)	Net migration average annual flow (000's) (61–66)
			Total	Male		
Northern Ireland	85	48·9	+ 1	− 2	7·0	− 6·9
Scotland	96	56·4	+ 3	− 1	3·9	− 38·8
Wales	90	47·1	+ 2	− 1	3·8	+ 1·9
North	91	51·8	+ 3	+ 2	4·1	− 7·1
Yorkshire and Humberside	88	56·1	+ 1	0	2·3	− 1·0
North West	96	58·1	+ 6	+ 4	2·6	− 5·7
South West	96	47·0			2·5	+ 24·8
United Kingdom	100 (£29·1)	56·2	+ 4	+ 2	2·3	+ 15·7
West Midlands	105	60·2	+ 6	+ 5	2·0	+ 7·1
East Midlands	97	56·3	+ 6	+ 4	1·9	+ 8·7
East Anglia	97	48·5	+ 13	+ 11	2·0	+ 11·9
South East	112	59·7	+ 5	+ 4	1·5	+ 20·8

SOURCES: *Family Expenditure Survey*; *Abstract of Regional Statistics*; *The Intermediate Areas*, Cmnd. 3998 (Appendix C.)

regional problems take many forms and no two regions are alike. Because of this variety, it of course follows that any finer classification is bound to be somewhat arbitrary, with any one region overlapping more than one category. Nevertheless it does seem possible to identify three broad categories of problem regions: the underdeveloped region, the depressed industrial region and the pressured region, each with its own distinctive set of problems.

1 *Underdeveloped/Sparsely populated regions.* Although such areas are more prominent in several other European countries, for example the Mezzogiorno of Italy, large areas of northern Scandinavia and the Massif Central of France, they are also found in the UK, where the Highlands of Scotland, the Scottish Borders and Mid-Wales would come under this classification. Such regions often cover a large proportion of the area of the countries concerned, although their populations may be quite small and scattered. The Scottish Highlands cover about 23% of the total land area of the UK, yet have less than 2% of the total population.

They are heavily dependent on primary occupations, especially agriculture, forestry, fishing, mining and quarrying, which may be suffering from a variety of factors such as a low income elasticity of demand for their main products, low levels of productivity, exhaustion of natural resources, outdated technology and so on. This situation is reflected in unemployment problems, low levels of income and rates of growth and, consequently, high levels of outmigration. This migration may be first to the larger centres within the region, but this is often only a stepping stone to movement completely out of the region. The migration tends to be selective taking the young and skilled, and this factor plus the poor service provision and geographical isolation of the regions makes the areas less attractive to modern industrial development, creating a typical Myrdal 'cumulative-causation' process.

2 *Depressed industrial regions.* In contrast to the first category, the UK probably provides the most widespread examples of depressed industrial regions. These are areas which went through the process of industrialisation in the nineteenth century and are now

169

suffering from an over-reliance on declining and stagnating industries. The decline may be caused by a general contraction in the demand for the products of such industries or because productivity is increasing rapidly through technological progress. As a result, the regional economic base is unable to utilise the regional resources to the full, and the regions display all the usual symptoms of high rates of unemployment and outmigration, and low activity rates, growth rates and levels of *per capita* income.

UK examples of depressed industrial areas are, with the exception of South Wales, found in the northern part of the country. The intensity of the problem tends to vary according to the narrowness of the industrial base. Central Scotland and North East England have suffered from an overdependence on coal and shipbuilding; the decline of the textile industry has been a major determinant in Northern Ireland, Lancashire and Yorkshire; and the problems of the iron and steel industry, and again coal mining, have been the major factors in the declining prosperity of West Cumberland and South Wales.

It should be added that, although the poor industrial structure with a lack of national growth industries may be the fundamental problem of these regions, they may also have locational disadvantages, as illustrated in the analysis of Chapter 5. Thus, if an area is peripheral to national markets and has problems of industrial dereliction, pollution, an ageing infrastructure and an ageing workforce, it may be less attractive to new growth industries. This suggests that a resolution of the problems may not only require industrial restructuring to widen the industrial base but also some investment in new infrastructure.

3 *Pressured regions.* These regions are found in most countries, and in the UK, large areas of the South East would fall into this category. The problems of the pressured regions are to some extent the reverse of the other problem regions. Because of an imbalance in their industrial structure in favour of growth industries and services, and the attraction of new industries to the agglomeration economies, these regions are developing at a rapid rate. Such growth brings undoubted benefits—full employment, high activity rates and high levels of income—but

there are also costs. There is too much development chasing too few resources and this is reflected in rising factor costs, congestion costs and the need for heavy investment in public infrastructure, (e.g. London's ringway system). In the long run, a wide range of social costs—noise, pollution and long journeys to work may effectively reduce the value of that ephemeral factor, the quality of life. The Barlow Commission recognised the existence of these problems in the South East as early as 1940, but it is only more recently that it has been recognised that the UK regional problems are not the monopoly of the depressed northern regions. It should also be recognised that the regional problems are interdependent. The growth of regions such as the South East is usually at the expense of the depressed industrial and underdeveloped regions. Conversely, any diversion of growth away from the pressured regions may have beneficial effects on the other problem regions.

There are of course alternative approaches to the 'underdeveloped/depressed/pressured' method of classification. Klaassen seeks to identify problem regions dynamically by means of a matrix approach as in Table 9.2. The criteria used here is regional income only, although multivariate analysis combining a range of socio-economic criteria can be used in a more comprehensive application. The advantage of the Klaassen approach is its emphasis on the dynamic characteristics of regional problems, identifying not only the prosperous regions and the 'hardcore' problem regions, but also regions that are developing out of problem situations and others that are facing potential decline. Policy characteristics would obviously vary according to the type of problem region, with for example an emphasis on the improvement of regional infrastructure to stimulate the continued growth of the industrial base of developing distressed areas; and a holding operation on the declining industrial base of potential distressed areas, while generally developing the growth of new light industries. Another classification by Friedman[3] similarly isolates the 'upward' and 'downward' moving regions, also stressing the relationship between 'core' regions and 'peripheral' problem areas.

The identification of problem regions is of major importance in inter-regional planning; but this identification, whatever the method adopted, does not in itself constitute a case to intervene to help the *whole* of any particular problem region. There may be a need for a more selective identification of particular areas of need and potential within the wider region. Nor of course, does the initial identification constitute a case for intervention at all.

Regional Income Level / National Income Level — Growth rate of Regional Income / Growth rate of National Income	High ($\geqslant 1$)	Low (< 1)
High ($\geqslant 1$)	Prosperity Area	Developing Distressed Area
Low (< 1)	Potential Distressed Area	Distressed Area

Table 9.2. *Klaassen's Typology of Problem Areas.*

SOURCE: Klaassen, L., Area Social and Economic Redevelopment, OECD (1965).

2 The case for intervention—goals and objectives

If the various regional problems were self-righting over a short period of time, there would be little case for intervention. However, Chapter 5 shows that regional growth may not be convergent. The diseconomies of prosperous regions may be offset by other economic and socio-psychological benefits; occupational immobility may hinder resource reallocation to more efficient growth sectors within the other problem regions; and inter-regional migration of firms and labour may be limited by economic and non-economic factors, such as uniform national wage rates for particular jobs and the strength of family ties. It must also be added that even if a *laissez-faire* approach was eventually self-righting, the inevitable distress of the intervening period would probably necessitate some form of intervention.[4] This suggests that there may be a case for intervention, but intervention is costly and there is a need for further evidence that such action is justified on economic and/or non-economic grounds. In particular, does intervention contribute to an achievement of the national economic goals of economic growth, full employment, price stability, a balance of payments and social equity?

Economic arguments figure prominently in the case for intervention. The indicators of the previous section reveal the imbalance between the depressed industrial and underdeveloped regions and the pressured regions. The former suffer from an 'under-utilisation' of scarce resources, reflected in high unemployment rates, low activity rates and a high level of outmigration; while the latter have an 'over-utilisation' of resources, reflected in immigration and high factor costs, congestion costs and levels of public expenditure. A reduction in this imbalance can have important implications for the regional and national economies.

The economic growth of the country could be substantially increased by utilising more fully the wasted resources of the depressed and underdeveloped regions. In the first British attempt at long-run national planning, the NEDC[5] estimated that a reduction in the differences between the problem region unemployment and activity rates and the corresponding national rates by half would add an extra 300 000 to the labour force. This represented a gain of 1·3% corresponding to an increase of £500m in GNP. Another constraint on economic growth is the rate of inflation. The regional imbalance tends to make the control of inflation difficult. Excess demand pulls up factor prices in the pressured regions, and these inflationary increases are passed on to the rest of the country via national agreements. In addition, the imbalance also limits government flexibility in the use of deflationary controls, as the latter have an exaggerated impact on the depressed and underdeveloped regions causing large rises in their unemployment levels. Thus, any reduction in regional imbalance will also facilitate a greater control over inflation, and likewise over the balance of payments situation.

Social arguments are also important in assessing the case for intervention. The cumulative process of regional growth increases

173

the gap between the rich and the poor regions. The latter are trapped in a 'vicious circle', a downward stagnation spiral. The lack of economic opportunities and poor environmental conditions encourage selective outmigration, leaving a top-heavy population distribution, poorer services and an overall reduction in the growth potential of the area. By intervening in these problems and reducing differences in per capita regional income levels, regional policy can make a substantial contribution to the national goal of social equality.

Finally, *political arguments*, although often not explicit, are nonetheless of considerable importance. Their importance stems from the fact that they are felt directly in the areas in question. People feel very strongly about problems such as unemployment. It follows that in democratic countries it is a sound policy to appease depressed areas because such areas if neglected for some time will invariably vote against the government. If the neglect extends over a long period, nationalist tendencies may develop. It is arguable that the poverty of Ireland coupled with the unwillingness of Britain to help, precipitated Irish independence in 1916. The revival of Scottish and Welsh nationalism provides a more recent illustration. Similarly, although the roots of the more recent Northern Ireland crisis are complex and much deeper, recent economic problems of the province do not help the situation.

Thus, there would seem to be a case that intervention to reduce regional imbalance makes useful contributions not only to the 'manifest' national socio-economic goals, but also to more 'latent' political goals. These general goals and such comprehensive aims as 'regional balance', as has been noted earlier, are necessarily vague and generalised. Inter-regional planning requires their translation into more specific, quantitative regional objectives against which the effectiveness of policy can be appraised. These objectives will vary according to the problems of each region, but since these problems stem largely from structural and locational conditions, objectives should preferably be related to such factors. In practice, however, the achievement of certain standards in the various socio-economic indicators outlined earlier—per capita regional income, activity rates, growth rates, levels of unemployment and net migration rates—are the most usual regional objectives.

Conflicts are inevitable between the mass of goals and objectives. The national goal of social equity may be in conflict with the achievement of a high growth rate. Regional objectives, such as the maximisation of the regional growth rate, may conflict with the national goal of maximising growth. Similarly, the objectives of one region may conflict with those of another. Short-run objectives may conflict with long-run objectives and so on. The effective integration of these various goals and objectives is a particularly difficult problem, but it is hoped that the development of techniques such as Planning-Programming-Budgeting Systems will facilitate the task.[6]

3 A choice of strategy—labour migration or industrial location?

A policy of intervention to alleviate the regional problems, particularly the imbalance in the supply and demand for labour, requires firstly a choice of broad strategy. This choice has tended to be between two alternatives, a policy of labour migration or a policy of industrial location. Migration is basically the *laissez-faire* approach, while the encouragement of investment in the problem areas involves more public intervention, although this is not to say that there cannot be a policy for labour migration also. There has been much written on the advantages and disadvantages of the alternatives (see: West, Needleman and Nevin[7]), but the policy of industrial location has been dominant in UK inter-regional planning and in most other countries and its relative merits require some investigation.

Political and social considerations are again of considerable importance. Fear of election reversals and the development of separatist movements not only means intervention, but intervention not unfavourable to the problem regions. One could imagine the uproar from the Welsh Nationalists if the policy for Wales was one of outmigration, rural depopulation, making the area into 'a playground for the English'! Similarly, a policy of moving workers out of the depressed and underdeveloped regions would be contrary to the equity arguments of equal opportunity in all areas of the country. It would also erode the variety of regional identities reflected in the range of customs, backgrounds, languages and dialects, and many would regard this as a major social loss.

The whole case for moving the work rather than the workers is on a much more secure foundation however, if it can be shown that the policy of industrial location has undoubted economic advantages. In this respect, three economic arguments which justify some examination are: that there are economic disadvantages in labour migration; that not all under-utilised labour will in fact migrate resulting in a perpetual unemployment wastage; and that the guidance of industrial location may not be harmful and may indeed be beneficial to the individual firms involved as well as to the regions and the nation.

It can be argued that outmigration has disadvantages for the three parties involved—for the individual migrant, and for the regions of 'departure' and 'reception'. Migration undoubtedly involves a high private cost to the individual, involving quantifiable factors such as house removal and non-quantifiable factors such as the costs of leaving friends and relations. Even if a person does migrate, he may be quickly disillusioned by his new location and return to his 'native hearth'. (Although this is not to suggest that migration is not without benefits to the individual, for in our increasingly mobile society it can at times lead to the introduction of new personal opportunities and the breakdown of social barriers.)

Migration may also impose wider social costs on the region of departure. The loss of the migrant's income and expenditure will have a negative multiplier effect on local services, and low activity rates will be reduced even more making the area less attractive to incoming industry. In the extreme cases of heavy outmigration, there may also be some waste of valuable social capital—houses, schools, hospitals and so on—although much of this often needs scrapping anyway.

The costs imposed by migration on the receiving region have been the subject of much debate. Needleman[8] has argued that migration to the pressured regions of the South East and the West Midlands increases the inflationary pressures. An additional worker will not only create a positive multiplier effect through his own expenditure, but through his need for social capital (housing) and economic capital (plant/machinery) will generate a derived

176

demand for more labour, thus encouraging rising factor prices, congestion costs and demand for expensive public infrastructure. Needleman in fact suggests that the movement of one worker may create an extra two jobs. The argument obviously depends on whether the migrant demands more than he supplies, and Richardson,[9] introducing a time element, takes a rather different view. He argues that the immediate effect is to increase labour supply with extra demand being soaked up by the more intensive use of existing services. By the time the effects of the migrants on investment is felt, the supply position will have readjusted.

Whatever the inducements to migrate out of the problem regions, there will always be a 'hard core' of unemployed who for some reason will not leave the region. They may be unskilled workers who are not as mobile as the skilled; young school leavers and others tied to relations; and those who just cannot afford the cost of moving, especially if they are moving from an area such as Scotland with its history of artificially low house rents. In addition, there are in many problem regions a large number of people, especially married women, who are available for work but do not register as unemployed. Nor will they wish to migrate as long as their husbands have jobs. This is part of the pool of 'hidden unemployment' reflected in the low activity rates in many regions. Only by bringing work to the workers can these unemployed resources be fully utilised, and although it has been claimed that such labour resources are often 'rusty' and less productive than those in the prosperous areas,[10] the argument has tended to carry some weight.

Against these reasons for an industrial location policy, it has been argued that interference in the locational freedom of industry is harmful leading to a fall in efficiency and a decline in national economic growth. If a firm is prevented from expanding in the South East or the West Midlands, it may not expand at all or may even move abroad. Further, subsidisation to aid industrial mobility may also lead to stagnation by keeping inefficient firms in business. The analysis of Chapter 6, however, suggests that such arguments can be effectively countered. It was shown that profits may vary only slightly over a fairly large area, allowing a firm to locate within fairly wide limits without too much concern. Within this range, the final location is usually a 'satisfactory'

177

rather than an 'optimal' location. Thus any guidance of a firm's location may impose little or no private costs to the firms. Indeed it may actually create benefits, breaking down socio-psychological barriers to certain regions and introducing more preferable locations not previously considered. The relocation of firms out of the pressured regions may also reduce social costs, provided that the new location avoids the equally congested urban areas in the other problem regions.

There would therefore appear to be some justification for the adoption of an industrial location policy in preference to one of labour migration. But the alternatives are not mutually exclusive and to completely rule out the migration of labour would be to oversimplify the situation. For some regions or parts of regions faced with a rapid decline in employment, the cost of moving in industry may be just too high, and a policy of encouraging inter-regional migration may be the only quick way of utilising otherwise wasted resources. As such, many countries include incentives to labour mobility as well as to industrial mobility in their tactics of inter-regional planning, although for political reasons the fact is not much emphasised.

4 The tactics of UK inter-regional planning

Britain was the first Western country to really come to grips with the problem of regional imbalance, and its history of intervention provides a good illustration of the various tactics of inter-regional planning and the associated problems.[11] Hence, this section seeks to outline the development of British policy, identifying the range of tactics used, prior to a discussion of their effectiveness and possible lines of improvement.

Any subdivision of policy over time is bound to be very arbitrary. However, there would seem to be four main periods with the first three providing the foundation for the rapid development of policy in the post-1960 period. These can be identified as:

a The Inter-war Period of the 1930's. This was the birth of the UK policy of intervention, and was mainly a response to the distressingly high levels of unemployment in the depression years. This was the only period when the strategy emphasis was more on moving the workers than the work.

b The Intermediate Post-war Years (1945–51). This post-war reconstruction period witnessed development of policy under a new Labour Government and the introduction of many measures, such as Development Areas and Industrial Development Certificates, which have been important ever since.

c The 1950's Lull. With the advent of a Conservative Government in 1951 and coinciding with a booming national economy, many regional measures fell into abeyance in the 1950's.

d The period from 1960 onwards. During this period a policy of intervention has been vigorously pursued under both Conservative and Labour governments, and a wide range of new measures have been introduced.

The measures can be subdivided into the various positive and negative tactics designed to facilitate industrial mobility; a series of measures to encourage labour mobility; and a more general but equally important range of measures designed primarily to improve the environment of the problem areas. Over time, these various measures have been largely administered by the central government through the Board of Trade, although the present responsibility now lies with the Department of Trade and Industry. Within this UK framework Northern Ireland has enjoyed a certain degree of autonomy with regard to policy measures.

THE EARLY FOUNDATIONS OF UK POLICY

The inter-war period

Although there had been problems of rural decline before, the incidence of depression in the old traditional industrial areas of Britain in the late 1920's and 1930's created a new dimension in regional problems. Unemployment rates varied between 20 and 30% and even in the prosperous South East were as high as 10–15%. Such problems created untold misery and hardship, as revealed by H. Powys Greenwood in a study of West Cumberland in the 1930's.

' . . . West Cumberland, a district as favoured by nature as any in Great Britain for scenery, climate and natural wealth, has been in the grip of intense depression ever since the War. Only seven miles from Seascale, at Egremont, the long line of derelict mining villages begins, where over 10 000 good men are eating their hearts out in idleness and, what is far worse, losing little by little the capacity for work if it should come. If we drive along the endless straggling streets of Cleator, Cleator Moor, Frizingdon and Arlecdon, we shall hardly see a smiling face, only little groups of men, and women too, hanging about at every street corner with soured, hopeless, expressions.'[12]

The first response to these problems was a policy to encourage labour migration out of the worst areas. Under the Industrial Transfer Act of 1928, centres were established to retrain men in new skills and removal costs were subsidised. Approximately 250 000 people moved under the scheme between 1929 and 1938, but many returned somewhat discrediting the 'workers to the work' strategy in Britain, and indelibly stamping on many people's minds the impression that the geographical transfer of labour was a 'bad thing'.

As an alternative approach, the government introduced the Special Areas (Development and Improvement) Act, 1934, which was the first legislative measure affecting the distribution of industry. Four particular problem areas were designated as Special Areas—Clydeside, West Cumberland, the North East coast of England and South Wales—and two Commissioners were charged with the duty of facilitating their 'economic development and social improvement'. Their particular aim was to attract expanding industries to the areas. Unfortunately they had little financial power, although the introduction of the Special Areas Reconstruction Association (SARA) and Special Areas Loans Advisory Committee (SALAC) to provide loan capital for small and large firms in the areas, somewhat improved the position. However, probably the most positive achievement of this period was the formation of trading estates in the problem areas, and towards the end of the 1930's, 12 000 people were employed in factories, mainly on the three large estates at Hillingdon, Team Valley and Treforest.

The symptoms of the regional problems disappeared during the war, with the demand for armaments and shipping reviving the traditional heavy industries. But the deep-seated problems were still there, and this had prompted the government to set up the Royal Commission on the Distribution of the Industrial Population in 1937. The Commission subsequently reported in 1940 (the Barlow Report),[13] although the war prevented any immediate consideration of its recommendations. The terms of reference of the Barlow Report fell into three sections: to examine the causes of the present distribution of industry, population and future trends; to investigate the social, economic and strategic disadvantages of this distribution; and to suggest remedial measures to be taken to improve the situation.

The Report showed the trend to the South East to be a result of many factors, including the decline in the traditional basic industries, the destruction of the locational monopoly of coal, the growth of high-value, market-oriented light industries and the improvement in communications. The concentration of the industrial population in the South East was seen to have many disadvantages. Social costs, especially the dangers to health from overcrowding, were particularly stressed. The various economies of scale were shown to be offset by a wide range of diseconomies, and at the time the report was prepared, the concentration of the industrial population in the South East was also regarded as a strategic risk.

As such, the Commission recommended that a national agency should be established with the objectives of redeveloping congested urban areas, encouraging the decentralisation and dispersal of both industry and industrial population from such areas, encouraging a reasonable balance of industrial development throughout the regions of Britain and checking the continued drift to the South East. The Majority Report believed that this agency should be a small body under the Board of Trade with mainly advisory and research functions but with some control over industrial location in the South East. The Minority Report was more positive in its recommendations advocating the setting up of a Ministry to deal with the problems, and the extension of controls of industrial location to the entire country with the simultaneous application of positive inducements to promote balanced industrial development.

The Barlow Report has rightly been hailed as the foundation

of post-war British planning. It is a document of tremendous importance and such foresight that only now are some of its ideas being developed. The report showed that the regional problem was an economic as well as a social problem. It emphasised the relationship of physical planning and regional economic planning, and showed the connections between the problems of congested conurbations and the depressed regions (although it should be noted that depressed regions also have their congested areas).

The immediate post-war years

The Beveridge White Paper on Employment Policy in 1944,[14] followed many of the recommendations of the Barlow Report. It pledged itself to full employment and believed that regional unemployment could be combated by a combination of influencing the location of new industries, revitalising existing industries, retraining the labour force in new skills and encouraging labour mobility. The legislation for this policy introduced the 'carrot' and 'stick' tactics.

Under the Distribution of Industry Act, 1945, supplemented by the Distribution of Industry Act, 1950, the four Special Areas were extended, increasing in population from 4 to 6½ million, and were renamed Development Areas. Smaller problem areas were added in 1946 and 1949. In the Development Areas the Treasury could make loans and grants to prospective and established firms on the advice of an independent advisory committee (Development Areas Treasury Advisory Committee), provided that the firms had no alternative source of finance and had good prospects of success. Other inducements included tax allowances on new investments and limited grants for environmental improvements. But by far the greatest inducement was the accelerated development of industrial estates and advanced factories in the Development Areas. The Board of Trade had powers to acquire land and build factories for lease, or sale, and to make loans to trading or industrial estate companies. £40 million were spent on this policy during this short period.

The negative aspect of the policy was first effected through the extension of wartime building licence controls. Between 1945 and 1947, licences were freely given for the Development Areas but were strictly controlled in other areas. However, in 1947, the Town and Country Planning Act introduced a new method of control, the Industrial Development Certificate (IDC), which, in amended form, has been effective ever since. Any application for industrial development in excess of 5000 square feet required a certificate. By granting or refusing the certificate, the Board of Trade could channel development to problem areas.

The 1950's lull

The post-war boom in the early and mid-1950's temporarily masked the regional problem. Pent-up war demand for the products of the traditional industries (coal, iron and steel, ships) at times resulted in the problem regions' growth rates being higher than the national average. In the face of this prosperity, many regional measures fell into temporary disuse. Very little was spent on positive inducements (£4–5 million p.a. compared with the £10–12 million average in the earlier period), and IDC's were freely given for development in the Midlands and the South East.

But by 1957–58 the situation began to deteriorate rapidly. The post-war boom was seen to be the last fling of many traditional industries facing secular decline, and this decline was further exacerbated by national deflationary measures to combat inflation and balance of payments problems. The regional problem symptoms reappeared with a vengeance, and the government was spurred into action, tightening IDC controls and introducing the Distribution of Industry (Industrial Finance) Act, 1958—the only regional legislation of any importance during the period. This Act extended the power of the Treasury to give financial assistance, and designated several new development areas. These were certain belts of specialised unemployment, such as Cornwall and North East Suffolk, which had suffered rates of unemployment over 4% for twelve months prior to designation. But this Act was typical of an approach which appeared to be more concerned with containing the symptoms of the problem rather than eliminating the root cause. It also added to the confusion caused by the varying availability of inducements in different areas.

Several factors, such as the ineffectiveness of the then existing policy, the increasing severity of the regional problems and the realisation that their alleviation might be in the interests of national economic growth as well as social equality, prompted some fundamental rethinking at the beginning of the 1960's. During the following decade both Conservative and Labour governments ploughed through a welter of legislation seeking to introduce more effective tactics, all of which was at times rather confusing to the industrialist. Policy was pursued particularly vigorously under the 1964–70 Labour Administration. At first, the return of a Conservative Government in 1970 suggested a more 'conservative' attitude, but recent legislation, the 1972 Industry Bill, marks a rather more positive approach. From the mass of legislation arising from this period, several important trends in the precise delineation of assisted areas and in the use of measures to aid these areas can be observed.

The delineation of assisted areas

In 1960, the Development Areas, evolved from the inter-war Special Areas and delineated almost exclusively by the criterion of unemployment, covered slightly less than 20% of the country with a population of approximately seven millions. By 1972, this 'blanket' approach had been replaced by a more sophisticated hierarchy of Special Development Areas, Development Areas and Intermediate Areas, based on multiple criteria including unemployment, and covering more than 50% of the country and including a population of approximately 25 millions (Figure 9.1).

However, the first stage in this replacement of the 'blanket' approach was rather a backward one. Under the 1960 Local Employment Act, the Development Areas were replaced by Development Districts. The criterion for delineation was basically the possession of an unemployment rate greater than $4\frac{1}{2}\%$ This unfortunately led to frequent re-scheduling as the unemployment in the areas improved or deteriorated. (Odber[15] provides an illustration of this situation in the North East). The policy also tended to aid those areas which had the least potential and were least attractive to industrialists.

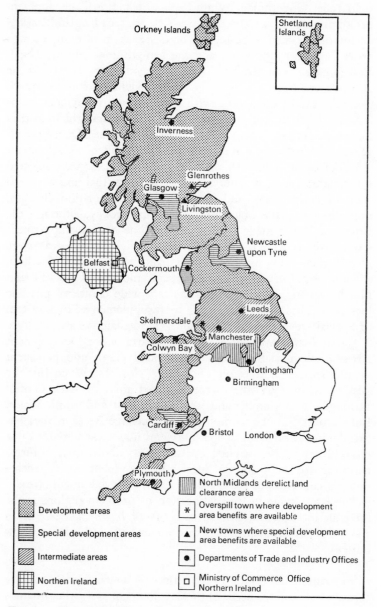

Fig 9.1 United Kingdom: the Assisted Areas (1972).

185

In 1963, Government White Papers on regional development programmes for Central Scotland and North East England marked an important turn in policy.[16] The designation of eight growth areas for Central Scotland and the growth zone for the North East (an area bounded by Tyneside, Teesside, the coast and the A1), allowed firms to choose the locations with maximum growth potential rather than those with hardcore unemployment problems and often limited prospects. But it was not until the Industrial Development Act (1966) that the narrowly defined Development Districts were finally abandoned and replaced by the Development Areas of today. Under this Act, *Development Areas* were selected on a wider range of criteria, including the actual and expected state of employment and unemployment, population changes, migration, and the objectives of regional policy, although the Board of Trade made it clear at the time that unemployment would still remain the main criterion. Five broad areas were identified covering most of Scotland and Wales, all the Northern Region and Furness, Merseyside and most of Cornwall and North Devon, allowing industrialists a wide choice of possible locations. These areas have since been supplemented by a system of Special Development Areas and Intermediate Areas.

Special Development Areas are those parts of the Development Areas likely to suffer from exceptionally high and persistent unemployment as a result of colliery closures. When initially designated in 1967, they were localised areas of West Central Scotland, West Cumberland, the North East and South Wales. But the addition of 71 Employment Exchange Areas in 1971 has greatly increased their scope and they now bear a remarkable resemblance to the original Special Areas of the 1930's. Firms choosing to locate in the Special Development Areas receive inducements extra to those locating in the Development Areas.

The latest stage in this delineation of problem regions is the introduction of an additional category of *Intermediate Areas*. In 1967, the Government established a committee (the Hunt Committee):

'to examine in relation to the economic welfare of the country as a whole and the needs of the development areas, the situation in other areas where the rate of economic growth gives cause (or may give cause) for concern, and to suggest whether revised policies to influence economic growth in such areas are desirable and, if so, what measures should be adopted.'[17]

On the basis of the following criteria:

a sluggish or falling employment
b slow growth in personal incomes
c slow rate of addition to industrial and commercial premises
d significant unemployment
e low/declining proportion of women at work
f low earnings
g heavy reliance on industry whose labour demand was growing slowly or falling
h poor communications
i decayed/inadequate environment
j serious net outward migration

the Committee concluded that quite large areas of the country, including the whole of the North West and the Yorkshire and Humberside regions, should be designated as Intermediate Areas and receive inducements proportional to those in the Development Areas. In the light of the Committee's Report, the Government decided to provide some additional assistance for industrial development to some areas, although they were much smaller than those recommended. These areas were Leith, North East Lancashire, the Yorkshire Coalfield, South East Wales and Plymouth. However, the 1972 extension of the 'Grey Areas' to include the whole of the North West and Yorkshire and Humberside represents an eventual triumph for the Hunt recommendations.

Measures directed at the individual firm

The *negative controls* over industrial mobility have been a constant feature of policy. The IDC policy has continued to the present day, although the severity of its application has varied from government to government. In 1965, the Labour Government lowered the limit above which it was mandatory to apply for an IDC to 1000 square feet. This low limit proved to be unduly

187

restrictive and in 1966 was raised to 3000 square feet in the West Midlands and South East and 5000 square feet elsewhere. The advent of a Conservative Government has subsequently raised the limit again. In 1972 it was raised to 15 000 square feet in all areas except the South East where it was raised to 10 000 square feet. The need for IDC's in the Development and Special Development Areas has been dispensed with.

But IDC controls apply only to manufacturing industry. Yet since 1960, while national employment in manufacturing has actually been falling, employment in the service sector has increased at a rapid rate. This service growth was concentrated in the prosperous areas of the country, especially the South East. But it was not until 1965, with the Control of Office and Industrial Development Act, that negative controls were applied to the service sector. Under this act, Office Development Permits (ODP's) are required for office developments of more than 3000 square feet in Greater London and 10 000 square feet in the rest of the South East and the urban parts of the East and West Midlands. Criteria considered in the granting of ODP's in these restricted areas include whether the firm can work elsewhere, whether satisfactory alternative accommodation is available, and the public interest.

The *positive financial incentives* to attract industrialists to the scheduled areas have, in contrast with the negative controls, become increasingly important over the period. The expenditure on such incentives increased from under £10 million in 1959–60 to £303 million in 1969–70. Although these absolute figures of gross exchequer costs can be rather misleading in that loans are repaid, guarantees are not called upon and factory rents may increase from their low 'introductory offers', the trend is nevertheless highly significant. Three main categories of direct financial incentives to industrial mobility have been used over the period.

a Subsidies to a firm's capital costs. At first, loans and grants towards the costs of a new firm setting up in a scheduled area were at the discretion of the Board of Trade and assistance was provided to industrialists dependent upon the level of estimated employment likely to be created. The discretionary nature

188

of such loans and grants was their very weakness for firms never knew exactly what they would receive.

There was a need for a standard form of grant available to any firm moving to a scheduled area. The 'cost/value' building grant of the 1960 Local Employment Act, whereby a firm moving to a scheduled area received 85% of the difference between the estimated cost and the estimated value of the proposed premises in the open market, was an early attempt at such a grant. It was rather complicated though, and was replaced in 1963 by standard grants designed to make assistance both more generous and more predictable. The standard grants were payable at the rate of 25% of the cost of building, and 10% of the cost of acquiring and installing plant and machinery. This direct subsidy to capital investment has continued ever since although at times it has applied to buildings only, and the rates have varied considerably.

The 1963 Local Employment Act also introduced 'accelerated depreciation'. This allowed new investment in plant and machinery in the assisted areas to be written off against profits for tax purposes at whatever rate the company chose. This had the effect of providing firms with capital in the early periods when they most needed it and providing an incentive to efficiency and growth by rewarding profitability. As such, the measure was popular with firms. Nevertheless it was still shelved between 1966 and 1970 in favour of increased standard grants on the grounds that the latter were more practicable and, being independent of current profitability, would be particularly helpful to new firms initially making little profit. Second thoughts and a change of government have since resulted in a reintroduction of accelerated depreciation, but unfortunately its extension to the entire country (1972) has reduced its value as a regional incentive.

A particularly interesting innovation is the recent establishment (1972) of an entirely new Industrial Development Executive within the DTI to be largely concerned with the promotion of industrial growth in the assisted areas. It is anticipated that the existing standard grants, the regional development grants, will be administered through the regional offices of this executive, which will also have considerable powers of selective financial assistance to industry in the assisted areas.

b Subsidies to variable costs. The first attempt at subsidising labour costs rather than capital costs was more an afterthought of a national policy measure rather than a direct regional measure. The Selective Employment Tax (SET) introduced in 1966 was a per capita tax of £1·25 per week payable by all employers for each of their full-time employees. A weekly sum of £1·62½ per capita was paid back to manufacturing industry, but service industry received nothing. This transfer between sectors was designed to aid the export manufacturing industries. In 1967, the repayment to manufacturing industries was lowered to £1·25, with the exception of Development Areas which still received the full £1·62½, and thus received a preferential subsidy.

A more specific attempt at subsidising regional labour costs was the Regional Employment Premium (REP) introduced in 1967. This involves a payment toward the labour costs of all manufacturing industry in the Development and Special Development Areas at the rate of £1·50 per week for males, with lower rates for women and juveniles. In 1968–9 REP and the SET regional premium involved an expenditure of £125 million.

c Industrial estates and advance factories. The provision of fully serviced industrial estates and advance or custom-built factories has been one of the constant measures in regional policy. Firms can usually buy or rent such factories on very reasonable terms and in certain circumstances rent-free periods may be available.

Until 1960, the estates were run by five trading estate companies—the North East Trading Estates Ltd. (formed in 1936); the Wales/Monmouthshire Industrial Estates Ltd. (1936); the Scottish Industrial Estates Ltd. (1937); and the North Western Industrial Estates Ltd. (1946). Under the Local Employment Act (1960) these were reduced to three Industrial Estate Corporations for England, Scotland and Wales, under the overall control of the responsible Ministry.

Measures directed at the re-employment and mobility of labour

Chapter 6 showed that the presence of a large pool of unemployed labour in an area isn't necessarily attractive to industrialists. The labour is often immobile between occupations. It may

190

be unskilled or skilled in the wrong trades and its utilisation requires considerable expense on retraining. *Government retraining grants* have been available since the Industrial Transference Act in the inter-war period, but have been developed considerably over the last ten years. The various schemes are co-ordinated by the responsible labour ministry—now the Department of Employment. They include national schemes operated by the Industrial Training Boards, established in 1964; and special training schemes for the scheduled areas. The various schemes provide a range of subsidies including a weekly per capita grant (£15 per man, £12 per woman) for 'on-the-job' training or 'off-the-job' training in one of the 33 Government Training Centres in the scheduled areas; financial assistance with training older workers, and grants to firms towards the cost of new machinery and equipment needed for training purposes.

The Government has also provided a *range of grants to encourage labour mobility between areas*. Grants to facilitate the movement of key workers into the problem areas have been available for some time. There has also been a Resettlement Transfer Scheme to give help to workers who are willing to move their homes to have a better chance of a satisfactory job. This remnant of a 'workers to the work' policy has recently been strengthened, and in 1972 the grant to a trainee to meet miscellaneous expenses, especially rehousing costs, involved in a move was increased from £100 to £600.

General measures

In addition to the various central government measures directed specifically at firms and labour, UK regional policy has also included a number of important more general measures. The importance of the preferential provision of infrastructure in the scheduled areas has slowly been recognised. The location of government establishments and the selective placing of government contracts has also been utilised as a policy tool. Finally, the whole gamut of central government measures are now being complemented by promotional bodies at the regional level.

Infrastructure and public investment. Many of the scheduled areas suffer from poorer than average social capital, for example education, housing and welfare facilities, reflected in criteria such as overcrowding, high pupil-teacher ratios, below average ratios of GP's to population and very much above average death rates. The severity of some of these social disparities contributes much to the cumulative process of regional imbalance. At last special urban programmes are being introduced to tackle the wider anomalies, and these will no doubt aid development in the areas.

Attempts are also being made to improve the inferior economic capital of many of the scheduled areas. In the 1960's, the 'growth policies' in the North East and Central Scotland involved considerable investment in 'promotional infrastructure'. The 1963 'growth zone' policy for the North East involved an increase in government public service investment in the area from £55 million (1962–3) to £90 million (1964–5), with 5½% of the nation's population receiving 7% of the public expenditure. This expenditure was earmarked for projects such as the building of the Darlington and Durham motorways, the expansion of new towns at Cramlington, Washington and Newton Aycliffe, and a new industrial estate on Teesside.[18]

Preferential investment has focussed heavily on the provision of communications (the 1972 White Paper on *Industrial and Regional Development* sees fit to provide for extra communications expenditure in the scheduled areas[19]). In contrast, there seems to have been less preference in the new town and expanded towns programme. Indeed there has probably been some bias towards the prosperous regions with the main aim being to accommodate the growing South East population.[20] Here, most of the new developments have taken place within or just over the borders of the region and overspill to the distant problem regions has been limited to small and isolated schemes (the GLC has overspill agreements with Bodmin and Plymouth in the South West and Burnley in the North West). The development of areas such as Severnside, Humberside and Tayside, identified as possible future major national growth poles, would provide more genuine counter magnets to the South East and aids to the scheduled areas. (Of course, all this investment in regional infrastructure is very much related to the field of *intra-regional planning* and this will be discussed more fully in the following chapter.)

The location of government establishments and the placing of government contracts. Government expenditure has also been used to aid the assisted areas by utilising the government's rôle as a major producer and purchaser of goods and services. The large nationalised sector and the numerous government offices mean that the government itself has effective control over many industrial location decisions. This control can be used in the interests of the assisted areas, although as yet there has been only limited interference in the locational decisions of public concerns perhaps reflecting the declining fortunes of many of them. Nevertheless, some investment programmes and 'run-down' programmes have been swayed. In addition, there is evidence of the increasing use of government offices in regional development, as witnessed by the establishment of the Royal Mint in Wales, the National Giro on Merseyside and the Post Office in the North East.

The public sector's position as a purchaser is a potentially most powerful policy tool. At present, the Department of Trade and Industry operates two relevant schemes. Under the general preference scheme, a firm in a scheduled area will receive preference over a firm from a non-scheduled area in tendering for a government contract where the tenders are equal. Under the contracts preference scheme, the firm from the scheduled area can still receive up to 25% of a government contract even if its original tender is not the lowest, provided that it can meet the price of the accepted tender.

Regional industrial development bodies. As the scheduled areas have increased in size, so a businessman influenced by the various central government measures to locate within them, faces, even subject to the locational considerations of his own particular industry, a wider and wider choice of final location. In an attempt to attract firms to their own particular location, many local authorities in the same region have sought to increase the expertise and financial resources available for the task by grouping together to form Industrial Development Associations. The major development bodies in Britain at present include the Highlands and Islands Development Board in Scotland, the North East Development Council, the Mid-Wales Industrial Develop-

193

ment Association, and the North West Industrial Development Association.

The principle objective of the development body is to assist industry to expand profitably in the localities that it represents. This involves aid to indigenous industry as well as attempts to attract new firms into the area. Indeed, in terms of jobs created the former is usually of more importance. With limited staff and financial resources, the aid provided by the development bodies is more in the form of co-ordination and regional information rather than financial support. This may involve publicity campaigns, industrial promotion and also parliamentary pressure. For example the North East Development Council has used TV documentaries; in 1970 organised promotional visits to Holland, West Germany and North America; and as the last General Election approached presented a paper to the Government entitled 'The Need for a Development Area Policy'.[21]

The Regional Industrial Development Boards of the new Industrial Development Executive, to be based at Billingham, Bootle, Cardiff and Glasgow may also be intended to co-ordinate tactics at the regional level. The 1972 White Paper states:

'a strong regional organisation based on the regional offices of the DTI will be an essential part of the new Executive in the assisted areas. This organisation will have a new positive rôle in promoting industrial expansion and modernisation, and in stimulating centres of growth. It will have an important degree of devolved authority. It will co-operate closely with local authorities and other bodies and agencies, and provide advice and assistance to industry across the whole field of responsibility of the DTI. It will have full and direct access to the industrial and financial expertise within the Industrial Development Executive.'[22]

(A brief summary of the major regional measures at present applicable (1973) in the Special Development Areas, Development Areas and Intermediate Areas can be found in Appendix B.)

5 The effectiveness of UK policy

An appraisal of policy measures should consider both their

194

effectiveness and their efficiency. A measure is effective if its execution has the desired effect, whereas its efficiency is assessed by way of its 'cost-benefit' ratios. The overall effectiveness of the 40 years of UK policy will first be discussed, and the effectiveness and efficiency of specific policy tools and possible improvements will be examined in the next section.

The comprehensive aim of UK regional policy has been to right the 'regional imbalance', reflected in the under-utilisation of scarce resources in the depressed industrial and underdeveloped regions and their over-utilisation in the pressured regions, to achieve certain economic, social and political goals. Such goals include a halting of the 'vicious circle' of social decline in some areas and a containment of the 'costs of growth' in others. More specific objectives have been to achieve certain standards in socio-economic indicators, such as the achievement of the national norm in unemployment rates and per capita income in the problem regions (although for certain indicators such as growth in output and/or income, a poor region must grow faster than the national norm if it is to achieve parity).

As regional policy generally has no specific end date, effectiveness must be assessed on the basis of trends in the various indicators. For example, is the gap between per capita income in the poor regions and national per capita income narrowing? This form of assessment is not without problems. There are, firstly, statistical problems. The numerous changes in the boundaries of the scheduled areas makes the observation of trends over a reasonable period difficult. A compromise approach is to observe the trends in the larger problem regions, such as the Northern Region, Scotland and Northern Ireland, although it must be remembered that trends for such broad regions may hide numerous sub-regional variations. In addition, trends in particular indicators may often be misleading, masking more subtle variations in other factors. Thus a falling unemployment rate may be a function of rising outmigration, a rise in hidden unemployment or a fall in activity rates; while the achievement of a balance on net migration may hide the fact that a region is losing skilled young people and gaining old people. The most difficult problem however is to distinguish the effects due to regional policy from those that would have happened anyway. The improvement in a region's position may be due more to social and economic policies at the national level and nascent growth trends within the region rather than to specific regional measures. Finally, even if indicators such as unemployment levels are used, their short run trends may not accurately reflect changes in the underlying industrial structure of the region which are so fundamental to long-run regional recovery.

However in spite of these problems it is still a useful exercise to observe the trends in a number of indicators to gain at least a general picture of the effectiveness or otherwise of UK regional policy. Tables 9.3–9.6 illustrate some of these trends.

Unemployment trends are still the most popular indicator. Table 9.3 illustrates the persistent nature of the regional imbalance in the utilisation of labour over a 20-year period. Unemployment rates in the Northern Region, Scotland and Wales have been between

Table 9.3. *Regional Unemployment Rates as ratios of national average (UK = 100).*

Region	1951	1956	1961	1966	1971
North	169	115	157	163	160
Yorkshire and Humberside	69	62	63	75	108
East Midlands	38	46	63	69	84
West Midlands	31	85	88	81	108
North West	92	100	100	94	111
East Anglia	} 69	69	63	{ 88	84
South East				{ 63	54
South West	92	100	88	113	92
Wales	207	153	163	181	127
Scotland	192	184	193	181	163
Northern Ireland	468	492	468	381	216
United Kingdom	100	100	100	100	100
	(1·3)	(1·3)	(1·6)	(1·6)	(3·7)

SOURCES: Hammond, E., *An Analysis of Regional Economic and Social Statistics.* University of Durham Rowntree Research Unit (1968).
Abstract of Regional Statistics
Ministry of Labour Gazette
Northern Ireland Digest of Statistics.

50–100% higher than the national norm, and in Northern Ireland the rates have been even higher. However recent figures do suggest some slight convergence in the disparity, and the 'hard core' problem regions appear to have withstood the national economic troubles of the late 1960's and early 1970's 'relatively' better than other regions, such as the West Midlands. A cynic might conclude from this some fulfilment of Churchill's view of regional measures as a means of 'equalising misery'. The unemployment figures also of course serve to illustrate the importance of a buoyant national economy in the pursuance of regional balance.

But as mentioned earlier a consideration of the unemployment indicator in isolation can be misleading, and other indicators must be considered. Many people in a region available for work but with no job may not show up in the unemployment statistics. These people, including a high proportion of married women who find it uneconomical to 'sign on', constitute the pool of *hidden unemployed*. Recent work by Taylor,[23] identifying 'cyclical' and 'structural' components of hidden unemployment, suggests that the recorded unemployment rate is on the whole, a poor guide to the unemployment situation in a region.

Table 9.4 summarises trends in *regional activity rates*. Over the period 1956 to 1966, national activity rates gradually rose but have recently fallen off sharply. This mainly reflects a fall in the male activity rate, although the impact of this fall has been partially cushioned by a rise in the female rate. The regional rates have tended to follow the national trend, although the decline has been more marked in the North West and Yorkshire and Humberside which are slowly losing their relative advantage. The other problem regions with much lower activity rates have generally failed to improve their relative positions.

Regional migration trends (Table 9.5) at first glance suggest a measure of success for regional policy.[24] The various policy controls appear to have halted the so-called 'drift' to the South East and the decline in the net annual loss from the Northern region is an encouraging sign. However, the South East reversal may be partly explained by trends in international migration. A closer examination of Table 9.5 also reveals increasing gains by

197

Table 9.4. *Regional Activity Rates as ratios of national average* (UK= *100*).

Region	*1956*	*1961*	*1966*	*1969*
North	95	94	93	93
Yorkshire and Humberside^a	104	103	102	100
East Midlands^a	99	99	99	100
West Midlands^a	110	108	109	107
North West	107	105	103	103
East Anglia ⎱	102	104	⎰ 87	89
South East ⎰			⎱ 104	104
South West	83	84	84	83
Wales	85	85	84	84
Scotland	100	99	99	101
Northern Ireland	84	84	85	88
United Kingdom	100	100	100	100
	(56·3)	(56·8)	(57·5)	(55·9)

[a] The figures for 1956 and 1961 refer to the previous regions—East and West Ridings, North Midlands and Midlands

SOURCE: *Abstract of Regional Statistics*

Table 9.5. *Regional Migration Trends (1951–69)—(000's and % of 1951 regional populations).*

Region	Ave. an. net migration			Total net migration 1951–69		Total natural change 1951–69	
	1951–61	*1961–66*	*1966–69*	*No.*	*%*	*No.*	*%*
North	− 8·0	− 7·1	− 5·8	−133	− 4·3	344	11·0
Yorkshire and Humberside	− 9·6	− 1·0	−13·5	−141	− 3·1	415	9·2
East Midlands	+ 3·9	+ 8·7	+ 4·5	+ 96	+ 3·3	453	15·6
West Midlands	+ 4·7	+ 7·1	+ 6·7	+103	+ 2·3	604	13·6
North West	−12·4	− 5·7	−15·1	−198	− 3·1	523	8·2
East Anglia	+ 2·7	+11·9	+16·1	+135	+ 9·7	134	9·7
South East	+43·8	+20·8	− 8·8	+515	+ 3·4	1510	9·9
South West	+ 9·9	+24·8	+16·6	+269	+ 8·3	234	7·2
Wales	− 4·9	+ 1·9	− 3·0	− 48	− 1·9	169	6·5
Scotland	−28·2	−38·8	−34·3	−579	−11·3	633	12·4
Northern Ireland	− 8·9	− 6·9	− 6·3	−143	−10·4	286	20·8
United Kingdom	−7·0	+15·7	−42·9	−121	− 0·2	5244	10·4

SOURCE: *Abstract of Regional Statistics* (1970).

neighbouring East Anglia and the South West in addition to the constant attraction of the Midlands. Scotland continues to lose annually almost the equivalent of its natural increase, including a high proportion of young males, and the constant net migration losses from the North West and Yorkshire and Humberside suggests that their recent designation as Intermediate Areas was not before time.

Trends in public and private investment are more encouraging. The increase in public spending in the period 1965–70 was 44% in the UK as a whole, 33% in the South East, 100% in the Northern Region and 150% in Scotland. In 1968, expenditure on trunk road projects was approximately equal in the South East, West Midlands, the Northern region and Scotland.

Figure 9.2 reveals the trends in industrial building (approved) over the period 1954–70. With the exception of the mid 1950's, the problem regions have fared rather better than their population size would justify in terms of gaining industrial floorspace. This

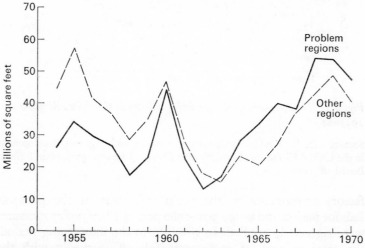

Fig. 9.2   Trends in industrial building (approved)
'Problem' regions: *North, Yorkshire and Humberside (East and West Ridings prior to 1960), North West, Scotland and Wales*
'Other' regions: *remaining British regions (northern Ireland excluded)*

SOURCE   *Abstract of Regional Statistics* (1965, 1971).

represents a major policy achievement. Much of this extra floorspace is attributable to new firms moving into the regions. In a valuable Board of Trade study[25] of the movement of manufacturing industry in the UK between 1945 and 1965, factory movements are subdivided into those destined for the 'peripheral areas' and those going to the 'remaining areas'. The peripheral areas are Northern Ireland, Scotland, Wales, the Northern Region, Merseyside and South West Lancashire and Devon and Cornwall. Figure 9.3 illustrates the large volume of

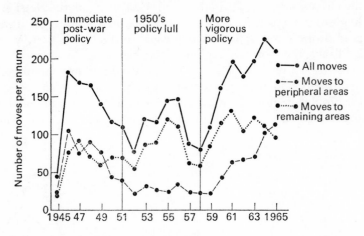

Fig. 9.3   The movement of manufacturing industry in the United Kingdom 1945–65

SOURCE   D. E. Keeble. 'Industrial movement and regional development in the United Kingdom', *Town Planning Review* (January 1972), page 6 (from Board of Trade 1968).

factory movements to the peripheral areas in the post-war Labour period and in the post-1960 period when policy measures were rigorously applied. In contrast, in the intervening period, the total volume of movements fell off markedly with the majority going to the Home Counties and the Midlands.

The number of factory moves however is not in itself a sufficient indicator of policy effectiveness. What types of moves are involved? Which industries are attracted to the problem regions?

Are the firms large or small and what of the employment created? The BOT study reveals that factories moving to the peripheral areas are mainly branch concerns. Of the 1101 complete transfers of factories recorded during the study period only 200 went to peripheral areas. Unfortunately branch concerns are usually more vulnerable in times of economic crisis, and this can have serious implications for the future economic stability of the problem regions. The factories moving to the peripheral areas include a wide range of industries, although the percentage of the total belonging to the faster growing manufacturing industry sectors (SIC IV, VI, VII and VIII, IX, XV and XVI) is only 60% compared with 75% for migrant establishments in the South East and East Anglia. But this is still quite substantial, and an application by Stilwell[26] of the proportionality modification shift variation of the shift-share analysis outlined in Chapter 5, indicates some improvement in the industrial structure of the North West, Scotland, Wales, the Northern region and the South West between 1959 and 1967.

Yet despite this large-scale public and private investment in the problem regions, the growth in employment has generally been less than the national average (see Table 9.1). The usual explanation is that much of the new development has been capital intensive.[27] There is undoubtedly some truth in this argument, although if a more long-run view is adopted, industrial relocation should be evaluated more in terms of future income growth and the creation of a sound industrial structure rather than simply in terms of jobs. Two other factors are perhaps of equal if not more importance in explaining this slow employment growth. Firstly, the South East has had a monopoly of the rapidly growing service sector, which remained largely uncontrolled until 1965. Secondly, the problem regions have faced an unprecedented decline in employment in their basic industries over the last 20 years, and this had to be offset by new jobs. Thus if one considers that Scotland, Wales and the Northern Region together lost more than 300 000 jobs in the traditional industries of mining, agriculture and shipbuilding alone in the decade 1956–66, the maintenance of the employment *status quo* is in itself something of an achievement.

The *change in regional income levels* is a final indicator of the effectiveness of policy tools. This is generally regarded as the acid test of regional policy—does it make people better off, reducing the regional imbalance? The evidence in Table 9.6 is not too encouraging. There might be very limited convergence but

Table 9.6. *Average Total Weekly Household Income: Regional Trends (Index of UK Average).*

Region	1964–66	1965–67	1967–68	1969–70
South East	113	111	112	113
West Midlands	110	107	105	102
East Midlands	99	95	97	95
South West	93	95	96	95
Yorkshire and Humberside	96	96	88	93
North West	96	96	96	98
East Anglia	94	91	97	93
Scotland	96	96	96	96
Wales	91	90	90	90
North	84	89	91	94
Northern Ireland	84	83	85	85
United Kingdom	100	100	100	100
	(£25·2)	(£26·7)	(£29·1)	(£33.9)

SOURCE: Family Expenditure Survey (1965–71)

the South East still remains well above the norm and problem regions, especially Northern Ireland, remain well below. There is also further evidence of a relative decline in the fortunes of the West Midlands; but no indicator is foolproof, regional cost of living variations may moderate the income differences. Nor do the latter necessarily reflect variations in the quality of life between the regions.

To conclude, this examination of a limited number of indicators offers little evidence to suggest that the regional imbalance will soon be a thing of the past. Policy to date has been basically a holding operation, running hard just to stand still. This in itself is a creditable achievement but there is still a long way to go and a relaxation of measures at this stage could be very damaging.

6 An appraisal of the tactics

Although it is difficult and perhaps not practicable to assess the effectiveness and efficiency of each regional measure, a general comparison of their relative merits can be useful. If certain measures have a much greater cost-effectiveness than others, it may be beneficial to increase their use, reducing the rôle of more dubious measures. There may also be policy tools as yet unused which have an important rôle to play. But the purpose is not to suggest the optimal policy measure or combination of measures, for obviously what is optimal for one region or industry will rarely be optimal for others.

THE CHOICE OF AREAS

Important lessons can be learnt from an examination of the UK approach to the actual delineation of assisted areas within the problem regions. In particular, there is the question of whether aid should be spread in blanket fashion over the depressed areas or concentrated in particular growth points or centres of potential.

Throughout the 40 years of UK policy there has been an undue emphasis on the level of unemployment as the major index, dividing the country into large development areas and the remainder. However, as Chapter 2 illustrates, homogeneous regions can be identified in a variety of ways using a range of criteria. Although the introduction of the two new categories of Special Development Areas and Intermediate Areas does suggest a more flexible approach, the unemployment factor remains dominant and the highest subsidies are still provided in the areas with the worst unemployment problems rather than in those with the most growth potential. In addition, the resultant areal spread of the assisted areas, although perhaps sound politically, raises the question as to whether the jam in the form of the available mobile industry is not likely to be spread too thinly to achieve any meaningful results in any particular area. An alternative approach would be a more areally selective policy—concentrating aid in more specific areas within the problem region—from which growth impulses could spread out to the rest of the region. (This, it must be added, is not synonymous

203

with the Development District approach of the early 1960's which often provided maximum aid to the areas with least potential and least attraction to new development.) Rather it involves identifying growth areas with potential, areas with natural advantages and strong inter-industry linkages, drawing on the concepts and analysis outlined in the earlier chapters.

Of course, there are problems in adopting such an approach. There is the fundamental political consideration that the choice of one locality as a growth point invariably rules out others, which then regard themselves as non-growth points deserted by the Government. In addition, although such a policy may narrow inter-regional variations it may contribute little to intra-regional equality. Yet the limited supply of mobile industry may eventually necessitate a more selective designation of specific growth areas within the assisted areas. A possible compromise approach could be the concentration of infra-structural investment in specific growth centres reaping the undoubted scale economies, but with the spread of industrial aid over wider growth areas reflecting the more disparate nature of inter-industry linkages.[28]

THE COST OF NEGATIVE CONTROLS

The UK system of control over the location of new projects or major expansion of existing firms via the use of IDC's is the most comprehensive in Western Europe. Of all the policy measures used by the Government to influence the location of industry it is probably also the most criticised. Much of this criticism centres around the administration of IDC control. The application for an IDC is judged in complete secrecy by the civil servants of the responsible government department (now the DTI), who themselves have been criticised for their lack of industrial experience and knowledge of the issues. The applicant is denied access to, and has little knowledge of the representation of his case and is thus incapable of correcting any misunderstandings that may arise. This situation makes it difficult for a firm to judge the reactions of the DTI and leads to the non-presentation of some potentially successful applications and to accusations of unfairness between cases.

Another major criticism is that the full cost of the measure is not explicit. It is argued that a firm faced with IDC controls may not expand at all, or may expand abroad or even if it does move to an assisted area may do so with a marked rise in costs and loss of efficiency. Evidence on these issues is difficult to collect and rarely conclusive. Luttrell,[29] in a study of 98 firms that moved to Development Areas in the late 1950's compared the production costs at the new branch location with the actual costs at the mother plant to determine whether there were (i) initial costs, and (ii) continuing extra costs, in the development area location. Results showed that although the cost of the move may be initially expensive, unit costs fall over time relative to the parent factory, with lower direct wage costs offsetting the higher over-heads. (Further, such a comparison is probably somewhat biassed by the scale economies at the mother plant.)

The issues were also examined by the Hunt Committee,[30] which concluded that the volume of expansion which might have been lost through IDC control could not be quantified, although it doubted on the evidence available whether it was large. It showed for example that between 1964 and 1967, only 17% of the floorspace applied for in the South East and West Midlands was refused, and of those firms refused 80% subsequently undertook expansion mainly in Development Areas.

Other criticisms relate to the operational difficulties of IDC control. There are loopholes. Firms may expand just beneath the IDC limit or may expand by building warehouses which have been exempt from control. Of course, some would regard these loopholes more as safety valves, allowing industry to expand in the West Midlands and the South East thereby maintaining economic growth and alleviating any development distress in the prosperous areas.[31] Finally, it has also been argued that IDC control may hinder self-help in the problem regions, developing a 'let's sit back and wait for the industry to come' attitude.

Balanced against these criticisms are several important advantages. The controls are in the narrow sense highly cost-effective, involving only the administrative costs of the DTI. They may also encourage a more rational locational choice by firms, forcing them to consider a wider range of locations and perhaps making them realise that there are a wide range of external diseconomies in the prosperous areas. The controls may also help to take some of the pressure off the labour situation in such areas, thereby reducing the wastage imposed by labour 'poaching' between competing firms.

There have been several suggestions to modify the existing system, including the introduction of a sliding scale whereby the smaller the firm the greater would be the area for which a certificate was not required, and the allocation of IDC's by a system of auction.[32] Politically, it would be very difficult to tighten the controls any further in face of increasing representation from the controlled areas, although one minor extension, used in Norway and Sweden, might be acceptable. That is, that *any* firm intending to set up or expand whatever the size of the proposed development should automatically consult the Government on possible locations.

THE EVALUATION OF FINANCIAL INDUCEMENTS

The use of financial inducements on an ever increasing scale has raised a number of important issues. What should be the scale of such inducements and what is their value to the individual firm? Should the emphasis be on subsidies to capital or labour, and should there be more flexibility in the allocation of such inducements?

The relative scale of financial inducements has increased at a rapid rate over the last 20 years. However the absolute value of such inducements to the individual firm is difficult to assess varying according to factors such as the ratio of a firm's variable to capital costs, and the period of lapse between the start of production and the start of profits. A recent EFTA study[33] estimated that in 1971 the cash values of investment incentive benefits during the first three years of a project in a Development Area could be as high as 57·1% of capital costs in industrial buildings and 42·5% of machinery and plant costs. Such a subsidy is obviously substantial although it appears less dramatic when considered relative to a firm's total costs. Wilson[34] estimated that in 1967 the value of subsidies to both capital and labour costs might typically account for little more than 5% of a firm's annual total costs. This is less impressive. If inducements are to be effective they must be large and available over a long period, at least ten years, to give the businessman confidence in them. But this is not to belittle the scale of recent UK financial subsidies. At the margin even a 5% subsidy may still be highly significant, perhaps offsetting the extra costs of moving to the assisted areas.

Capital cost subsidies have been the predominant form of financial inducement in the UK although the introduction of the Regional Employment Premium in 1967 marked a certain shift of emphasis. Capital subsidies have the advantages of usually being simple and explicit, of being a 'once and for all' subsidy rather than continuing subsidisation, and of encouraging new investment in buildings, plant and machinery and thereby improving the capital stock of the region. But they also have disadvantages. They have been validly criticised for encouraging capital intensive development. The new capital stock is often supplied from outside the assisted areas generating only a limited intra-regional spin-off. Similarly, although a capital intensive firm may sometimes 'trigger off' linked development in the depressed region, it often has a rather low multiplier effect with many of its complex components coming from outside the region.

Many of these problems can be overcome by the use of a labour subsidy such as the Regional Employment Premium (REP). Such a subsidy encourages labour intensive development, has less spillover effects to other regions, and may still have the same effect as capital subsidies in making the assisted areas more competitive. However the impact on employment of such a measure is difficult to forecast. It was estimated that the annual injection of £100 million into the assisted areas via REP would reduce labour costs by $7\frac{1}{2}\%$.[35] This would lead to a reduction in the price of goods produced in these areas, leading to an increased demand, increased industrial expansion and a rise in employment by 100 000 over a seven-year period. Such an estimation assumes that the demand for the goods of the assisted areas is price elastic, that firms can substitute between labour and capital and that firms, many of them branches of larger firms, can actually reduce prices. Many of these assumptions are undoubtedly dubious. It is probable that much of the subsidy will leak into profits and/or wage and salary increases. This in itself may generate more employment via the income multiplier and, in the profits case by attracting more firms to the area. But the total increase in employ-

207

ment may be considerably less than 100 000, reducing the cost effectiveness of the measure. A labour subsidy may also encourage labour hoarding, and its interference with a firms variable costs may lead to permanent subsidisation and the shoring up of inefficient concerns.

The flexibility in the allocation of the UK financial inducements in the assisted areas is limited. Capital grants are automatically available to manufacturing firms engaged in new developments in the assisted areas (although the grant rates do vary between the types of assisted areas) and labour subsidies are available to all manufacturing firms in the Development and Special Development Areas. This contrasts markedly with several other European countries. In theory, there could be more flexibility in UK inducements with measures designed to attract firms which could best contribute to an achievement of the regional objectives. Thus, in an ideal situation an area suffering from male unemployment and the decline of the traditional base, would benefit from measures designed to encourage a range of labour intensive, male employing, growth industries. One development of this approach is the payment of firms according to results, usually the creation of employment. However, there are certain problems not the least of which is that the achievement of the results may be dependent upon the receipt of the initial payment.

In practice, there are several constraints on greater flexibility. The situation would inevitably be more complex, less fair, more time consuming and perhaps tie a government too closely to the success or otherwise of an enterprise in a particular locality. Nevertheless, UK policy would benefit from a more flexible approach in one particular area—the extension of positive inducements to service industry. Since 1960, employment in the service sector has increased by 1 000 000 jobs, yet incentives to attract such jobs to the problem areas are minimal. Under the Local Employment Acts (1960–70), offices moving into Development Areas and creating more than 50 new jobs could apply for discretionary assistance, in the form of removal and training grants and a 25% building grant if the move involved the firm building its own premises. But such aid was poorly publicised and very low in comparison with that available to manufacturing industry. Rhodes and Kan[36] estimated that a capital intensive manufacturing

208

industry moving to a Development Area between 1967 and 1970 might well have received around £4900 per new job provided. The figure falls to £1900 per job for a labour intensive manufacturing industry, but is as low as £625 for office development. This constitutes a major failure of regional policy to date. Rhodes and Kan believe that if office employment is to be attracted to the Development Areas on a reasonable scale, incentives will have to be increased to at least £1500 per new job to cover the costs involved and provide the necessary stimulus.

THE RÔLE OF THE PUBLIC SECTOR

In addition to incentives and disincentives to development in the private sector, use can also be made of the public sector in inter-regional planning. This has slowly been realised and as outlined earlier, public investment in infrastructure, the location of government establishments and contract preference schemes are now being used as policy tools.

Public investment in infrastructure has been used in several countries—in Languedoc in France, in the Mezzogiorno in Italy for example—as an instrument of regional policy. Investment in economic overhead capital such as roads, ports and public utilities can make an area economically more attractive; while investment in social overhead capital such as housing and recreational facilities can break down many social and psychological barriers. However the extent to which infrastructural investment can be the central instrument of inter-regional planning is not too clear. Very little is known of the ability of superior infrastructure to attract new industry. Improved inter-regional roads, for example, may open up a problem region to dangerous competition rather than encouraging new development.[37] The Hunt Report suggests that infrastructural investment may not be as cost effective as direct measures.[38] Therefore perhaps infrastructural investment should be regarded, as the French say, more as *accompagnement* rather than *entrainement*—that is accompanying growth rather than inducing it.

It contrast it has been suggested that more use could be made of public companies and the location of government establishments in the initiation of growth points in the problem regions.

This could be in the form of government support for the development of industrial complexes, as in Bari–Taranto in Southern Italy;[39] or through the specific location of public sector industry.* The Labour Party[40] note that much of the large demand for goods and services created by the public sector is at present privately supplied—electrical equipment for the GPO, surgical supplies for the National Health Service, school supplies, breathalysers etc. More public control of these supplies could provide a source of mobile industry for the problem regions. An alternative approach is to extend the use of the distribution of public contracts as an instrument of regional policy. In 1972, total public sector purchasing was approximately £12 000 million (at current prices), representing 25% of GNP (UK). The public sector's position as a purchaser is a most powerful government weapon; used as an instrument of regional policy it could be revolutionary.

7 Summary

Despite the fluctuating fortunes during its 40-year history, inter-regional planning now appears to be well established in the UK. The case for intervention to help the problem regions, particularly the depressed industrial areas is now firmly based on economic, as well as social and political reasoning.

With the exception of the early inter-war period, the broad strategy has been predominantly one of 'work to the workers', but the range of tactics for implementing this strategy has shown some interesting trends. The delineated areas have evolved from the original Special Areas based almost exclusively on unemployment criteria and covering less than 20% of the country, to a hierarchy of Special Development Areas, Development Areas and Intermediate Areas, based on multiple criteria and covering more than 50% of the UK. To attract employment to these areas,

* A report *The Dispersal of Government Work from London*, Cmnd 5322, HMSO (1973) now recommends the dispersal of 31 000 London-based civil service posts, in addition to the 7000 already in the pipeline. However, much of the additional dispersal would be within or on the periphery of the South East (e.g. Milton Keynes), with perhaps only 50% of the posts going to certain concentrations in the assisted areas—Cardiff, Plymouth, Liverpool, Central Lancashire new town, Manchester, Teesside, Newcastle and Glasgow.

the financial 'carrot' has become progressively larger, and more attractive, primarily through increased aid to a firm's capital costs. But the 'stick' in the form of IDC control has also constantly loomed menacingly in the background. Policies directed at the re-employment and mobility of labour have progressed quietly, and the rôle of direct public involvement via infrastructural investment and the use of the public sector's position as a producer and consumer of goods and services is slowly being recognised.

Yet in spite of this impressive array of measures, UK interregional planning has failed as yet to achieve anything more than a holding operation. Of course, this in itself can rightly be considered to represent some degree of success but there is still a long way to go. The process is long-drawn-out and premature relaxation could undo much good work.

'the economy of a less prosperous area is not static and while new employment is being introduced, job opportunities in other sectors may be lost. Indeed in areas suffering from deepseated problems, the need for industrial renewal may extend even to a "second generation" of industrial mobility, with enterprises introduced some years before primarily to offset the decline in the traditional industries themselves having to adapt to changing circumstances, thus increasing local need for new employment.'[41]

Hence, the efficiency and effectiveness of existing measures must be kept constantly under review, and the possibility of new directions such as the greater use of the public sector and service industry must be fully investigated.

References

1 Friedman, J. F., *Regional Development Policy: A Case Study of Venezuela*, MIT Press, Camb. Mass. (1966).
2 Coates, B. E., and Rawstron, E. M., *Regional Variations in Britain*, Batsford (1971).
3 Friedman, J. F., *op cit*, page 41 ff.
4 Allen, K., and Hermansen, T., in *Regional Policy in EFTA; An examination of the Growth Centre Idea*, page 32, EFTA Secretariat,

Geneva (1968), note 'that it was Joan Robinson who once made the pun that the trouble with the lazy fairies is that they are too lazy!'

5 National Economic Development Council (NEDC), *Conditions Favourable to Faster Growth,* page 16, HMSO (1963).

6 EFTA Economic Development Committee, *Regional Policy in EFTA; Industrial Mobility,* pages 68–74, EFTA Secretariat, Geneva (1971).

7 West, E. G., Regional Planning—Fact or Fallacy, *Lloyds Bank Review,* pages 33–49, April 1966;
Needleman, L., What are we to do about the regional problem? *Lloyds Bank Review,* January 1965;
Nevin, E. T., The Case for Regional Policy, *Three Banks Review,* December 1966.

8 Needleman, L., *op cit,* pages 46–7.

9 Richardson, H. W., *Regional Economics,* pages 393–7, Weidenfeld and Nicolson (1969).

10 Davies, G., Regional Unemployment, Labour Availability and Redeployment, *Oxford Economic Papers,* May 1967.

11 See: Odber, A. J., Regional Policy in Britain, Part 6 in *Area Redevelopment Policies in Britain and the Countries of the Common Market,* US Dept. of Commerce (1965);
McCrone, G., *Regional Policy in Britain,* Allen and Unwin (1969). The text by McCrone provides the most comprehensive study of policy up to 1967, Odber's paper provides an excellent summary up to 1963.

12 Greenwood, H. P., *Employment and the Depressed Areas,* page 88, Routledge (1936).

13 *Report of the Royal Commission on the Distribution of Industrial Population,* Cmnd. 6153, HMSO (1940).

14 *Employment Policy,* Cmnd. 6527, HMSO (1944).

15 Odber, *op cit.*

16 *Central Scotland: A Programme for Development and Growth,* Cmnd. 2188, HMSO, Edinburgh (1963);
The North East: A Programme for Development and Growth, Cmnd. 2206, HMSO, London (1963).

17 *Report of the Committee on the Intermediate Areas* (The Hunt Report), Cmnd. 3998, HMSO (1969).

18 Cmnd. 2206, *op cit.*

19 Secretary of State for Trade and Industry, *Industrial and regional development,* Cmnd. 4942 HMSO, (1972).

20 South-East Joint Planning Team, *Strategic Plan for the South-East,* HMSO (1970).

21 NEDC, *Tenth Annual Report, 1970–71.*

22 Cmnd. 4942, *op cit.*

23 Taylor, J., A Regional Analysis of Hidden Unemployment in Great Britain, 1951–66, *Applied Economics,* pages 291–303, **3** (1971).

24 For a fuller discussion, see: Eversley, D. E. C., Population Changes and Regional Policies since the War, *Regional Studies,* pages 211–28, **5,** (1971).

25 Board of Trade, *The Movement of Manufacturing Industry in the UK (1945–1965),* HMSO (1968).

26 Stilwell, F. J. B., Regional growth and structural adaptation, *Urban Studies,* June 1969.

27 Bray, J., *Decision in Government,* Garden City Press (1970).

28 McCrone, G., *op cit.*

29 Luttrell, W. F., *Factory Location and Industrial Movement* (2 Vols), NIESR (1962).

30 Cmnd. 3998, *op cit,* paragraph 346.

31 Smith, B. M. D., Industrial development certificate control: an institutional influence on industrial mobility, *Journal of the Town Planning Institute,* February 1971.

32 Townroe, P. M., Industrial Development: What Alternatives?, *New Society,* 18/2/71.

33 EFTA, *Industrial Mobility, op cit,* pages 111–12.

34 Wilson, T., Finance for Regional Industrial Development, *Three Banks Review,* September 1967.

35 Brown, A. J., The 'Green Paper' on the Development Areas, *National Institute Economic Review,* May 1967.

36 Rhodes, J., and Kan, A., *Office dispersal and regional policy,* Occ. Papers 30, University of Cambridge, Dept. of Applied Economics (1971).

37 Gwillam, K. M., The Indirect Effects of Highway Investment, *Regional Studies,* pages 167–76, **4** (1970).

38 Cmnd. 3998, *op cit,* pages 155–65.

39 Newcombe, V., Creating an Industrial Development Pole in Southern Italy, *Journal of the Town Planning Institute,* April 1969.

40 Labour Party, *op cit.*

41 EFTA, *Industrial Mobility, op cit,* page 108.

10 Intra-regional planning in the United Kingdom

1 The aims of intra-regional planning

Intra-regional planning is concerned with the planning of individual regions such as metropolitan South East England and the industrial North West and their constituent sub-regions. It has evolved out of the local land-use planning tradition and its objectives are social, economic and possibly also aesthetic.

The starting point of intra-regional planning in many countries is to be found in the problems resulting from urbanisation and population growth. This process has resulted in the growth of major metropolitan conurbations such as London, Paris, Randstad Holland and the Ruhr. But it is also a process which is affecting more than capital and major cities and can be observed in smaller towns and cities throughout the country. Such urban growth is invariably accompanied by a wide range of general social costs and increasing economic inefficiency within the urban/metropolitan regions themselves because of factors such as congestion costs and strains on public services. To cope with these problems there is a need to look beyond the existing urban area to the wider regional or sub-regional context. This need for a wider view is also reinforced by the increasing mobility of the population.

Intra-regional planning can also be seen as a necessary complement to the primarily economic based inter-regional planning geared largely to promoting economic development in the depressed industrial and under-developed regions. It is here that the relationship between regional economic planning and regional physical planning is most clearly seen, for economic regeneration depends not only on labour supply and financial incentives to industry but also on the adequacy of the physical infrastructure such as roads, public utilities, housing and schools. A modernisation of industrial activity needs to be accompanied by a modernisation of the general physical and social environment and this requires careful planning.

Intra-regional planning usually involves the preparation of a plan for a region. The primary aim of this plan is to provide a framework for the region showing what it can do to improve the economic and social conditions and the quality of the environment . . . to achieve a satisfactory relationship between people, jobs and the environment within the region. In addition it can also be seen as providing an input into national planning and a basis for co-ordinating more local plans.

Suggestions for the contents of such a plan vary, but most usually involve a target for the future in the form of a definitive plan—with proposals for the location of population, employment, major recreational and cultural facilities, the communications network and so on—and a programme of planned development towards that future. In their report on *Regional Planning Policy*, the Labour Party Study Group suggested the following as the approximate contents of a regional plan:[1]

a study of the region's resources—land and natural resources, population and manpower, capital and entrepreneurship—together with its regional and inter-regional industrial linkages, input–output relationships, travel-to-work patterns and so forth

b analysis of problems and needs, such as shortages of jobs and particular sorts of jobs, of manpower and particular skills, of transport facilities, housing, education and other social service provision, water and power resources, and so on

c working in existing plans and programmes for the future, e.g. for roads, hospitals, new towns, universities, together with the plans of the nationalised industries

d gathering information on the future plans of the private sector both directly and from known future investment plans, from share of the market targets, from analysis of regional, national and international growth rates and trends, from input–output linkages and so on

e examination of changes that are likely to affect the present structure, e.g. demographic trends, changes in education, technology, social habits, investment

f working out the likely rates of expansion in sectors at given growth rates on the basis of examined linkages, and the consequences of this for job creation, public expenditure etc.

g analysis of the necessary action to be taken on incentives to industry (including guidelines on the types of industry and employment most needed), retraining, infrastructure development and the like

h land use pattern—agricultural land, water, areas of natural beauty and tourist attraction, communications, areas suitable for population and industrial growth.

The remainder of this chapter now examines the evolution of intra-regional planning in the United Kingdom, the regional planning process, emerging strategies and selected case studies. However, the vital question of administration and alternative forms of administrative machinery is left to the next chapter.

2 The evolution of intra-regional planning in the United Kingdom

The evolution of UK intra-regional planning followed a course somewhat similar to that for inter-regional planning. Although the original impetus dates back to the late nineteenth century, it was not until the inter-war years that planners became concerned about the conurbations and inter-urban development. This was followed by significant progress in the immediate post-war years, but then a lull in the 1950's. However since the early 1960's there have been considerable advances and the development of several alternative approaches to regional and sub-regional planning. [Appendix C lists the major UK Regional and Sub-Regional Studies by Economic Planning Region.]

THE EARLY DEVELOPMENT OF INTRA-REGIONAL PLANNING

The history of intra-regional planning can probably be traced back to Ebeneezer Howard. In his *Garden Cities of Tomorrow* he proposed the establishment of a cluster of new towns linked to a central city to deal with the rapidly expanding nineteenth-century city. These multi-centred regional clusters were to be separated from the existing cities, such as London or Glasgow, by means of green belts and were to contain both homes and jobs. But, apart from the early garden cities such as Letchworth and Welwyn, there was little immediate development of Howard's ideas. The most significant development in the inter-war years was the establishment of Joint Advisory Committees of Local Authority Planning Departments to attempt to co-ordinate the growth and interaction of towns. Unfortunately such bodies achieved little primarily due to the parochial infighting between the various County Boroughs and County Councils.

Towards the end of the Second World War there were more encouraging signs. The Barlow Report[2] realised the advantages of regional planning and the Scott Committee,[3] concerned with the problem of industrial development in rural areas and its effect on agriculture and rural amenities, recommended that planning should be carried out regionally as well as nationally so that local authority land-use plans conformed to national priorities. Out of this background emerged a series of advisory regional plans, the most notable being those for Greater London and the Clyde Valley. The *Greater London Plan 1944* was prepared by Professor Patrick Abercrombie for the Standing Conference on London Regional Planning, constituted in 1937; and the *Clyde Valley Plan 1946*, was prepared by Abercrombie and Matthew for the Clyde Valley Regional Planning Advisory Committee, composed of constituent local authorities and established in 1943.

These advisory urban regional plans were documents of considerable vision motivated by the social aims of accelerated redevelopment and dispersal and by the aesthetic concept of new regional forms against a background of green belt and countryside. But they were primarily physical planning documents with little economic content. In addition, their immediate implementation was limited by the lack of resources and inflationary pressure in the post-war years. Nevertheless they did have considerable influence on government decisions and local authority plans. From this period stems much of the important post-war physical planning legislation—the New Towns Act (1946), the Town and

217

Country Planning Act (1947) and the Town Development Act (1952)—all of which provided important tools for the implementation of urban regional planning. In the late 1940's, a number of new towns were designated including the eight London new towns and East Kilbride and Glenrothes in Scotland. Many of these were located in accordance with the principles laid down in the advisory plans. A start was also made in the preparation of development plans to cover the whole country. These also were influenced by the advisory plans.

With the advent of a Conservative Government in the 1950's, this early enthusiasm soon waned. Planning fell into disrepute and the political disinterest was reflected in several ways. There was a lack of a national lead on matters of overall policy, the regional offices of the Ministry of Town and Country Planning were abandoned, there was a failure to extend, revise and implement the advisory regional plans, and only one new town, Cumbernauld, was designated during the decade. The antiquated local government units continued to undermine the effectiveness of any form of regional planning, and the 'overspill controversies', such as that between Manchester County Borough and Lancashire County Council over the use of Westhoughton as an overspill location, were a typical result.

Only in Scotland was there any commendable progress. The *Clyde Valley Plan* was published in 1946 and was later adopted as the framework for resolving the general problems of the Clyde Valley and the congestion problems of Glasgow in particular. The designation of the new town of Cumbernauld in 1955 provided early evidence of the acceptance of the plan and, in spite of taking many hard knocks, it has continued to underpin the planning policies of the area. Scotland has also continued to figure prominently in both the practice and theory of UK regional planning, and this no doubt stems to a large extent from the degree of Scottish administrative independence in many matters, including planning.

A REVIVAL OF INTRA-REGIONAL PLANNING

A revival of interest in intra-regional planning was stimulated by a re-emphasis of the regional imbalance in the country at the beginning of the 1960's. The symptoms of economic distress became more marked in the problem regions and the Government was forced to take action. As outlined in Chapter 9, one response was the production, in 1963, of two White Papers on regional development programmes for Central Scotland and North East England designating eight growth areas for Central Scotland and a growth zone for the North East. These areas were to benefit from considerable investment in promotional infrastructure. This action implied a large degree of government commitment and represented an important fusion between the economic and physical aspects of inter- and intra-regional planning.

The government also took a renewed interest in the major conurbations where the problems of congestion were becoming worse and worse. A major stimulus came from the need to accommodate a far greater population growth than had originally been anticipated. A new generation of new towns, including Dawley, Redditch, Skelmersdale and Runcorn were designated to take the overspill of Birmingham and South Lancashire, and a new series of major regional studies were commissioned—the first since the *Clyde Valley Plan*. The *South East Study (1961–1981)* was produced in 1964. The proposals in this document introduced a new scale of planning, but they were essentially physical, seeking to accommodate the population growth of the area, and there was little economic content. The study was regarded primarily as a basis for discussion and implied no government commitment.

An interesting contrast at this time was the situation in Northern Ireland. In 1963, the government commissioned Professor Thomas Wilson to prepare a comprehensive plan for future economic development in Northern Ireland. The Wilson Report of 1965 provides a detailed programme of action covering the location of industry in centres of growth, amenity and tourism, transport services, training, inducements to industry, agriculture and the general investment programme. This Report was accepted by the Government, and together with Sir Robert Matthew's physically oriented *Belfast Regional Plan* (1963), has since formed the basis for the development of the province.

Following these initial developments, the 1960's and early 1970's have witnessed the production of a whole range of intra-regional studies, reports, plans and strategies which can be broadly divided into regional and sub-regional categories. The

219

distinction between the two categories is bound to be somewhat arbitrary with wide areas of overlap, but for the purposes of discussion the regional studies are taken to relate to the large Economic Planning Regions and are primarily sponsored by departments of central government; whereas the sub-regional studies relate to smaller areas and have been more in the sphere of local planning authorities.

The regional level

The creation of a new Ministry, the Department of Economic Affairs (DEA), in 1964, and the establishment during 1965 and 1966 of a series of Regional Economic Planning Councils and Boards for eight English planning regions and Scotland, Wales and Northern Ireland marked the advent of a new phase of regional studies. The Councils of nominated members were given the tasks of studying the needs and potentialities of their regions, giving regional advice to the government, and preparing broad strategies for future development. The Boards of civil servants were to assist the Councils in their tasks and to co-ordinate the work of central government departments at the regional level.

The first studies, for the North West and the West Midlands, were produced by central government under the DEA. Later studies were produced by the respective regional councils and by 1968 were available for each region. The studies vary greatly in quality but overall have not matched up to many people's expectations. They have been criticised on several counts—for being descriptive studies rather than positive strategies, for their inability to link the physical and economic aspects of regional planning, and for their inward-looking nature and lack of integration.

It is certainly true that many of the studies have been more concerned with regional stocktaking seeking to clarify the regional planning problems rather than to put forward policies and propose solutions. Thus the aim of the *East Midlands Study* was:

'to present to the public an account of the region as it is, and as it is changing; it draws attention to problems and opportunities, with an indication of what is involved in them. It is hoped that the study will form an adequate basis for the public discussion out of which the main lines of the region's planning will emerge, until adequate opportunity for that discussion has been provided it would be presumptuous to go further.'[4]

Similarly, *A Review of Yorkshire and Humberside*

'does not attempt to produce a regional plan, either economic or physical. It is the report of the Regional Economic Planning Council's first survey of the area, based mainly on information collected and analysed by the various departments of central government, constituting the Economic Planning Board. For the most part it presents a statement of the main demographic, economic and social circumstances of the region as a whole and of its sub-divisions.'[5]

This approach however can be partially justified by the fact that in many regions, particularly in the newly constituted Yorkshire and Humberside Region, there was at the time little in the way of official regional statistical data on which plans could be based.

This first round of studies was followed in the late 1960's by an attempt by the Economic Planning Councils to produce preliminary regional strategies. Outline strategies with an economic emphasis were produced for the North, North West and Yorkshire and Humberside, and a more physically oriented strategy was produced for the South East. But such strategies did not constitute firm plans, accepted by the Government. They were more initial sketches of the future principles of strategic planning to be discussed and amended with central government, local authorities and any other public agencies involved in large-scale regional investment. In contrast, the White Paper for Scotland *The Scottish Economy 1965–70. A Plan for Expansion* published in January 1966 by the Scottish Office carried more political commitment. The White Paper included an interesting survey of the existing situation and future potential of Scotland, and although it did not have the scope of a comprehensive regional plan, did deal in detail with proposals for immediate investment over a five-year period. It also provided a framework for more detailed sub-regional plans such as those for Central Scotland, Grangemouth–Falkirk, and South West Scotland produced by the Scottish Development Department.

Over the last few years, the work of the Regional Economic Councils and Boards in regional planning has been paralleled by that of the local authorities. Indeed, the formation of the Councils and Boards probably stimulated some coming together of local authorities within the same economic planning region, in the form of Standing Conferences, to push along the preparation of regional strategies. In the South East, this pressure resulted in the commissioning by the Standing Conference on London and the South East, the South East Economic Planning Council and the Government, of a new *Strategic Plan* for the region. The terms of reference of the strategy were:

'to report on patterns of development for the South East . . . with the objective of providing a regional framework for the local planning authorities to carry out their planning responsibilities . . . and for government decisions on investment and economic and social policies relating to the region's future development.'[6]

The comprehensive report, prepared by a team under the Chief Planner of the Ministry of Housing and Local Government, was published in 1970. In October 1971, it was accepted in principle by the Government as the framework for regional planning in the South East.

In the West Midlands, the Planning Authorities' Conference took the initiative into their own hands and in 1971 published *A Developing Strategy for the West Midlands* as a basis for consultation with individual local authorities, the Economic Planning Council and other interested bodies prior to the submission of proposals to the Government.

Such developments have prompted Government support for the joint preparation of regional plans.

'It is the Government's intention that future regional strategies should be prepared on a tripartite basis in collaboration between the regional economic planning councils, the local planning authorities, and central government. Ultimately, it is hoped to cover all the English regions in this way, but detailed arrangements and timing will vary from region to region.'[7]

Planning teams are already at work in the North West and East

Anglia, and their strategies are expected towards the end of 1973. Preparatory work for regional strategies is being undertaken in other regions.

The sub-regional level

The late 1960's have also witnessed the development of a whole range of supra-urban studies. The origins and objectives of these studies are diverse, but two major groups can be identified which are now conventionally regarded as constituting the new breed of sub-regional studies. The first group are studies carried out for local planning authorities to co-ordinate the future natural growth or interaction of large towns and cities. Included in this group are the sub-regional plans for Teesside, Leicester and Leicestershire, Nottinghamshire and Derbyshire, North Gloucestershire and Coventry–Warwickshire–Solihull. The Teesside study published in 1969 dates from the transportation planning era of the early 1960's and can be regarded as a bridge between the transportation and sub-regional plans. The other studies originate from an awakening of the sub-regional idea by Richard Crossman, who as Minister of Housing and Local Government in 1965

> 'believed that in advance of, and without prejudice to any subsequent reform of local government functions and boundaries, co-operative planning ventures could begin between the towns and their surrounding authorities. His initial aim was to persuade the authorities in a small number of selected areas to come together and set up ad-hoc teams to prepare long term "broad-brush" plans for land uses and transportation. These were to be called 'sub-regional studies.'"[8]

Leicester City Council and Leicestershire County Council set up one of the earliest of these studies in 1966, and the report was published in 1969. This was followed in quick succession by three other studies, the most recent one for *Coventry–Solihill–Warwickshire* being published in 1971. All the studies have been produced by independent study teams set up for the purpose, with the exception of the *North Gloucestershire Sub-Regional Study* which was produced primarily by the local authority planning departments. The studies have introduced many technical innovations in the planning process, with each study building on the work of its predecessors, and will no doubt have a major impact on planning in the 1970s. Indeed, under local government re-organisation (discussed in Chapter 11), the new county structure plans will no doubt take on many of the attributes of the recent sub-regional studies. But sub-regional planning will still have a useful rôle to play. Many issues will continue to overlap local authority boundaries and the 1971 Town and Country Planning Act makes provision for joint studies. Here, sub-regional planning can perhaps be viewed as strategic planning at the scale of the whole or parts of at least two authorities, providing a link between the regional framework and the structure plans.

The second group of studies are concerned with an examination of the feasibility of the large-scale planned expansion of selected areas of the country. They were commissioned by the central government and have been undertaken either by consultants or directly by government departments. Important studies in this category include those for South Hampshire, Humberside, Severnside and Tayside. The objective of the *South Hampshire Study* was to investigate the feasibility of large scale expansion of the area and its suitability for receiving some of the anticipated population increase of the South East in the form of overspill in the order of 250 000. The study, undertaken by Colin Buchanan and Partners, was completed in 1966 and makes an important contribution to the study of urban form. The three estuarial studies for Humberside, Tayside and Severnside arose out of the *Interim Report of the Long Term Population Distribution Group*, which raised the need to investigate possible reception areas for part of the then anticipated population increase of 20 million by the end of the century, and for industrial/maritime purposes. The objective of the studies was to investigate the physical possibilities and economic prospects for accommodating population increases in the order of 175 000–300 000 for Tayside, 300 000–750 000 for Humberside and 650 000–1 000 000 for Severnside by the end of the century. The *Humberside Study*, published in 1969 and the *Severnside Study*, published in 1971, were undertaken by a special Central Unit for Environmental Planning established under the DEA, with some local authority assistance. The Scottish Study, published in 1970, was undertaken by a joint team from the

224

Scottish Development Department and the University of Dundee. The collective consideration of both economic and physical planning aspects is a major strength of this group of studies.

Other sub-regional studies are at various stages of progress in several areas of the country.

3 The regional planning process

The process of producing regional and sub-regional plans and strategies has been well documented elsewhere (see: McLoughlin; Jackson; Boyce, Day and McDonald)[9] and this brief section seeks only to outline the main stages in such a process, as used in recent British and American studies.

Over the last few years, and particularly in the recent spate of British regional and sub-regional studies, the planning process of 'survey-analysis-plan' first formalised by Geddes has taken on a new terminology. The planning process is now seen as a sequence of operations involving the survey and analysis of the study area examining its needs and potential for development, the formulation of goals and/or objectives and the generation and testing of alternative strategies. However, although there may be some correlation between the main stages of the processes of recent studies, in detail they vary considerably, each geared and tailor-made to the requirements of its study area. Figures 10.1 and 10.2 provide simplified flow diagrams of the main stages in the processes used in the preparation of the *Coventry–Solihull–Warwickshire Sub-Regional Study* (CSW), and the *Strategic Plan for the South East* the most recent of the British sub-regional and regional studies.

The broad aims of a regional/sub-regional study are usually implicit in the initial terms of reference. From this starting point, generalised goals relating to factors such as social and economic balance and prosperity, choice and flexibility can be developed. But an assessment of how far alternative strategies might actually achieve these goals requires the definition of more specific objectives. Such objectives usually evolve from the survey and analysis stage which throws up identifiable problems. This may involve multi-stage development and refinement and the breakdown into sub-groups such as primary, secondary and tertiary

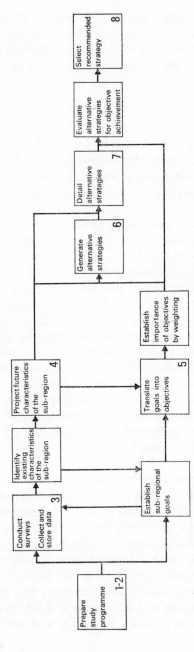

At these stages special reports were presented to the Planning Authorities viz:-

1. A sub-regional primer   3. Data report   5. Report on intended evaluation procedure   7. Detailing report
2. Study programme   4. Brief for the plan   6. Alternatives report   8. Draft final report

Fig. 10.1 Simplified flow diagram of main stages in study process: Coventry–Solihull–Warwickshire sub-regional study

SOURCE *Coventry–Solihull–Warwickshire: A Strategy for the Sub-region*, Coventry City Council, Solihull County Borough Council and Warwickshire County Council (1971).

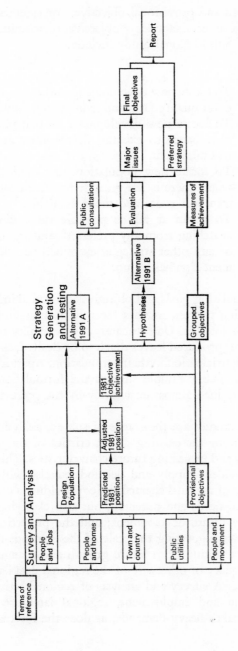

Fig. 10.2 Summarised diagram of process: Strategic Plan for the South East

SOURCE C. L. W. Minay, Department of Town Planning, Oxford Polytechnic (based on text of study report, *Strategic Plan for the South East*, HMSO (1970)).

objectives, grouped and provisional objectives, or essential and discriminatory objectives. Examples of objectives (discriminatory) used in the CSW Sub-Regional Study include:

Objective Number

2   To locate new development so that the loss of good quality farmland is kept to a minimum.

7   To locate new development so that physical disturbance to existing development is kept to a minimum.

16   To locate new population and employment where there is the greatest possible choice of transport route and mode available.

20   To retain as far as possible the option of switching from any preferred strategy to one of any other strategies examined once implementation has begun.

This stage of formulating goals and objectives is of vital importance in the planning process and has recently been assuming a much more significant rôle. Unfortunately the generality of the goals and objectives produced leaves much to be desired, as does the lack of public participation in their formulation. Apart from a limited number of public sample surveys the formulation has tended to be determined almost exclusively by the professional planning team.

Basic to all the studies are the stages of survey, analysis and forecasting, identifying the existing characteristics of the study area and exploring and projecting future characteristics. This can be seen as a two-sided, supply and demand exercise with the survey and analysis of regional characteristics providing a picture of existing regional needs and potential, but also clarifying the constraints on any future development; and the projection of future characteristics suggesting the scale of the demands to be made on the area resulting from future growth and change. At this stage, the adequacy or otherwise of the regional data base is of vital importance. A survey and analysis of regional activities such as population and employment, regional land use and communications makes heavy demands, as does the forecasting

228

involved. Projections of population trends, changes in industry and employment, housing and shopping and many other associated activities are made on the basis of a variety of assumptions about natural population change and migration, trends in the major industrial sectors, rates of household formation and so on. The methods used vary in their complexity from simple trend projections to the use of complex mathematical models. But the length of the projection period (often greater than 25 years), the lengthy chains of reasoning and uncertainty about the future leave much room for inaccuracy and make forecasting extremely hazardous.

Given the projection of future characteristics and the formulation of specific objectives, the next stage involves the generation of alternative strategies. The contemporary approach to plan generation has been to produce a wide range of competing alternatives in an attempt to achieve the best solution. Although all studies consider factors such as the location of employment, housing demand and work–home relationships, there is no standard approach to plan generation and a variety of different methods can be identified:*

1. the use of simple, hypothetical concepts of urban form—linear cities, grid cities, growth corridors are examples
2. urban extensions determined primarily by land form and physical factors and problems using a simple 'sieve map' technique
3. trend growth—continuing the established pattern of development
4. sensitive analysis of the internal economic and social system which would be extended by the growth being planned—especially the distribution of basic employment
5. the construction of strategies derived directly or indirectly from the planning objectives emerging from survey and analysis.

The generation of a range of alternative strategies necessitates the need for choice and most studies now identify a distinct evaluation stage in their planning process. It is the stage at which

* This classification is based partly on 'A background paper on the Coventry–Solihull–Warwickshire Sub-Regional Study.' *CES Next Stages in Sub-Regional Planning Conference,* pages 10–11, January 1972.

an identification is made of the comparative advantages and disadvantages of the alternatives. It logically follows the stage of analysis and alternatives generation and precedes decision making, although in practice there may be some blurring between them. For example, evaluation may provide new insights which may lead to recycling and the generation of a set of superior alternatives.

A wide variety of evaluation techniques are now available and have been used in regional and sub-regional planning (see: Lichfield[10]). They can be broadly subdivided into partial and comprehensive techniques. Of course, to some extent all evaluation techniques are partial in that they fail to include all the repercussions of a particular action. However, certain techniques make little attempt to be comprehensive. Narrow financial appraisal, cost effectiveness and cost-minimisation are the major categories of partial evaluation. The cost minimisation approach of threshold analysis is of particular interest and has been used in several studies.[11] However, most studies prefer a more comprehensive form of evaluation such as Cost-Benefit Analysis (CBA). CBA involves taking a wide view and a long view of the repercussions of a particular action—the adoption of a strategic plan for an area. The method involves the identification, enumeration and evaluation of all relevant costs and benefits and their discounting to a standard base. This involves problems, not least the enumeration problems of defining the 'cut-off' point and dealing with intangibles, the problems of evaluating intangibles and considering equity factors, and the choice of discounting technique and interest rate.[12]

In this evaluation stage, the use of developments of CBA such as the Planning Balance Sheet (PBS)[13] and the Goals Achievement Matrix (GAM)[14] overcome some of the problems and may present more useful tools. The GAM Method involves the evaluation of alternative strategies against the stated goals and objectives and in some studies has been developed into a complex evaluation procedure. The existence of many diverse goals and objectives usually necessitates a system of weights as an input into the technique. This provides another opportunity for public participation which has largely been neglected to date. Similarly, there has been little attempt to incorporate the impact of alternative strategies on community groups.

The evaluation stage inevitably leads to a preferred strategy. But evaluation is not decision making, it is only an aid to the decision makers. If the plan is accepted by the responsible authorities it then remains to be implemented, for 'a form of planning which does not comprehend within itself the resources and means of implementation is not planning in any effective sense.'[15] This stage of the regional process constitutes a major stumbling block in the UK at the present time and the administrative questions involved are explored more fully in the next chapter. But this is not the end of the process. Planning, as envisaged in contemporary studies, has no end-product. It is part of a continuing process which must be kept under review and amended where necessary in the light of the monitoring of the key indicators of the region's condition.

4 Growth centre policies

A recurrent feature of contemporary regional and sub-regional plans and strategies in this country and abroad is the concentration of growth and development in a limited number of centres. The advantages of such a policy relate back to the theoretical discussion of growth poles in Chapter 8. There it was suggested that such concentration brought industrial advantages (the various economies internal and external to the firm); urban advantages (economies of scale in the provision of social and economic infrastructure, reflected in factors such as good services and communications); and a nucleus from which growth could spread into the rest of the region. In addition, development in a limited number of growth centres may also bring 'rural' advantages, with concentration facilitating the retention of recreational and agricultural open space.

Growth centres have been liberally sprinkled over many of the contemporary British regional and sub-regional plans and strategies and it is interesting to briefly examine their use and misuse within the framework of the policy typology outlined in Chapter 8, prior to a more comprehensive discussion of strategies for the South East and North West. Growth centres have been advocated as remedies for the whole range of regional problems, although their suggested rôle is primarily twofold—firstly as centres of relief for congested urban areas and secondly as vehicles to secure regional development.

In the so-called *sparsely developed/underdeveloped* regions of Britain, growth centres have been proposed as a means of breaking out of the vicious circle of decline. In the North of Scotland, the Highlands and Islands Development Board has identified three areas as being capable of substantial growth based on industrial development—Fort William with a present population of approximately 16 000; Caithness (30 000); and the Moray Firth sub-region (75 000). A recent planning scheme[16] suggested that the latter could be raised to 300 000 with high standards of amenity preserved. Yet there would seem to be little or no adequate foundation for such an increase for, although each of the three areas has been the scene of interesting new industrial developments over the last few years, there is little evidence as yet of comprehensive development. However, North Sea oil may provide the necessary catalyst for major industrial development, but at what price?[17] The areas identified in the Highlands represent growth centres of development with the main function being one of at first stabilisation and then generation of growth; they also represent a 'passive' or 'reinforcing' strategy, accepting the rationality of the existing system of centres and concentrating on the most promising within them. In contrast, a plan for the Central Borders[18] proposed an 'active' or 'initiating' growth centre policy with the concentration of expansion in the area of the small community of St. Boswells, near to Galashiels. The application of threshold analysis suggested that this area would be one of the least expensive to develop, reaping economies of scale in the provision of public utilities. In the event, the plan was politically unacceptable, was rejected and growth was spread around the existing settlements. A similar proposal for a major new centre in Mid-Wales,[19] a linear settlement of 70 000 at the head of the Severn Valley based on the small centre of Caersws, met a similar fate, although a more limited scale of development has since been approved at nearby Newtown.

In the *depressed industrial regions*, growth centre policies have been clearly proposed for Northern Ireland, Central Scotland and the North East. In Northern Ireland, the problem is one of imbalance between east and west with overcrowding and congestion in the Belfast conurbation in the east and the lack of opportunities, decline in agriculture and population loss from the western counties. Yet even Belfast is not too prosperous, therefore the policy required was to establish strong relief centres to Belfast within the Belfast region, as well as the inauguration of development centres in the more remote western areas. It was recognised that 'in a region which had less than 1·5 million people, the number of centres must be limited'.[20] As such future growth is to be concentrated in three Major Centres of Accelerated Growth. The most important, Craigavon, lies 20–25 miles south-west of Belfast, centred on the towns of Lurgan and Portadown. The aim is a population increase from approximately 60 000 to 100 000 by 1981—and there have already been major infrastructural investments and industrial development. In the other growth centres, Antrim–Ballymena and Londonderry, proposed expansion is on a rather smaller scale but still quite substantial. All the centres represent primary developments in the Northern Ireland context. All also have development functions aimed at regenerating the south and west of the province, although Craigavon and Antrim–Ballymena can also be seen as centres of relief for Belfast. At a lower level in the settlement hierarchy, a number of smaller key centres have also been identified for the concentration of infrastructural investment.

In Central Scotland, the rôle of growth centres is again to act as relief centres to the older industrial congested centres like Glasgow and to serve as vehicles for regional development. Since 1947, a number of new towns have been developed for overspill purposes, but it was not until 1963 that eight growth centres were designated at Irvine, Vale of Leven, East Kilbride, North Lanarkshire, Cumbernauld, Grangemouth/Falkirk, Greater Livingston and Central Fife. The total population increase of the growth areas is expected to be in the order of 500 000. The growth areas are intended to 'form focal points of growth benefiting much wider districts'[21] through their initial relief of unemployment, followed by the spreading out of development into the surrounding areas. Such benefits, it was realised, could be enhanced by a policy which would encourage 'industrial complexes . . . to build up around them'. It is with regard to the latter that the growth centre policy in Scotland differs from almost all other UK contexts, for since 1963 a deliberate policy of attracting science-based industry to the growth centres has been encouraged. The foundation of this policy was the existence at East Kilbride of the National Engineering Laboratory, the presence of the universities of Glasgow and Edinburgh, and the urbanisation economies of the growth centres themselves. There is, in fact, now commencing the birth of an industrial complex around the larger electronic firms, and

'Scotland now boasts an unrivalled concentration of electronic plants . . . its electronics and associated industry has mushroomed from one firm to a host of more than 80 companies with a labour force now getting on for 40 000.'[22]

In the North-East, two growth centre policies have been produced. The 1963 proposals[23] reinforced the existing settlement hierarchy proposing main centres of expansion at the conurbations of Tyneside and Teesside and the Darlington/Aycliffe area. In contrast, the 1968 Outline Strategy by the Northern Economic Planning Council[24] proposed a hierarchy of major growth, growth and secondary growth centres and appeared to be an attempt to restructure the city system in the area. Growth centres have also been proposed in the two 'intermediate' depressed industrial regions of the North West and Yorkshire and Humberside. In the North West, the proposals for the Central Lancashire New Town (Preston–Leyland–Chorley) constitute a primary development in the regional settlement hierarchy, and are particularly interesting in that the area is seen not only as a centre for concentrated infrastructural investment, but also, as in Central Scotland, as a suitable location for an industrial complex development. In Yorkshire and Humberside a series of 'primary' growth centres have been proposed[25] for Dinnington/Maltby, Adwick/Bentley and 'Five Towns' (Castleford–Pontefract–Featherstone–Knottingley–Normanton). All the locations have good access to existing and proposed motorway interchanges and are aimed primarily at relieving the problems of the coalfield area. In the Five Towns development which is to be given some priority, it is anticipated that the population will almost double to approximately 200 000 by the end of the century.

In the *pressured regions* there has been the gradual evolution of a strategy of 'concentrated decentralisation' to deal with the problems of population growth and overcrowding in particular urban areas. At first, growth was accommodated on the periphery of existing urban areas increasing the concentration at the centre and this will no doubt still be the inevitable approach for many smaller centres. But more recently there has been a deliberate attempt to create a better balance between the central urban areas and the surrounding hinterlands, leading to less confused regional structures and combining growth with less rather than more congestion. This was first reflected in the dispersal of growth into small/medium sized towns not too distant from the major urban centre, such as the early overspill new towns for London. Unfortunately, such centres, with populations of less than 100 000 may not be large enough for the growth involved. In addition, at distances of less than 30 miles from the central city, they may also lack functional independence. This has led to another alternative, the accommodation of growth in major new growth centres generally at much greater distances from the centre and with much larger populations. In the late 1960's, plans for expansion at Telford in the West Midlands and Northampton in the South East suggested ultimate populations in excess of 200 000, and the latest plans for growth centres in the South-East have much higher estimates still. Such centres can be expected to have a greater degree of functional independence than the smaller new towns.

This brief survey gives some indication of the many and varied uses of growth centre policies in contemporary UK regional plans. The centres have been used for purposes of relief and as vehicles for regional development and often both at the same time. Their population size varies greatly from a few thousand in remote rural areas to figures in excess of 0·25 to 0·5 million in the most populous regions. Their importance in the regional settlement hierarchy also various although most tend to be major centres at a primary or secondary level. Many centres seek to build on existing central places, a passive approach reinforcing the existing settlement structure, and tend to rely primarily on infrastructural investment to provide the necessary growth catalyst.

The survey also provides examples of the misuse of growth centres. A typical failing is the designation of too many centres which limits the concentration of investment in any one. This reflects the basic dilemma of a growth centre policy—the need to reconcile economic efficiency with social and political pressures. Areas not designated as growth centres tend to regard themselves as 'non-growth centres' and rebel accordingly. Another problem is the concentration on 'growth centre' policies and the failure to develop industrial 'growth poles'. A growth pole policy is much more likely to establish a state of self-sustaining growth in an area because of its stress on interlinkages between activities, and growth centres lacking a pole focus lose many of the benefits of concentration.

5 Regional planning in the metropolitan South East

THE SOUTH EAST IN PERSPECTIVE

The South East occupies a unique position both in the United Kingdom and in a wider international context. This uniqueness stems from the general strength and vitality of the economic base of the region, from the particular importance of London as the capital and seat of government and its rôle as a world centre of business and financial activity. Many of the political, financial and business decisions taken in the South East have important repercussions far beyond the region. Within the UK, one result of this high degree of interdependence is to make the actual definition of the South East a difficult task. It also reinforces the need to plan on an inter-regional as well as on an intra-regional basis.

Unfortunately however, the South East is also unique in the country in the scale of its problems, the various diseconomies of growth. These problems have existed in various guises for a long time and unrelated policies seeking to deal with them date back hundreds of years. But, as the previous chronology showed, it is only since the turn of the century that there have been any serious attempts to deal with them at the regional scale. At first these attempts were rather unco-ordinated, taking place as they were in a period of largely unconscious planning. Howard and his

236

disciples pioneered the road to decentralisation policies by the early establishment of the satellite new towns in the 1920's, and Raymond Unwin and the London Society were largely instrumental in fostering the Green Belt Act of 1938 to restrain the outward growth of London. But it was not until the advent of Abercrombie's *Greater London Plan 1944* that a more comprehensive view was taken of the planning of the region. Although even here it is interesting to note that at the same time the then London County Council was asked to prepare a plan for London itself, which was published in 1943 as the *County of London Plan*. This duality seems to suggest that the interrelationship between London and its region was still not fully realised. Nevertheless these documents formed the framework for strategic planning in the metropolitan region for the next 20 years until they were replaced by a spate of more sophisticated studies and strategies— the *South East Study* in 1964, *A Strategy for the South East* in 1967, and the *Strategic Plan for the South East* in 1970.[26]

DEFINING THE SOUTH EAST

A review of regional planning from pre-Abercrombie times shows that the region has been continuously growing in a vain attempt to catch up with its problems. In 1937, the Standing Conference on London Regional Planning took the London Traffic Area as its field of study, an area roughly coinciding with the old LCC boundary. Abercrombie defined his region as roughly 30 miles in radius from Central London although he was wise enough to qualify this by stating that the region consisted of:

'the one and indivisible Metropolis, whose boundaries are invisible to the naked eye, unrealised by the normal citizen— save when indicated by rate demands—and unmeaning to the planner.'[27]

The *South East Study* extended the region well beyond Abercrombie's original conception, taking in a massive area east of a line drawn from South Dorset to the Wash. This included the whole of the East Anglian and South Coasts, an area 100 miles north of Central London and beyond Oxford in the north west.

The 1967 *South East Strategy* took a rather more conservative view contracting the boundaries in the north east and south west, and the most recent *Strategic Plan* takes a similar area defined on a grid basis.

THE REGIONAL PROBLEMS—TO GROW OR NOT TO GROW?

The growth of population and jobs is the major influence on regional planning in the pressured region of the South East. This growth has continued apace despite all attempts to restrain it and has imposed a severe strain on the resources of the region. Housing, communications and amenities such as attractive countryside are particularly vulnerable, and in the long run a wide range of social costs result.

The *Greater London Plan* was prepared in a climate of antipathy towards any further growth of the London region. Growth in itself, rather than its form was considered undesirable. This clearly influenced Abercrombie's proposals which were based on a number of assumptions which were clearly stated in the plan. The first assumption was that, in conformity with the recommendations of the Barlow Report, no new industry would be admitted to London and the Home Counties, except in special cases. The second assumption was that there would be a decentralisation of persons and industry from the congested centre to achieve better environmental standards both inside and outside London. The third assumption was that the total population of the area would not increase, but on the contrary be somewhat reduced. All these assumptions, especially that of a static or declining population, were soon proved to be unrealistic. Growth continued and by not planning for it a situation arose where the pressure for land resulted in many *ad hoc* planning decisions and development completely unrelated to the objectives of the plan.

In contrast, the more recent regional plans have adopted a more realistic approach. They all start from the premise that growth in the South East, at least that part attributable to natural increase, is inevitable and must be planned for. The *South East Study* estimated a population increase of approximately 3.5 million on the base population of 17 million between 1961 and 1981 and the *Strategic Plan* recognised a probable growth of approximately

238

5 million between 1966 and the end of the century.* This acceptance of a high level of growth in the South East is seen by many as conflicting directly with the objectives of inter-regional planning and hastening the decline of the economically less fortunate regions. There are of course also those who are convinced that national economic welfare would benefit most by 'letting the South East rip!'[28]

TOWARDS A REGIONAL PLANNING STRATEGY FOR THE SOUTH EAST

In spite of the fundamental difference in attitude to the idea of growth in the South East, the concepts of the regional plans and strategies reveal a remarkable similarity over time. Two concepts are particularly dominant. These are the division of the region into a series of concentric zones with varying problems and the need for the concentrated decentralisation of population and employment from the inner zones to the outer zones to achieve a 'drawing-off' of influence from Central London.

Abercrombie divided the superficially apparent amorphous sprawl of the London region into the Inner Urban Ring, the Suburban Ring, the Green Belt Ring and the Outer Country Ring, all of which had quite different characteristics and problems. The Inner Urban Ring was characterised by serious environmental problems, with unhealthy, overcrowded development and a high level of sub-standard housing. The Suburban Ring was characterised by rapid, but anonymous and jumbled, growth which was beginning to leap the Green Belt creating a similarly undesirable pattern of development in the Outer Country Ring, destroying its rural and agricultural quality. The remedy for these problems, as Abercrombie saw it, was to decentralise industry and the overcrowded population from the problem areas such as the Inner Urban Ring to carefully chosen locations in the Outer Country Ring. This would both improve the environment of the inner areas and co-ordinate development around London into a limited number of towns providing good housing and job opportunities. He therefore proposed a policy of developing a series of

* Although a report by the Monitoring Group on Strategic Planning in the South-East (DOE, HMSO, 1973) suggests that there could be a shortfall in this projected increase of 1·25 million.

satellite new towns and the enlarging of existing suitable towns in the Outer Country Ring to accommodate a possible overspill population of approximately one million. Just over a third of this number would be accommodated in eight new towns, which were to be finite self-contained communities of 40–60 000 population at about 30 miles from London. A further 250 000 would be accommodated in the expansion of existing towns in the Outer Country Ring, 125 000 would be in quasi-satellites and 250 000 would be dispersed in areas beyond the metropolitan influence. All this was against a background of an assumed static or even declining population.

The new town programme was implemented and has been a considerable success. But the rapid population growth after the Second World War demanded a reappraisal of policy. The *South East Study* was set up to examine the growth and movement of population in the region, to lay down a broad strategy to deal with it, and to suggest ways and means of implementation. The Study again identified four concentric rings forming the region. These were labelled the London Conurbation, the Inner and Outer Country Rings which constituted the Outer Metropolitan Region, and the Remainder of the South East. Once again the suggested policy was one of decentralisation from the congested centre and the accommodation of the regional population growth in the outer rings, but the scale of the proposals was much larger. The London conurbation was to be stabilised at a population of eight million, with the one million moving out offset by natural increase, and the whole of the population growth of 3·5 millions between 1961 and 1981 was to be housed in the outer areas, (Figure 10.3). It was suggested that a large proportion of this likely growth should be diverted into planned 'counter-magnets' between 50 and 100 miles from Central London. New cities were proposed for the Southampton–Portsmouth, Bletchley and Newbury areas, and six other places were named, including Swindon, Ipswich and Northampton, where there might be substantial expansion, each with an import population of 50–100 000. Another twelve places were identified as possible locations for smaller expansion, each with an import population of at least 30 000. These schemes, plus the new and expanded towns programme, which was to take another 250 000, would account for 1–1·25 million, and it was anticipated that the remaining increase of approximately two millions would be accommodated under the normal development plans of local authorities outside the London conurbation. The *South East Study* enlarged the scale of regional planning in the South East, the rings had become wider and the 'counter magnets' were to be

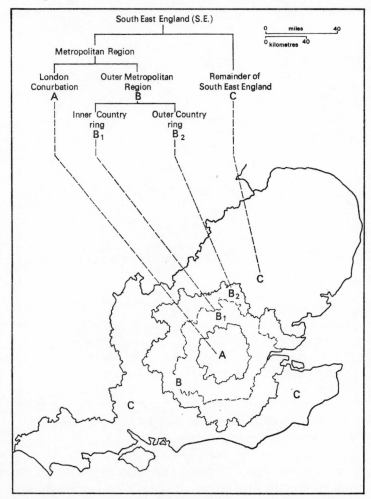

Fig. 10.3(a)   Regional planning in the South East: South East Study (1961–81) *Sub divisions of South East England*

much larger and more distant from Central London, but in principle the underlying policy of decentralisation remained unchanged.

A *Strategy for the South East*, produced by the Regional Economic Planning Council, varied the pattern only slightly (Figure 10·4). Three basic zones were defined—Greater London, the Outer Metropolitan Area and the Outer South East. Within this

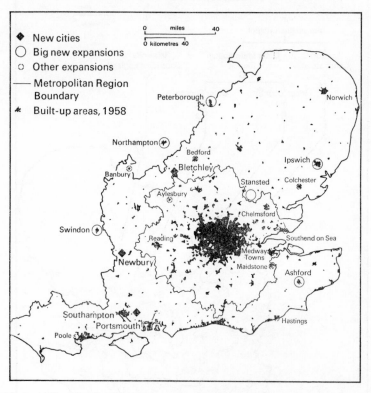

Fig 10.3(b)   Regional planning in the South East: South East Study (1961-81) *Areas suggested for expansion*

framework it was again proposed that there should be no significant increase in the population of Greater London beyond eight million. All growth was to be accommodated in other parts of the region or nearby, taking account of existing plans for

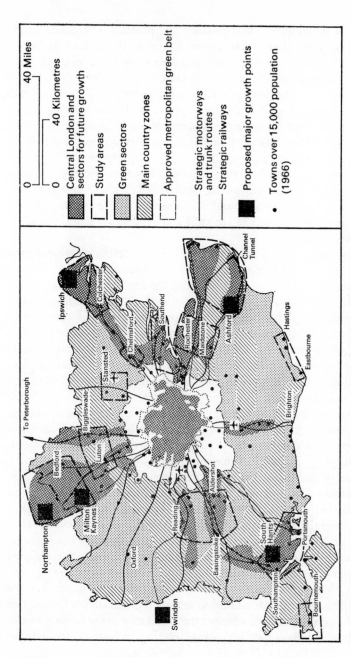

Central London and
sectors for future growth

Study areas

Green sectors

Main country zones

Approved metropolitan green belt

Strategic motorways
and trunk routes

Strategic railways

Proposed major growth points

Towns over 15,000 population
(1966)

Fig. 10.4 Regional planning in the South East: A Strategy for the South East

243

further development and existing and planned investment in the region, particularly in transport facilities. A number of 'major growth points' were recommended to form large 'counter magnets' such as Southampton–Portsmouth, Northampton–Milton Keynes and Ipswich–Colchester at the outer ends of 'growth sectors' radiating from the metropolis. In all nine such sectors or corridors were proposed following major transportation radials such as express inter-city rail links, motorways and trunk roads programmed for major investment (although in effect, they could be combined into four major groups radiating from the central hub to the north and north west, the east and north east, the south east and the west and south west). However, the strategy was not well received and in 1968 a new planning study was set in motion.

The South East Joint Planning Team undertaking the preparation of the most recent *Strategic Plan* was required by its terms of reference to take as a starting point the strategy proposals of the South East Economic Planning Council. As such, in many ways, the resultant plan follows a similar pattern to its predecessor, with the same definition of concentric zones and the recommendation of growth points to accommodate the population and employment increase. Ten diverse patterns of population and employment distribution were designed and examined by the team and two of the alternatives for 1991 were considered in detail. 1991A suggests counter magnets 40–80 miles away from London, and 1991B suggests development closer to London. The result is 1991C, a compromise between the two hypothetical patterns identifying major and medium growth points (Figure 10.5). Three of the major growth points, South Hampshire, Reading–Aldershot–Basingstoke, and South Essex are each identified as locations for populations in excess of one million by the year 2001. The populations of the medium growth points vary between 0·25 and 0·5 million. As noted earlier, this strategy has been accepted in principle by the government as the basis for regional planning in the South East.

At this most recent stage, it is interesting to note that the duality in planning for London and its region still continues. For on the central issue of whether the spontaneous outflow of households and jobs, especially manufacturing industries, from Inner

244

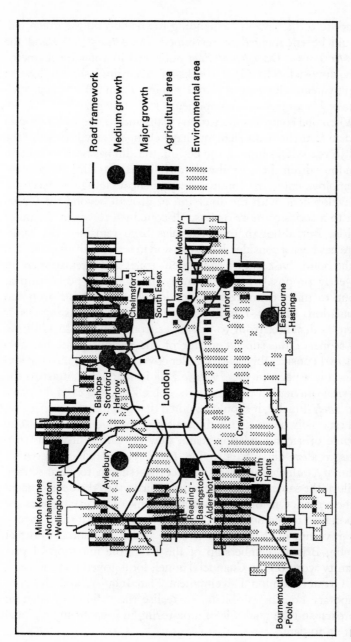

Legend:
— Road framework
● Medium growth
■ Major growth
▤ Agricultural area
░ Environmental area

Milton Keynes
-Northampton
-Wellingborough

Aylesbury

Reading-
Basingstoke-
Aldershot

Bournemouth
-Poole

South Hants

Crawley

London

Bishops
Stortford-
Harlow

Chelmsford

South Essex

Maidstone-Medway

Ashford

Eastbourne
-Hastings

Fig. 10.5   Regional planning in the South East: Strategic Plan for the South East—preferred strategy

245

London to the new and expanding towns beyond the green belt should be encouraged or restrained, the *Strategic Plan* and the *Greater London Development Plan* published in 1969 are diametrically opposed. The GLC speaks of 'retarding' the outflow of employment, whereas the Joint Planning Team believes that such dispersal is an essential component of its strategy.

When one compares the various plans and strategies it becomes evident that the main elements have changed very little over the last 30 years. Throughout the period, the aim has been to contain London within the area already developed, arresting the growth of employment in the conurbation and encouraging the necessary redevelopment, with the diversion of growth beyond the Green Belt to a series of more or less self-contained towns in the outer region. But although the principles have remained the same, there has been a considerable expansion in scale, with an extension of the South East and its constituent zones and a replacement of the early proposals for new towns of 40–60 000 population at about 30 miles from Central London, by cities with proposed populations of 0·25–1 million, usually based on existing major towns at distances from 50–100 miles from London. In addition, the scope of the subject matter of the various plans has also widened considerably, with a fuller coverage of both physical and economic aspects in the *Strategic Plan* in marked contrast to the physical orientation of the Abercrombie Plan, and even the *South East Study*. Finally, it should be noted that planning for any region and especially one with the dynamism of the South East, must be capable of accommodating major new developments. The 1970 *Strategic Plan* aims to provide for a considerable degree of flexibility, which earlier experience has shown to be essential, while at the same time giving a firm guidance to the development of the region. One only needs to note some of the events of major importance to the South East that have taken place since 1970—the government decision to site the Third London Airport at Maplin, British membership of the EEC, the initiation of preparatory work on the Channel Tunnel, local government reform, the Greater London Development Plan Inquiry, and the contemporary housing problem—to realise the validity of such an approach and the vital rôle of monitoring in keeping any regional plan up to date.

246

6 Regional planning in the industrial North West

WHAT IS THE NORTH WEST? [29]

In marked contrast to the South East, the North West embracing the geographical counties of Lancashire and Cheshire, and the High Peak of Derbyshire, covers less than 5% of the country and is the smallest UK region. On the other hand, with 6·7 million people it contains 14% of the total population of the country. Understandably it therefore has some of the highest population densities in the country as evidenced by the 9200 people per square mile on parts of Merseyside. Marked by hills and mountains to the north and east, by fine agricultural land to the south and by the Irish Sea to the west, it also has a much more defined physical identity than the sprawling South East and is much more of a 'natural' region. Within this framework there is a great sub-regional variety, including two major conurbations, a large number of major towns and beautiful and remote rural areas, and areas of growth and decline. The North West is in many ways a microcosm of the country. Yet it can also be seen as a functional unit, as a single city with many centres, large and small. Aspects such as these, plus the attempts of this first major industrial region in the world to undertake major economic readjustments, make the tentative attempts at regional planning in the North West of particular interest.

STRATEGIC ISSUES—THE NORTH WEST'S LEGACY

Most of the problems of the North West stem from its industrial heritage. It was the cradle of the Industrial Revolution and in the nineteenth century the region's 'cotton–coal' economy boomed, population grew at a tremendous pace, towns doubled and re-doubled their size, and Manchester was the centre of gravity of industrial Britain. But such growth was achieved with nineteenth century machinery and sources of power and little thought for the environmental consequences, and even by 1900 the region had begun to regret and to pay for its reliance on a narrow industrial base and it has been paying for it ever since. As evidenced in Chapter 5, this decline in the traditional industries in the face of the changing internal and external factors of resources and

247

markets, plus the region's rather disappointing record in the new growth sectors, have created major structural problems. A decline in the numbers employed in the Lancashire textile industry from over 600 000 at the turn of the century to a present figure of less than 100 000 has reduced the rôle of this major industry to one of secondary importance. Such economic malaise breeds all the usual symptoms, including high unemployment, falling activity rates and net outmigration. The incidence of economic problems of course varies and they have been particularly persistent in the North East Lancashire and Merseyside sub-regions.

Intrinsically linked with these economic problems are fundamental environmental problems. The region is seen by many as 'drab, dirty, dismal and dark'. As the oldest of the world's industrial regions it has an unwelcome legacy of dirty air and filthy rivers, of scarred and derelict land, and congested towns crammed with old and worn houses and factories. Housing problems are particularly acute. 20% of the 2·5 million poorest dwellings in the country are in the North West, the worst problems being in the two conurbations where urban renewal will continue to generate large overspill problems. But not all of these poor dwellings are necessarily ripe for demolition. Many of the houses are solid and capable of improvement although there may now be too much reliance by twentieth century planners on the improvement of nineteenth century houses to provide a twenty-first century environment. Houses thought at present 'too good to knock down' may be millstones around the necks of future generations. The problem is a vicious circle—the economic structure creates environmental problems, which in turn are not conducive to economic regeneration, and similarly environmental improvement. Nor is the situation helped by the apparent acceptance by the North West residents of low environmental standards and the 'image' of the North West by the British public at large.

The drabness of the local environment plus the lack of employment opportunities are the major causes of the long-standing problem of outmigration in the region. This factor plus the relatively low rate of natural increase makes the rate of population growth in the North West slower than that of any other English region. However, this does not mean that the area is not without

248

population problems. In the period 1961–71, the total increase was approximately 200 000 persons and it has been estimated that the increase over the 1971–91 period may be in the order of 450 000. This of course means building more houses and finding more room in an already congested region. There are also specific sub-regional population problems, for although the region as a whole may be growing in population, areas in the major conurbations and North East Lancashire have suffered from an absolute decline. Thus, in addition to the fundamental industrial and environmental problems, the region also has to cope with population growth and redistribution.

Yet although the problems are many and widespread and cannot be ignored, they must not be overemphasised. The economic problems are balanced by rapid developments in major growth sectors such as chemicals, oil, glass and vehicles—perhaps heralding the birth of a new industrial revolution. The problem of large-scale environmental obsolescence, which in itself presents important opportunities for a fresh start, is partly offset by factors such as the excellent road system, new docks at Seaforth and a prosperous airport at Manchester. Over the years, such problems and opportunities have attracted a great deal of professional attention at the local level by local planning departments and consultants, and more recently at the regional level.

A MOVEMENT TOWARDS REGIONAL PLANNING

Prior to 1965, the North West had no overall regional planning body. Planning was in the hands of 24 independent planning authorities established under the 1947 Planning Act, each pre-occupied with its own internal problems. The only authorities with any possibility of taking a wider view were the counties of Lancashire and Cheshire, but even here the problem was one of planning 'for a blanket with holes in', (see Figure 10.6). As a result, the early approach to strategic issues was dealt with on an unco-ordinated and piecemeal basis. Approaches to the overspill problems of Liverpool and Manchester included peripheral expansion on the fringes of the Liverpool city boundary, the promotion of a large number of small overspill expansion schemes

249

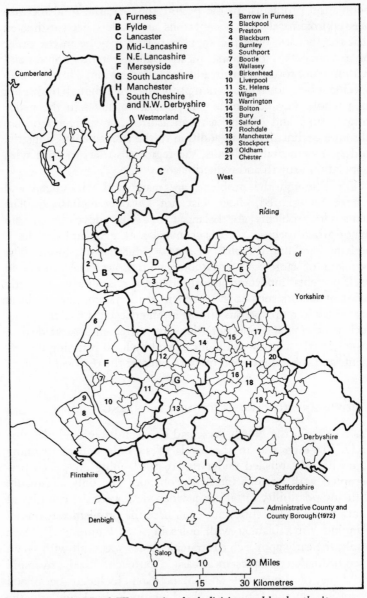

A Furness
B Fylde
C Lancaster
D Mid-Lancashire
E N.E. Lancashire
F Merseyside
G South Lancashire
H Manchester
I South Cheshire
  and N.W. Derbyshire

1 Barrow in Furness
2 Blackpool
3 Preston
4 Blackburn
5 Burnley
6 Southport
7 Bootle
8 Wallasey
9 Birkenhead
10 Liverpool
11 St. Helens
12 Wigan
13 Warrington
14 Bolton
15 Bury
16 Salford
17 Rochdale
18 Manchester
19 Stockport
20 Oldham
21 Chester

Cumberland

Westmorland

West

Riding

of

Yorkshire

Derbyshire

Flintshire

Staffordshire

Denbigh

—— Administrative County and
    County Borough (1972)

Salop

0   10   20 Miles

0   15   30 Kilometres

Fig. 10.6   The North West: regional sub-divisions and local authority boundaries (1972) (Lancashire and Cheshire)

by Manchester County Borough, and the initiation of new towns at Skelmersdale and Runcorn.

Since 1965, the North West Economic Planning Council and Board have been established and there have been a series of modern studies looking at the region as a whole. The *North West Study* was produced by a multi-department government team in 1965, and *An Economic Planning Strategy for the NW Region* (*Strategy I*) and *Strategy II: The North West of the 1970's* were produced in 1966 and 1968 by the Council.[30] Unfortunately, not one of these documents can as yet be said to constitute a regional plan, and they all rightly disclaim any pretensions of being such.

The *North West Study* was basically a factual survey of the region prepared by a group of civil servants as the basis for evolving a regional planning strategy. It included discussions of the population, employment, housing, transport and the general physical environment situation, highlighting major problems. Housing obsolescence was seen as the most important single problem. The study was particularly concerned with the physical accommodation of the population increase in the region, which, even with the continued net outmigration was estimated to be in the order of 800 000–930 000 between 1964 and 1981. But it was markedly lacking in considered proposals merely stating that the existing new towns at Skelmersdale and Runcorn plus the major proposals for the development at Warrington and Preston–Leyland–Chorley (Central Lancashire New Town) would probably be adequate to meet the needs of at least the near future. The development of major new complexes in North Lancashire and South Cheshire were suggested as possible long-term locations. The study was also weak on economic content with little discussion of the fundamental industrial problems of the region as a whole and of the depressed sub-regions in particular.

Strategy I was similarly concerned with the accommodation of population in the area, and, rejecting the assumption of continued net outmigration as the probable course of future events, suggested that there could be a population increase of one million by 1981. This would certainly require the development of the two long-term growth areas in North Lancashire and South Cheshire. However it was left to *Strategy II* to introduce some economic realism into these suggestions. It realised that the

251

region's future depended on its ability to provide good locations for the growth industries. One of its main conclusions was that 'the influence on the location of industry in the Region should be where it can operate most efficiently within a broad planning framework'. *Strategy II* also considered the problems and proposals of the nine regional sub-divisions in much more detail than its predecessors. Yet it was still 'only a stage in our thinking' and was quite some way from a regional strategy.

It is debatable whether the Planning Council and Board would have had the resources to produce the required strategy, and even more debatable whether such an advisory document would have been heeded by the local authorities. As it is, recent events are more encouraging. Following a series of studies of the region's main economic and social problems, such as land use and transportation problems in Merseyside and Greater Manchester, the costs and benefits of barrages across Morecambe Bay and the Dee Estuary, and the impact of Central Lancashire New Town (CLNT), a more detailed *Strategic Plan for the North West* (SPNW) is now being produced on a tripartite basis through the Planning Council, local authorities and government departments. The SPNW Study is seen as a companion volume to the *Strategic Plan for the South East* and will hopefully provide more positive guidelines for future action. It is urgently needed, for, with the designation of Warrington and CLNT as major urban developments and the spread of the motorway net, major strategic decisions are at present going by default. The study team are due to submit their final report to the commissioning body in 1973. A preliminary *Issues Report* outlines the main problems at the regional level, the adopted regional planning process, provisional objectives and alternative hypothetical strategies.

SPATIAL STRATEGIES AND ECONOMIC REALISM

Two of the main elements of a regional strategy are economic growth and spatial distributions. A spatial strategy for the North West is immediately constrained by a wide range of predominantly physical factors. Within such constraints, three alternatives appear to be viable—a 'trend' alternative with peripheral expansion on the perimeter of the Manchester and Liverpool green

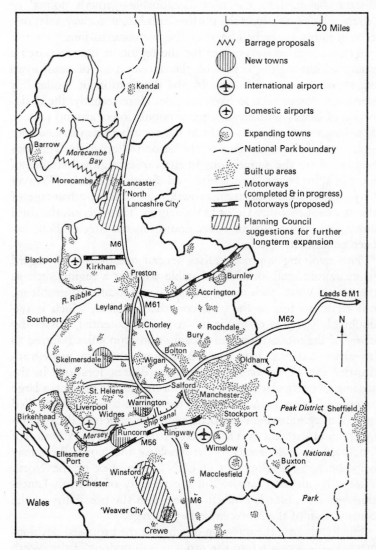

Fig. 10.7 The North West: regional planning proposals and commitments (1973)

belts and limited overspill to new and expanded towns; more distant dispersal to the now fashionable 'growth points' or 'counter magnets' along the north–south M6 motorway axis; or a concentration in the belt between the two conurbations.

The various *ad hoc* policies for the region at first favoured a policy of limited dispersal with the development of small town expansion schemes followed by the designation of moderately sized new towns such as Skelmersdale. More recently, the designation of CLNT with an anticipated population of around 500 000 at a distance of 20–30 miles from the conurbations marks a confirmation of some changes to the second alternative. This was reinforced by the suggestions in the earlier regional studies of locations in North Lancashire and South Cheshire ('Weaver City') as possible long term growth points taking advantage of the excellent mobility factor in the region. Throughout, the third alternative, the policy of concentration in the Mersey Belt, has been continually rejected.

This evolving approach raises several questions with regard to economic realism. It is debatable whether a region such as the North West, with major structural and locational problems, can afford to ignore the inter-conurbation zone, which is undoubtedly the area of maximum economic potential, possessing many of the localisation and urbanisation economies referred to in earlier sections. It is also debatable whether new growth industries can be attracted to the more distant locations in the absence of particular inter-regional incentives. At present, a large amount of the new investment in the region is being channelled into Merseyside which has benefited from preferential Development Area treatment over a period of many years. The extension of 'intermediate area' status to the whole of the North West may help the new development at CLNT—the apex of the North West's 'Randstad' triangle. But the viability of a North Lancashire growth point is doubtful, even with the possibility of the construction of the Morecambe Bay Barrage.

Finally, there is the question of whether the proposed developments will inject life into the problem sub-regions of the North West. Consultant's studies suggest that the development of an industrial complex in CLNT might generate favourable economic impulses into the economy of surrounding areas, especially

North East Lancashire. From input-output matrices, metal-based industries were selected as the most desirable basis for the industrial complex, as they possessed the highest degree of linkage benefits. However, vociferous elements from towns such as Blackburn, Accrington and Burnley in the North East Lancashire sub-region are not as optimistic and would favour a shift of the new town site eastwards towards Blackburn—even further away from the Mersey Belt. In the absence of more preferential regional location controls and incentives, the demands on nationally mobile industry would also seem to be excessive.

Economic factors are at the root of many of the North West's problems. Similarly, any future regional planning strategy for the North West must be economically realistic.

7 Summary

British intra-regional planning has quite a long history dating back to the beginnings of the century. Yet it has only really come to the fore in the last decade with the production of a variety of regional and sub-regional reports, plans and strategies. The studies originate from varied sources reflecting the various pressures from above and below for regional planning. The regional level studies have largely been produced by central government and the regional arms of central government, and more recently by standing conferences and on a tripartite basis by local authorities, central government and the regional councils and boards. In contrast, sub-regional studies relating to smaller areas have been more in the sphere of local planning authorities. The studies also vary in their content with the early 'stocktaking' documents contrasting with the later strategic plans. An interesting trend in the more recent and positive documents is the increasing sophistication in the process of producing regional and sub-regional plans, with the studies introducing many technical innovations. There is also a growing use, and quite often misuse, of growth centre policies. Such developments are reflected in the regional planning response to the regional problems of the metropolitan South East and the industrial North West. Yet however complex the process, and however satisfying the preferred plan, there cannot be effective regional planning without the necessary administrative framework.

References

1 Labour Party, *Regional Planning Policy,* pages 96–7 (1970).
2 *Report of the Royal Commission on the Distribution of Industrial Population,* Cmnd. 6153, HMSO (1940).
3 *Report on the Committee on Land Utilisation in Rural Areas,* Cmnd. 6378, HMSO (1942).
4 East Midlands Economic Planning Council, *The East Midlands Study,* HMSO (1966).
5 Yorkshire and Humberside Economic Planning Council, *A Review of Yorkshire and Humberside,* preface, HMSO (1966).
6 South-East Joint Planning Team, *Strategic Plan for the South-East,* HMSO (1970).
7 *Hansard,* 19 January 1972.
8 Leicester City Council and Leicestershire County Council, *Leicester and Leicestershire Sub-Regional Planning Study,* page 2, 1 (1969).
9 McLoughlin, J. B., *Urban and Regional Planning—A Systems Approach,* Faber and Faber (1969);
   Jackson, J. N., *The Urban Future,* Allen and Unwin (1972).
   Boyce, D. E., Day N. D., and McDonald, C., *Metropolitan Plan Making,* Regional Science Institute, Philadelphia (1970).
10 Lichfield, N., Evaluation methodology of urban and regional plans: A review, *Regional Studies,* **4,** 2 (1970).
11 See: Scottish Development Department, *The Central Borders: A Plan for Expansion,* **1,** HMSO (1968).
   Scottish Development Department, *Grangemouth/Falkirk Survey and Plan,* **2,** HMSO (1968).
12 See: Pearce, D. W., *Cost-Benefit Analysis,* Macmillan Studies in Economics (1971).
13 Lichfield, *op cit.*
14 Hill, M., A goals-achievement matrix in evaluating alternative plans, *Journal of the American Institute of Planners,* **34,** 2 (1968).
15 Smith, P. M., What Kind of Regional Planning?, *Urban Studies,* **3,** 3 (1966).
16 The Jack Holmes Planning Group, for the Highlands and Islands Development Board, *Moray Firth: A Plan for Growth* (1968).
17 See *Guardian,* 13 December 1972.

18 Scottish Development Department, *The Central Borders: A Plan for Expansion, op cit.*

19 Welsh Office, *A New Town in Mid-Wales* (Economic Associates), HMSO (1966).

20 Government of Northern Ireland, *Development Programme (1970–75)* 1970.

21 *Central Scotland: A Programme for Development and Growth,* Cmnd. 2188, HMSO, Edinburgh (1963).

22 Hamilton, D., The Scottish Miracle, *New Scientist,* 42 (1969).

23 *The North-East: A Programme for Development and Growth,* Cmnd. 2206, HMSO, London (1963).

24 Northern Economic Planning Council, *Outline Strategy for the North* (1968).

25 Yorkshire and Humberside Economic Planning Council, *Yorkshire and Humberside: Regional Strategy,* HMSO (1970).

26 See Appendix C for references.

27 Abercrombie, P., *op cit.*

28 Heywood, P., Letting the South-East Rip, *Town and Country Planning,* September (1970).

29 For a comprehensive picture of the North West, see: Smith, D. M., *Industrial Britain: The North West,* David and Charles (1969).

30 See Appendix C for references.

11 UK regional planning—an administrative problem

Throughout their history the two forms of UK regional planning have tended to follow separate paths. There has been very little attention paid to the impact on intra-regional planning of inter-regional planning and vice versa. Growth point programmes in prosperous regions may limit the effectiveness of programmes to attract mobile industry to the assisted areas; conversely their viability may be threatened by high development area inducements attracting industry to the assisted areas.

This situation reflects, in large measure, the administrative gap between central and local government. Central government sees regional planning primarily as the correction of economic imbalance between one region and another. There is little consideration of the location of investment within regions, which is of course of crucial importance. Local government on the other hand interprets regional planning in terms of comprehensive long-term strategies for economic and physical development within regions. Co-ordination between the two approaches is essential. But the gap will not be bridged until there is effective machinery at the intermediate level for distributing resources within regions on the basis of a comprehensive strategy.

Interesting trends towards bridging this gap can be observed in the emergence of two new intermediate levels of administration. The inadequacy of the existing local government structure to deal with supra-urban problems has recently led to a range of proposals for the scale enlargement of local government. These

258

proposals, such as those contained in the Report of the Redcliffe-Maud Commission,[1] involve the replacement of the myriad of local authorities by more simple systems based on between 40 to 60 major authorities. At the same time attempts to improve the efficiency of economic planning have led to some limited devolution of central administration to the Regional Economic Planning Councils, established in 1965–6. But many regard the latter as unsatisfactory and of limited effectiveness, and there has also been a wide range of proposals to reform this larger scale of regional machinery on the basis of between 10 to 15 major authorities with more wide-ranging functions and powers. Both of these trends will now be examined in more detail.

1 The reorganisation of local government

The recognition of the need to plan on a supra-urban scale has been paralleled over the last few years by a series of proposals for local government reform. The hotch-potch of 79 county boroughs, 45 counties, 227 non-county boroughs, 449 urban districts and 410 rural districts in England, and similar systems in Northern Ireland, Scotland and Wales, raised a host of problems. Many of the authorities were too small to carry out efficiently the services required of them, and the overall pattern of authorities no longer corresponded to the contemporary pattern of work and life. Increasing personal mobility has led to an increasing interdependence between town and country. More and more people now live in the countryside but go into the towns for work, shopping, education and entertainment. Similarly, people in towns go out into the countryside for recreation, and towns and cities with overspill problems look to the surrounding areas to provide a solution.

That such problems existed had been realised for some time, but it was not until the mid 1960's that the government decided to investigate the possible form of a completely new administrative structure. Prior to this, there had been Local Government Commissions charged with the duty of reviewing the structure of local government and of making changes considered desirable in the interests of effective and convenient government, but they were only tampering on the fringes of the problem. In 1966, the Royal

Commission on Local Government in England was set up under the chairmanship of Lord Redcliffe-Maud:

'to consider the structure of Local Government in England, outside Greater London, in relation to its existing function; and to make recommendations for authorities and boundaries, and for functions and their division, having regard to the size and character of areas in which these can be most effectively exercised and the need to sustain a viable system of local democracy; and to report'.[2]

A similar commission under the chairmanship of Lord Wheatley was established to consider the situation in Scotland.

THE MAUD REPORT (1969)

The Redcliffe-Maud Commission produced its report in 1969. During its deliberations it received evidence on a variety of alternative solutions. One solution, strongly supported by the government departments, was to establish a primarily single-tier system of between 25 to 45 city regions which would perform all or nearly all the services of local government. A second solution, advocated by the County Councils Association, predictably proposed 40 or 50 modified counties, with a lower tier of enlarged urban or rural district councils. This two-tier system was very similar to the present division between the counties and county districts. In contrast, a third solution supported by the Association of Municipal Corporations, proposed a two-tier system with a greater number of city regions, between 60 and 140, and a limited number of regional or provincial bodies.

To choose between the alternatives the Commission formulated and applied certain general principles. Amongst others, these principles stressed that areas must be based upon the interdependence of town and country, all services concerned with the physical environment (planning, transportation and major development) must be in the hands of one authority, and all personal services must also be in the hands of one authority. In the interests of efficiency, the minimum population of the areas should be around 250 000; but in the interests of democracy it should not be much more than 1 000 000. The new local government pattern should also stem as far as possible from the existing one.

From the application of these principles a three-tier solution emerged, but with the emphasis strongly on the intermediate 'unitary' tier, (Figure 11.1). This involved the creation of 61 new local government areas—somewhat similar to the third alternative above—each covering town and country. Fifty-eight of these were unitary areas with one authority responsible for all services; and three (Greater Merseyside, Greater Manchester and the Birmingham conurbation) were metropolitan areas, with services divided between three metropolitan authorities and 20 metropolitan district councils. The metropolitan authority was to be responsible for planning, transportation and also the major development functions. Above the intermediate tier were a limited number of provincial councils, and below them a series of local councils.

The Maud proposals brought about the unification of town and country and had much to commend them, allowing the planning and transportation problems of the urban regions to be tackled as a whole. They also did much for the big cities extending their boundaries far beyond the built-up areas and the constricting green belts. But they were not acceptable to everyone, least of all to one of the Commissioners, Derek Senior.

SENIOR'S ALTERNATIVE PROPOSALS

Senior first set out his ideas for local government reform in 1965.[3] He believed that the right approach to reform was to analyse functional and democratic needs in relation to the patterns of settlement, activity and community structure in which a motor age society organises itself. It is argued that people look for services to the nearest large urban centre, and thus the best unit for providing services, planning them and rallying local involvement is a city region. Senior saw this city region as 'a marriage between the built up core and its socially and economically dependent areas'.

Four types of city region were distinguished by Senior in 1965, dividing the whole of Britain into 42 areas:

a The mature city regions were well defined areas already looking

towards a major city of regional importance, with total populations of at least two million people. These were London, Birmingham, Liverpool, Manchester, Leeds, Newcastle and Glasgow.
b The emergent city regions had hinterlands of over one million people, but their centres were not as well defined and developed

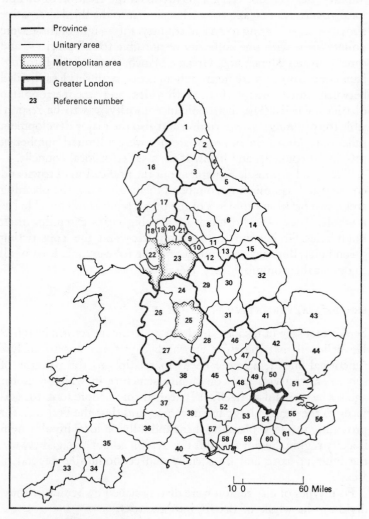

Fig. 11.1   Proposals of the Redcliffe-Maud Commission (1969)

as in the previous category. This type included Cardiff, Bristol, Southampton, Nottingham, Sheffield, Preston and Edinburgh.

c The embryonic city regions were based on cities not yet of regional importance but of considerable local influence, with hinterlands of 300 000 to 800 000 people, such as Exeter, Brighton, Coventry, Middlesbrough and Aberdeen.

North East province
1. Northumberland
2. Tyneside
3. Durham
4. Sunderland and East Durham
5. Teesside

Yorkshire province
6. York
7. Bradford
8. Leeds
9. Halifax
10. Huddersfield
11. Mid-Yorkshire
12. Sheffield and South Yorkshire
13. Doncaster
14. North Humberside
15. South Humberside

North West province
16. Cumberland and North Westmorland
17. Furness and North Lancashire
18. The Fylde
19. Preston-Leyland-Chorley
20. Blackburn
21. Burnley
22. Merseyside metropolitan area
23. SELNEC metropolitan area

West Midlands province
24. Stoke and North Staffordshire
25. West Midlands metropolitan area
26. Shropshire
27. Herefordshire and South Worcestershire
28. Coventry and Warwickshire

East midlands province
29. Derby and Derbyshire
30. Nottingham and Nottinghamshire
31. Leicester and Leicestershire
32. Lincoln and Lincolnshire

South West province
33. Cornwall
34. Plymouth
35. Exeter and Devon
36. Somerset
37. Bristol and Bath
38. North Gloucestershire
39. Wiltshire
40. Bournemouth and Dorset

East Anglia province
41. Peterborough-North Fens
42. Cambridge-South Fens
43. Norwich and Norfolk
44. Ipswich, Suffolk and North-East Essex

South East province
45. Oxford and Oxfordshire
46. Northampton and Northamptonshire
47. Bedford and North Buckinghamshire
48. Mid-Buckinghamshire
49. Luton and West Hertfordshire
50. East Hertfordshire
51. Essex
52. Reading and Berkshire
53. West Surrey
54. East Surrey
55. West Kent
56. Canterbury and East Kent
57. Southampton and South Hampshire
58. Portsmouth, South East Hampshire and Isle of Wight
59. West Sussex
60. Brighton and Mid-Sussex
61. East Sussex

d The potential city regions referred primarily to large rural areas with at present only limited links with central towns and cities, such as Plymouth, Peterborough, York and Carlisle. In some of these potential areas the population was as low as 250 000.

It was accepted that the latter two groups did not form regions readily, but it was thought that they could if given the opportunity.

When the Maud Commission came out in favour of the unitary authority in preference to the city region solution, Senior restated his views in a voluminous Memorandum of Dissent[4] accompanying the majority report. He believed that the Maud proposals suffered from a theoretical approach to the problem of local government re-organisation, with boundaries determined more by the population requirements for administrative efficiency and democratic control rather than by the facts of social geography. His proposals for a system of 35 English city regions (Figure 11.2) deviated little from his earlier views, with the exception of the creation of several new areas on the periphery of Greater London. The city regions would have directly elected regional authorities responsible for functions such as planning, transportation, development and capital investment programmes. Beneath them there would be 148 directly elected district authorities responsible for the more personal services.

The city region solution has undoubted attractions. It would end the division between town and country, create authorities large enough to handle the functions of local government, and receive the support of government departments. But it also has fundamental problems the most obvious being that not all of the country fits neatly into a city region pattern. In many of the rural areas of the South West, the Wash Fens of East Anglia, the remoter Pennines and the Lake District, there is not the same emphasis on city life and there may be no one acceptable centre. In areas such as these Senior's proposals appear contrived, ironically lacking the basic clarity of the majority proposals they sought to replace.

THE NEW FRAMEWORK

Overall, the Maud proposals were widely welcomed. They redrew local government boundaries in a way that was particularly

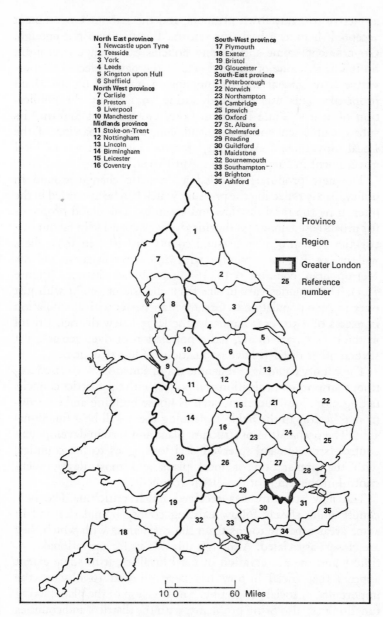

North East province
1 Newcastle upon Tyne
2 Teesside
3 York
4 Leeds
5 Kingston upon Hull
6 Sheffield
North West province
7 Carlisle
8 Preston
9 Liverpool
10 Manchester
Midlands province
11 Stoke-on-Trent
12 Nottingham
13 Lincoln
14 Birmingham
15 Leicester
16 Coventry

South-West province
17 Plymouth
18 Exeter
19 Bristol
20 Gloucester
South-East province
21 Peterborough
22 Norwich
23 Northampton
24 Cambridge
25 Ipswich
26 Oxford
27 St. Albans
28 Chelmsford
29 Reading
30 Guildford
31 Maidstone
32 Bournemouth
33 Southampton
34 Brighton
35 Ashford

Province
Region
Greater London
25 Reference number

10 0   60 Miles

Fig. 11.2   Senior's alternative proposals (1969)

265

attractive to many town planners, and the Labour Government accepted them as a basis for reform. But that was not enough. Governments come and go and policies can change overnight. So it was that one of the first acts of the newly elected Conservative Government was to announce a standstill on the Maud proposals. This was followed during 1971-72 by the publication of a new White Paper on Local Government Reform,[5] its subsequent discussion and amendment, and the passing of the Local Government Act (1972)[6] for the administration of local government in England from 1 April 1974.

The new proposals revealed a dramatic change around in policy, partly reflecting the pressure which had been exerted in the interim by the rural districts and counties. The Maud proposals for urban-based unitary authorities were swept aside in favour of a two-tier system of counties and county districts. In 1974, there will be 39 English counties with 296 new districts, and six Metropolitan counties with 36 metropolitan districts (Figure 11.3). The counties vary in size from the Isle of Wight with just over 100 000 population to Greater Manchester with a population in excess of 2 500 000. Similarly, the largest new district, Bristol in the new Avon county, has a population of over 400 000, yet several other districts have populations of less than 40 000.

The county councils will handle major functions such as education, transport co-ordination and police, with the district councils taking more local functions such as house building and environmental health. In the field of planning there will be a functional split. The preparation of structure plans and certain development control (strategic and reserved decisions) goes to the counties, with the preparation of local plans and most development control in the hands of the district councils.

The new structure has received much criticism. The new county units closely follow existing county boundaries and in some areas separate towns from the rural areas with which they are closely associated. Although this allows for operational continuity and the preservation of local loyalties, it to some extent appears that social history has been allowed to obscure the importance of social geography. The division of the plan-making function may also bring problems, with the districts and counties having to agree on a 'development plan scheme' ('who does

266

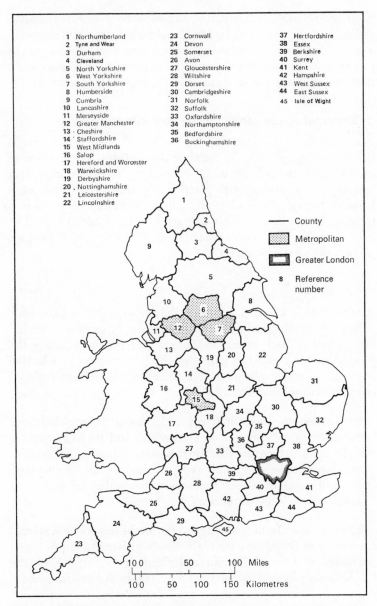

1 Northumberland	23 Cornwall	37 Hertfordshire
2 Tyne and Wear	24 Devon	38 Essex
3 Durham	25 Somerset	39 Berkshire
4 Cleveland	26 Avon	40 Surrey
5 North Yorkshire	27 Gloucestershire	41 Kent
6 West Yorkshire	28 Wiltshire	42 Hampshire
7 South Yorkshire	29 Dorset	43 West Sussex
8 Humberside	30 Cambridgeshire	44 East Sussex
9 Cumbria	31 Norfolk	45 Isle of Wight
10 Lancashire	32 Suffolk	
11 Merseyside	33 Oxfordshire	
12 Greater Manchester	34 Northamptonshire	
13 Cheshire	35 Bedfordshire	
14 Staffordshire	36 Buckinghamshire	
15 West Midlands		
16 Salop		
17 Hereford and Worcester		
18 Warwickshire		
19 Derbyshire		
20 Nottinghamshire		
21 Leicestershire		
22 Lincolnshire		

—— County

Metropolitan

Greater London

8 Reference number

Fig. 11.3 Boundaries in the Local Government Act (1972)—to be implemented in April 1974

what and when?'). Nevertheless, although the proposals are not as radical as those proposed by Maud and Senior, they still represent a real step forward allowing large supra-urban areas to be considered as a whole for purposes of planning and transportation. But such areas still require a larger regional framework.

2 Regional economic planning councils and boards

The UK Regional Planning Councils and Boards were established during 1965–66. At the time this attempt to introduce an intermediate tier of planning seemed to mark an important turning point in regional planning heralding the start of a brighter future. The bodies are still in existence today and it is interesting to examine their operation in the interim period to assess whether in retrospect the early euphoria was either justified or perhaps a little premature.

THEIR RÔLE

After the 1964 General Election, the Department of Economic Affairs was established with the general aim of putting 'muscles' into planning, and more specific responsibilities including the production of a national plan and the introduction of effective regional economic planning. The Government defined regional economic planning as having:

'two main purposes: first to provide for a full and balanced development of the country's economic and social resources; and secondly to ensure that the regional implications of growth are clearly understood and taken into account in the planning of land use, of development—in particular of industrial development—and of services'.[7]

The regional planning rôle led to the establishment of Regional Councils and Boards for the eight English planning regions, and Scotland, Wales and Northern Ireland. The purpose of the Councils was defined by the First Secretary in 1964 as follows:

'The economic planning councils will be concerned with broad strategy on regional development and the best use of the

268

region's resources. Their principal functions will be to assist in the formulation of regional plans and to advise on their implementation. They will have no executive powers.'[8]

In addition the Councils were subsequently required 'to advise on the regional implications of national economic policies'. Their membership consists of about 25 unpaid members, with a paid Chairman. The members are all chosen by the responsible Minister and are not electorally responsible. They are chosen to represent a wide range of experience in the region, and include people with experience in local government, industry and social service, together with members drawn from universities in the region. The Chairmen include prominent citizens from various walks of life—industrialists, trade unionists, academics and local politicians. The Councils meet at roughly monthly intervals and most have found it necessary to appoint sub-committees to tackle particular aspects of regional planning in their areas.

The Regional Boards were seen as providing the technical backup to the Council's work and the:

> 'machinery for co-ordinating the work of Government Departments concerned with regional planning and development ... their creation will not affect the existing powers and responsibilities of local authorities or existing Ministerial responsibilities'.[9]

They consist of civil servants from the regional offices of departments concerned with aspects of regional planning and development. In England, the Chairman was an official of the DEA.

In practice, the Councils have sometimes been consulted by central government on national policy affecting the affairs of their regions—such as the regional implications of railway closures and the effects of the reorganisation of the coal industry. But their advice has often had little impact and at times, where decisions have been dictated by national considerations, they have been bypassed completely. Within the regions the Councils have mounted limited 'ginger campaigns' such as 'Operation Springclean' in the North West, but above all their main work has been in the preparation of regional plan documents. In the period

269

since 1965, a range of documents has been prepared for most of the regions. (Appendix C). Yet as noted in Chapter 10, many of these documents have come under much criticism, particularly for their descriptive, stocktaking approach outlining the region's structure and amenities, forecasting population and employment changes and spelling out problems rather than identifying solutions. In their reports, the Councils have also tended to adopt an introverted approach ignoring other regions and the aims of inter-regional planning in selfish bids on the nation's resources.

AN ASSESSMENT

In their short life the Regional Councils and Boards have run into many problems and there have been some notable resignations of members. One initial difficulty has been the weakness of the national planning body—the DEA until 1969—and the lack of a national planning framework; but there have also been fundamental problems specific to the Councils and Boards.

Basic problems of the Councils stem from their lack of executive powers and elective responsibility. Only if their advice commands general support in the region and is based on rigorous analysis can they exert any substantial influence on the major policy decisions. Yet their structure is not conducive to such an approach. They were set up on an amateur basis in the hope that they would function in the form of corporate consultants with their collective wisdom having more standing than the recommendations of individual advisers. But the Council members are busy men in other walks of life and, with limited support facilities, it was certainly unfair to expect much progress at an early stage.

The Regional Boards have given rise to less criticism although here also there are some fundamental problems. One problem is how to get members of government departments to switch from a vertical ministry view to a horizontal regional view when 'their objective is not to win praise for putting the region's case possibly against the views of their masters in Whitehall but to please these masters so that they can return from exile in the provinces'.[10] The Boards have also suffered from staff shortages, limited regional statistical data and knowledge of up-to-date regional planning techniques; although it should be added that substantial progress has been made in these areas over the last few years.

Partly as a result of these problems, the relationships between the Councils and Boards and central government on the one hand, and local government on the other have always been problematic. If a Regional Council objects to a particular aspect of national policy it can raise the matter with the responsible ministry in Whitehall, but it carries very little weight to press its case for it represents no one and has little public support to fall back upon. Indeed the only communication with the regional public tends to be via the statements of the Chairman, and through the publication of regional studies. Similarly, the recommendations of the Council are not binding on the constituent local authorities of the region. The local planning authorities may exercise their statutory power to suit their own ends merely paying lip-service to the ideas of regional consultation. Alternatively they may organise their own regional consultation through the establishment of Standing Conferences of Local Planning Authorities.

Associated with this lack of power of the existing machinery is the lack of a political focus. This contrasts with Scotland, Wales and Northern Ireland, where there is a Secretary of State specifically concerned with the problems of the region. The introduction of some form of political focus might help to lift the Councils and Boards out of their present limbo.

Many of these difficulties facing the Councils and Boards are reflected in the regional studies produced, which probably provide evidence more of regional thinking than of regional planning. But it would be wrong to think that this new machinery has not achieved anything. It has at least established bodies for clarifying and analysing the problems of a region and for assessing the implications of various policies. Nothing like this existed before and it surely represents an advance, even if it is on the typically amateur basis beloved of the British. It also marks the formal acceptance by government of the concept of government action on a regional basis in Britain. The fact that there are certain fundamental problems and that questions are being asked about the effectiveness of the existing machinery however, suggests that it would be premature to regard the present form of regional machinery as the final solution.

3 Reform at the regional/provincial scale

If the existing regional machinery is not to become yet another 'false dawn' in the long history of British regionalism, there must surely be some changes. In the true spirit of the regionalist movement, there has been no shortage of alternative suggestions, ranging from the retention of the existing Councils and Boards with only minor modifications to the introduction of a fully fledged system of regional government, with multi-purpose regional authorities backed by representative assemblies directly elected, with full executive powers. The alternatives, including those raised in the Redcliffe-Maud Report, those raised by Senior, the Liberal Party and others, can be usefully examined with regard to their attitude to the functions, boundaries and power of the proposed regional institutions. Many of the alternatives refer to this large scale of regional organisation as 'provincial'. The relative merits of terms will not be discussed here and throughout this section *province* and *provincial* will be used interchangeably for *region* and *regional*.

FUNCTIONS

The various alternatives suggest a wide range of functions for the new regional tier, including some derived from existing regional bodies—such as regional economic planning councils and standing conferences; others taken from central government or its agencies; and some which local authorities have been increasingly unable to cope with (the extent of the latter are obviously influenced by the state of local government and local government reform).

The Redcliffe-Maud Commission on Local Government in England included proposals for provincial councils,[11] and believed that their main function should be in the making and continual updating of the provincial framework of land use and economic strategy within which planning authorities must operate. Key elements in this framework would include the changing distribution of population, inter- and intra-regional migration, the location of major new growth points, the broad division of the province into urbanised, agricultural and recreational areas, major industrial developments, the provincial pattern of road and rail communications, the siting of airports, the future of seaports and the siting of cultural and recreational facilities. The provincial councils would have limited development functions, with such power remaining in the hands of the local authorities and central government. But reserve powers would be available to allow the council to act if such action was necessary to ensure the success of the provincial plan, and for the development of projects of benefit to the region as a whole (the development of a barrage could be one example of the latter). The provincial councils would also assess provincial priorities in certain specialist areas such as further education, child care, cultural and recreational services and tourism. In addition, they would ensure that central government was fully aware of provincial needs and aspirations, and would consider the impact on the province of national decisions and policies. The Association of Municipal Corporations included a similar range of functions in their proposals, mentioning that provincial councils would also provide something which is at present lacking, namely a regional machinery for co-ordinating sub-regional studies.[12]

The Redcliffe-Maud proposals represented a limited advance in the functional responsibilities of the intermediate tier. Yet to some even this was excessive. Senior, in his Memorandum of Dissent[13] on the Maud proposals believed that the important functions of a provincial body should be to advise the government on the implications of government policies on the well-being of the province; to assist in the preparation of national plans; to monitor the progress of the regional economy; to help local authorities interpret the significance of a provincial strategy; and to provide a forum for confrontation on regional priorities. These functions are mainly advisory in nature, and although Senior did accept the need for a strategic provincial plan to comprehend and resolve the interlocking spatial, social and economic problems that arise at the provincial scale, its contents would be necessarily flexible and it would not carry any formal statutory approval.

273

In contrast, there have been many suggestions for a much wider range of provincial functions than those suggested by Maud. Mackintosh[14] proposed a series of regional councils with wide-ranging functions such as regional planning (with the planning of major communications), highways (construction and maintenance), housing (large-scale redevelopment, overspill, new towns), countryside amenities, police, fire services, water supplies, higher education, regional transport and many others. A Liberal Party Report[15] similarly suggested a wide range of functions for the regional body including, amongst many others, the co-ordination of all forms of transport and the control of certain public utilities and services such as gas and electricity area distribution boards and regional hospital boards.

BOUNDARIES

The existing Economic Planning Regions correspond closely to the earlier Standard Regions and, in shape and number, appear to have been delineated by the consideration of primarily administrative factors. The regional capitals each required about 80,000 square feet of office space which was available in centres which had been regional headquarters in the past. They also required specialist staff, and with a greater number of regions, the limited number of staff available would have been thinly spread. In addition, there was a reluctance to cross the boundaries of local planning authorities which might result in some local planning authorities being divided between two Economic Planning Regions.

Administrative viability is undoubtedly a major factor in the delineation of regions, and the administration of the variety of functions outlined in the previous section has been a major consideration in suggestions of alternative regional boundaries. But Chapter 2 illustrates that regions also have formal and functional characteristics which must also be considered. Regional boundaries should be chosen so as to interfere as little as possible with the economic unity of an area. They should also pay due regard to physical boundaries, and should preferably reflect the range of social, economic, political and informational relationships between the hierarchy of centres within the region, paying due regard to any sense of regional identity.

Discounting the extremes such as Senior's proposals for only five major English provinces (Figure 11.2), or the division of the country into only two provinces—prosperous Metropolitan England and depressed Industrial England, most of the alternative proposals include between 10–15 major regions. The variations between them are explained mainly by alternative proposals for the difficult areas in the South West, the South East and the 'area in between', and there is much agreement on many of the remaining regional boundaries.

The Maud Commission[16] believed that the existing Economic Planning Regions provided an appropriate model for the provinces, arguing that not only do they provide areas of suitable size for the administration of the provincial functions but also reflect some sense of provincial identity. The Commission also believed that the economic and geographical composition of the country fell broadly into the pattern of the existing planning regions, and that there was advantage in building on areas already familiar to people. Therefore, their proposed provinces only depart from the existing boundaries where it was thought there would be clear advantage in so doing (Figure 11.1). The most notable changes are the reduction in size of the Northern Economic Planning region with Cumberland and Westmorland joining the North Western province and most of the North Riding joining the Yorkshire province. The East Midlands Economic Planning region gains parts of Lindsey but loses Northamptonshire to the South Eastern province and small areas to East Anglia.

Other proposals were rather more radical, particularly in their approach to the South West and South East. The Economist Mark I Plan,[17] put forward as early as 1963, proposed the division of Britain into 16 large regions, with Scotland and Wales subdivided, the reduction in size of the South East and South West and the creation of two new South Central regions—Hampton based on Southampton and Cotswold based on Bristol (Figure 11.4a). The Liberal Party Report[18] proposed the subdivision of England into twelve provinces. Here the dominance of the South East was reduced by its subdivision into Anglia, Greater London, Weald and Thames Valley, and the South West was subdivided into West Country, Severnside and Solent. The

275

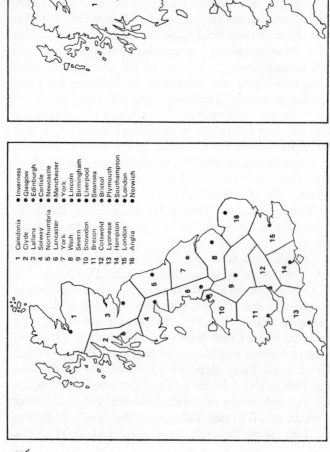

1 Caledonia	● Inverness
2 Clyde	● Glasgow
3 Edinburgh	● Edinburgh
4 Solway	● Carlisle
5 Northumbria	● Newcastle
6 Lancaster	● Manchester
7 York	● York
8 Wash	● Lincoln
9 Severn	● Birmingham
10 Snowdon	● Liverpool
11 Brecon	● Swansea
12 Cotswold	● Bristol
13 Lyonesse	● Plymouth
14 Hampton	● Southampton
15 London	● London
16 Anglia	● Norwich

1 Scotland
2 Northern
3 North West
4 Yorkshire & Humberside
5 Wales
6 West Midlands
7 East Midlands
8 Anglia
9 South West
10 South Central
11 South East

Fig. 11.4 a The Economist Mark I Plan for sixteen British regions   b Mackintosh's proposals for eleven British regions

SOURCE *The Economist*, 18 May 1963
J. P. Mackintosh, *The Devolution of Power*, page 192. Penguin (1968).

Association of Municipal Corporations[19] similarly recommended that the South West and the South East provinces recommended by the Redcliffe-Maud Commission should be recast to make four or five provinces. One final and interesting proposal was made by Mackintosh.[20] He contracted the South West and South East regions to leave a residual South Central region (Figure 11.4b). The latter, with Bristol, Oxford and South–ampton Portsmouth within its area, has little functional unity but may offer the most satisfactory solution to this thorny problem.

FORM AND POWER

The range of proposals for regional functions and boundaries has been accompanied by a variety of suggestions for the form and power of the regional machinery. One approach favoured by Senior is to maintain the existing non-executive/non-elected 'advisory' form of body. Such a body has the advantage of having no electoral inhibitions in preparing and presenting strategies for the region, being able to take a regional view and to consider what is best for the region rather than what is politically accept-able. But the experience of the Regional Economic Planning Councils suggests that much of their impotence stems from this advisory rôle. Without executive power and/or elective res-ponsibility, they exert only limited influence on local and central government. Senior[21] seeks to counter this argument by attribut-ing their ineffectiveness more to the failure of central government to complement the regional machinery with machinery for the exercise of its own executive powers, and hypothesises on the possibility of a Minister of Regional Development with Ministers of State and support staff in each of his five provinces.

The recent association of the 'advisory' councils with local planning authority standing conferences and central government in the form of tripartite bodies to initiate regional strategies is an interesting development in the existing situation, which has prompted some government support. But a joint arrangement tends to be problematical and the South East Joint Planning Team frankly states the present limitations and difficulties. The matter was put rather succinctly by Aneurin Bevan when he said that a joint board 'has no biological content, it has no mother and it has no progeny, it is a piece of paperwork'.[22]

One approach to increasing the power of the regional machinery is through the creation of regional development bodies with executive powers. Over the years there have been several proposals for regional development commissions, regional planning commissions and regional development corporations. One of the most notable was presented in the report of the Steering Group to the *Traffic in Towns* study.[23] The group, under the chairmanship of Sir Geoffrey Crowther, recommended the setting up of a number of Regional Development Agencies for each of the recognisable 'urban regions' in Britain. Such bodies, similar to huge new town development corporations, would 'oversee the whole programme of modernisation in their regions', and 'should be given far-reaching legal powers'. In addition to co-ordinating and encouraging the work of local and national authorities at the regional level, they would have powers to act in their own right, reviewing plans, controlling grants and acting 'like a gigantic property development company'.

The Highlands and Islands Development Board provides an isolated example of this type of executive body in the UK. The board is a statutory body responsible to the Secretary of State for Scotland. It was set up in 1965 with the task of assisting the people of the seven counties of North West Scotland to improve their economic and social conditions, and to enable them to play a more effective part in the economic and social development of the nation. For these purposes it has been given finance and a wide range of powers. Although the financial resources are not excessive, it does have the power to borrow money, acquire land and business by compulsory purchase, to enter into partnership with commercial and industrial concerns and to broaden the capital structure of a company. The Board has had notable economic successes, but as with all the suggested forms of regional development bodies, there is no electoral responsibility. Members of development bodies are nominated by central government— by the Secretary of State for Scotland in the case of the Highlands and Islands Board—and although their freedom of action may benefit from the resultant lack of democratic control it may also suffer by not having the strength of democratic authority.

278

The alternative is to have a democratically elected regional council, and this idea has been popular throughout the history of UK regionalism. Proponents of the idea claim that it would reintroduce the democratic principle into many spheres which were too complex for local authority control and have now been either centralised under central government control or taken over by regional *ad hoc* bodies. It has also been suggested that it would attract greater public interest and participation than local government has ever done. But the approach is not without its problems. How will the councils be financed; can an electoral system be devised to avoid the domination of the councils by the more powerful local authorities; and is there indeed popular interest at the regional scale?

The Redcliffe-Maud Commission[24] opted for a limited form of provincial council to replace the existing regional economic planning councils. It proposed that council members should be indirectly elected from the constituent authority councils in the province (unitary and metropolitan authority councils). To prevent the swamping of the councils by members from the larger authorities, it was proposed that each authority should have two council members for the first 250 000 of its total population and one further member for each additional 250 000 or part of 250 000. On this basis, omitting the South East province, the number of provincial council members would range from 14 in East Anglia to 41 in the North West. In the South East, the same principles would apply except that there would be a limit of 20 on the Greater London members. The councils would also co-opt between 20% to 25% of their total membership from outside local government thereby complementing the democratic element with particular experience and expertise of relevance to the region. In pursuing their functions, the councils would not be heavy spenders and would cover their mainly administrative costs by precepting on the main authorities.

In contrast, Mackintosh[25] suggested a more radical change with English regional councils and Scottish and Welsh assemblies directly elected for a fixed period of three years. The councils and assemblies would have between 100 to 150 members with an executive consisting of a prime minister and cabinet. The members would continue with their normal occupations, but the executive would have to be full time and be paid a full salary. To carry out the wide range of functions proposed by Mackintosh, the councils would each receive a share of national taxation calculated on a per capita basis but with deficiency allowances for special problems. The Liberal Party Report[26] referred to earlier similarly suggested this 'federal' form of approach, with twelve provincial assemblies of 60 to 120 full-time elected members. Such a high degree of regional autonomy represents the most fundamental alternative to the present system of regional machinery.

TECHNICAL SUPPORT

An improvement in the existing machinery demands not only an alternative political organisation but also an alternative technical organisation. This might, for example, be in the form of the Office of the Regional Plan or the Regional Technical Unit. The staff of such bodies should be recruited directly by the provincial authority. This would not only help to foster a primary loyalty to the province, but would also mean that careers would depend on the performance of the staff in the authority's service. The functions of the organisation obviously depend on the range of functions and powers of the provincial authority, but would probably include the preparation and maintenance of the regional plan, continuously monitoring change and the effects of policy.

The range of functions will also determine the number of technical staff. The Redcliffe-Maud Commission[27] believed that the work at the provincial level would not call for large staffs, and suggested that, where appropriate, use should be made of the services of consultants, short-term contracts and the placing of work with universities. This may be somewhat optimistic, for planning at the regional scale is complex and if it is to be efficiently carried out may demand a large team with a wide range of techniques of analysis and data processing at their disposal.

4 Regional reform and national administration

The shape of the future UK regional machinery is at present being considered by the Commission on the Constitution set up in 1969—

'to examine the present functions of the central legislature and government in relation to the several countries, nations and regions of the United Kingdom.

To consider, having regard to developments in local government organisation and in the administrative and other relationships between the various parts of the United Kingdom and to the interests of the prosperity and good government of our people under the Crown, whether any changes are desirable in those functions or otherwise in present constitutional and economic relationships.'[28]

The Commission has yet to report. It may recommend a greater degree of regional autonomy, especially in the 'Celtic fringe' regions, but a full federal system seems highly unlikely. Therefore whatever the functions, boundaries power and technical support proposed at the intermediate level, the final responsibility for planning will still remain in the hands of the central government. As such it is essential that there is more co-ordination between central government departments concerned with aspects of regional planning and development.

The dichotomy in UK regional planning has been mirrored and perpetuated by a split in central administration, with for many years the Board of Trade handling the economic inter-regional aspects and the Ministries of Housing and Local Government and Transport concentrating on the more physical intra-regional aspects. It was hoped that the creation of the Department of Economic Affairs, in the mid-1960's, with the Ministry of Housing and Local Government working within its general directives, might bridge the gap, but its powers of execution were limited and with its demise, the split continues.

Today, regional functions are split between the two new 'super' Ministries, the Department of the Environment (DOE) and the Department of Trade and Industry (DTI), created in a major rationalisation of the machinery of government in 1970. The DOE, which includes the former Ministries of Housing and Local Government, Public Building and Works, and Transport, has the overall aim of improving the physical environment and has most of the powers necessary for the implementation of regional policies. However, it is the DTI, created by putting together the

Board of Trade, most of the Ministry of Technology, and some functions from the Department of Employment and Productivity, that exercises the collective responsibility over industrial development—the key to regional prosperity. Co-ordination between these two super Ministries at the centre is essential if regional planning is to be more effective. Whether this will be in the form of increased inter-departmental consultation, or perhaps via the creation of a new Ministry of Regional Development remains to be seen.

5 Summary

Government and administration in the United Kingdom, polarised as it is at the central and local levels, is not conducive to planning at an intermediate level. Therefore if regional planning is to be planning in any effective sense, rather than just regional thinking, there must be a more effective regional machinery. Over the last few years, there have been some interesting trends in this direction. At the lower end of the scale there has been a series of suggestions for the scale enlargement of local government, evolving through the Maud and Senior proposals and culminating in reform on the basis of 45 counties. At a higher level, there has been the creation of the Regional Economic Planning Councils and Boards, which, although they have their problems, do at least represent a start—a base from which to develop a more effective system. The possible functions, boundaries, form and power, and indeed the very desirability of such a system, awaits the Report of the Commission on the Constitution. But it is arguable that if the regional machinery is to be a major force, it must be democractically elected with the powers, finances and technical support to carry out its functions effectively. Even then, more co-ordination at the national level will be an essential complement to effective regional planning.

References

1 *Report of the Royal Commission on Local Government in England 1966–69.* (Chairman: Lord Redcliffe-Maud), **I,** Report. Cmnd. 4040 (1969).

2 *Ibid.*
3 Senior, D., 'The City Region as an Administrative Unit,' *Political Quarterly*, **36,** January–March 1965.
4 *Report of the Royal Commission on Local Government in England 1966–69,* **II,** Memorandum of Dissent by Mr. D. Senior, Cmnd. 4040–1 (1969).
5 *Local Government in England—Government Proposals for Re-organization.* Cmnd. 4584 (1971).
6 *Local Government Act (1972),* HMSO (1972).
7 Statement in the House of Commons by the First Secretary of State for Economic Affairs, The Rt. Hon. George Brown, MP, 10 December 1964.
8 *Op cit.*
9 *Op cit.*
10 Mackintosh, J. P., *The Devolution of Power,* Penguin (1968).
11 *Royal Commission, Vol* **I,** *op cit,* Chapter X.
12 Association of Municipal Corporations, *Reorganisation of Local Government in England,* London, November 1970.
13 *Royal Commission, Vol* **II,** *op cit,* Chapter V.
14 Mackintosh, *op. cit.*
15 Liberal Party, *Power to the Provinces* (1967).
16 *Royal Commission, Vol* **I,** *op cit,* Chapter X.
17 Federal Britain's New Frontiers, *The Economist,* 18 May 1963.
18 Liberal Party, *op cit.*
19 Association of Municipal Corporations, *op. cit.*
20 Mackintosh, *op. cit.*
21 *Royal Commission, Vol* **II,** *op cit* Chapter V.
22 From Robson, W. A., *The Development of Local Government,* Allen and Unwin, 3rd edition (1954).
23 Ministry of Transport, *Traffic in Towns,* HMSO, London (1963).
24 *Royal Commission, Vol.* **I,** *op cit*
25 Mackintosh, *op. cit.*
26 Liberal Party, *op cit.*
27 *Royal Commission, Vol* **I,** *op cit.*
28 *Hansard,* Written Answers, Col 290, 11 February 1969.

Note: A publication by the International Union of Local Authorities, *Regional Planning and Regional Government in Europe,* E. Kalk (ed.), provides an interesting discussion of the relationship between regional planning and regional government in the wider European context.

Much can be learnt from regional planning experience elsewhere and interesting examples can be drawn from all over the world. Each example would merit a text in its own right rather than the few pages that are available here. Hence, if the study is not to be too superficial, it is only possible to take a very limited number— and even then this may be only scratching the surface of each one. Of particular relevance to regional planning in Britain is the experience of other neighbouring countries in Western Europe. Thus this chapter examines the practice of regional planning in France and the Netherlands, set in the wider context of the EEC. The chosen countries vary greatly. France has an area of over 200 000 square miles and a population of over 50 millions, com- pared with the smaller but more densely populated Nether- lands, which has an area of only 14 000 square miles and a population of approximately 13 millions. But both face major regional problems which have given rise to interesting and often contrasting experience in inter- and intra-regional planning.

1 Regional planning in France

Regional planning is a recent phenomenon in France. Prior to the Second World War there were neither regions nor plans, but since that period there have been many interesting developments. Some of these developments are similar to those that have been taking place in the UK and some have directly influenced British thinking. Others, such as the development of French regional planning within the framework of an established system of national planning, are fundamentally different. (Useful references on French regional planning include those by Allen and Maclennan,[1] Boudeville,[2], Hansen[3] and Hall[4] (on the problem of the Paris Region).)

REGIONAL PROBLEMS IN FRANCE

Paris et le Désert Français

As in the UK, regional planning in France is a response to two types of problems—the problems of socio-economic disparities between the regions of the country and the physical environmental problems of growing urban areas which can only be tackled effectively on a supra-urban scale.

The regional disparities in economic and social development are particularly acute in France and nowhere are they more marked than in the contrast between the Paris region and the rest of the nation. Paris dominates France and the life of the country is centralised around it. This centralisation has a long history stemming back to the days of Louis XIV and Napoleon. Today, Paris is not only the political and intellectual capital of the country but also the industrial and business capital, with one quarter of all industrial workers and over a half of the country's business turnover. This dominance is reinforced by the lack of other large metropolises, with the only other major urban agglomerations at Lyons and Marseilles. This is in marked contrast to the situation in other Western European countries such as the UK and West Germany where there are several major conurbations counterbalancing the attraction of the centre.

The disparity between the Paris region and the rest of the country is however not the only one. Another major cleavage can be identified between the east and west of the country. An imaginary line drawn from Le Havre in the north-west to Marseilles in the south-east roughly divides France into a 'prosperous' eastern industrial zone enlivened by the influence of Paris and a 'poor' western agricultural zone. The latter has over 50% of the area of the country but less than 40% of the population and less

285

than 30% of its labour employed in industry. It furnishes many clear examples of the underdeveloped problem region although there are exceptions to the general rule with pockets of growth and prosperity in centres such as Toulouse, Lacq and Rennes. In contrast the eastern zone, even excluding the Paris region, has about 43% of the area of the country, 44% of the population and almost 50% of its labour employed in industry and is relatively much more prosperous. Nevertheless here also there are exceptions to the rule, with areas of the Nord Coalfield and Alsace-Lorraine providing examples of depressed industrial regions.

The east–west disparity is a function of both structural and locational factors. In contrast to the industrially based economy of the eastern zone, industrial activity in the west is restricted to a small number of individual centres and there is a high degree of dependence on agriculture—a sector where increased mechanisation and land reform are leading to a progressive decline in employment opportunities. In addition, the physical structure of the area and its peripheral nature (especially within the context of the EEC) constitute additional locational problems, as do the conservative culture and political traditions prevalent in such areas.

This threefold division of France into the Paris region, the eastern zone and the western zone has been evident for many years. Yet there was, perhaps not surprisingly, some reluctance to interfere especially in the growth of Paris for fear of jeopardising French economic development which in such a highly centralised country was closely linked to the fortunes of the Paris region. However, the widening of the disparities plus the recognition of the need for the second aspect of regional planning to deal with the environmental problems of growing urban areas, especially Paris, on a large scale, finally began to have some effect. It was the publication of a book entitled *Paris et le Désert Français* by J. F. Gravier[5] in 1947 which probably lit the fuse. This book, which in its impact on public opinion was the French equivalent of the UK Barlow Report, focussed attention on the regional problems and particularly the effects of excessive centralisation and the growth of Paris.

Out of an appraisal of these problems emerged the objectives of French regional planning which can be briefly summarised as the reduction of regional disparities, with the control of the growth and excessive centralisation around Paris, the development of the under-developed west and south, and the regeneration of problem industrial areas. The achievement of such objectives however requires an efficient regional planning machinery.

The French administrative framework of the early post-war period was not at all well fitted to the task of regional planning. With 90 *départements* and 38 000 *communes* it was a relic from the Napoleonic era. But over the next 20 years, with the development of regional planning, this framework was to undergo major changes resulting in the development of a regional planning machinery of great administrative complexity. This development stemmed from two sources—the spontaneous efforts of private regional committees concerned with the future of their areas and the need for a regional tier in the French national planning machinery.

In 1955 local regional pressure was finally recognised by the government and local representatives were encouraged to set up 'regional expansion committees' in 21 embryonic regions. In 1959, after studying the boundary problem for four years, the government formally set up 21 planning regions (*régions de programme*). The regions contained between two and eight *départements* and populations of roughly two million inhabitants. The regional boundaries (see Figure 12.1) were very much a compromise delimited to correlate as closely as possible with the existing administrative boundaries of government agencies and taking little account of functional associations. Even so, central government was loath to adopt them until a decree of 1960 enforced 30 government agencies to do so. For each region a social and economic plan was to be drawn up by an interdepartmental conference of civil servants chaired by the co-ordinating prefect and in consultation with the regional expansion committees.

The regional administrative machinery continued along this path until 1964 when there were far-reaching reforms creating a completely new system. In each of the 20 regions outside Paris the administration is headed by a Regional Prefect responsible for co-ordinating development programmes within his region. The prefect, assisted by a technical team, the *Mission Économique Régionale* is responsible for the preparation of five-year regional programmes for economic development. He is supported by a *Conférence Administrative Régionale* (CAR) similar to the UK

Fig. 12.1   France: planning regions

Regional Economic Planning Boards, and a new consultative body the *Commission de Développement Économique Régionale* (CODER), similar to the UK Regional Economic Planning Councils. In addition, in six regions, there are also new sub-regional planning bodies known as *Organismes d'Études*

288

d'Aménagement d'Aires Métropolitaines (OREAM), created in 1966 to prepare plans for metropolises including two cities—Lille–Dunkerque, Nantes–St. Nazaire, Nancy–Metz, Lyons–St. Etienne and Marseilles–Aix. In the Paris region, a separate body—the *District de la Région de Paris*—was set up in 1961 to deal with planning problems. This body is distinct from the others in that it is headed by a full-time director. *Délégue-Général*, and has a budget of its own raised through Parliament by the levying of taxes on the Paris region. The District has a consultative regional assembly and being a financial power also has a board consisting of elected local council members and government appointees. The annual budget is not great but is useful for initiating schemes of regional importance.

To meet those developments at the regional level, the government introduced new co-ordinating bodies for regional planning at the national level.[6] Underneath the main body for national economic planning, the *Commissariat Général du Plan* (CGP), two further institutions were formed—the *Délegation à l'Aménagement du Territoire* (DATAR) and the *Commission Nationale d'Aménagement du Territoire* (CNAT). DATAR is a small body charged with co-ordinating regional plans in the short run and pushing them along. It can draw upon the resources of a regional development fund, amounting to 1·5% of the public investment budget to facilitate its tasks. CNAT is a much larger body concerned with the preparation of long-term perspectives (up to 20 years ahead) for urban and regional development. It produces long-term guidelines on matters such as population and employment trends and the distribution of jobs and people. In 1967 CNAT and CGP merged to form a single medium/long run planning institution, successfully integrating spatial and economic planning at the national scale.

INTER-REGIONAL PLANNING IN FRANCE

In contrast to the UK, inter-regional planning in France has the advantage of a well tried, accepted and effective framework of national planning. Such a framework, perhaps at first sight somewhat alien to the French *laissez-faire* attitude, developed shortly after the end of the Second World War in response to the need for some central direction to rebuild the country. French national planning is of the indicative form with the government setting down guidelines for economic growth and seeking to effect their achievement by the use of the range of economic tools at its disposal. The plan is produced by a sophisticated planning machinery centred on the CGP, and since 1947 five major plans have been produced and implemented with ever increasing levels of success, and the sixth is now in operation.

At first, inter-regional planning was regarded as more of a social and political necessity than an essential input into the strategy for national economic growth. During the 1950's attempts were made to divert growth from the Paris region to a number of critical zones defined primarily by the criteria of unemployment, using a system of financial incentives and controls. This industrial location policy had some success although most of the decentralisation tended to be to a zone within 70 to 200 km of Paris. Towards the end of the decade however, ever widening regional disparities prompted a fresh look at the regional level. The administrative reforms already outlined were effected and during the 1960's inter-regional planning was pursued more vigorously within the framework of the Fourth and Fifth National Plans.

Industrial location policy was continued, but in 1964 sweeping changes were made in an attempt to make it more effective. The system of critical zones was replaced by the division of the country into five zones, each with a different kind of financial aid (Figure 12.2). The first zone covers the under-industrialised western and south western periphery—over one third of the area of the country. Within this area investment grants for new establishments are available (1969) ranging from 25% in certain specific localities such as Cherbourg, Bordeaux and Toulouse to 12% for the majority of the area. Grants for the extension of existing factories range from 15% to 6%. Fiscal exonerations—involving the exemption or reduction in taxes on land purchase, local taxation, and capital gains taxes—plus training and resettlement aid, are also available. The second zone, a 'conversion zone', is a more fragmented area of eastern France, where the traditional mining and textile areas are in a state of decline. Here an equally wide range of incentives are also available, but whereas in zone 1

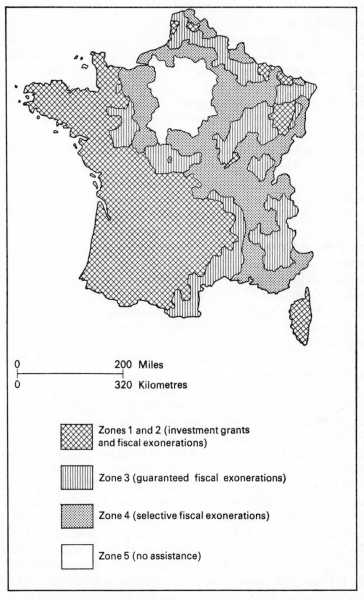

Zones 1 and 2 (investment grants
and fiscal exonerations)

Zone 3 (guaranteed fiscal exonerations)

Zone 4 (selective fiscal exonerations)

Zone 5 (no assistance)

Fig. 12.2   France: zones of financial aid for industrial development

they are available over an indefinitely long period, in zone 2 the availability is determined by the persistence of the structural problems and the number of jobs created. Zones 3 and 4 are more extensive and constitute the 'grey areas'. In the third zone expanding firms automatically qualify for tax exemptions. In the fourth zone, the procedure is more selective. Finally in the fifth zone, the region around Paris, no government assistance is available and industrial development is actively discouraged by the use of a system of development controls. Overall, this system has much in common with the UK approach, although the fact that the French system of incentives and controls applies more rigorously to the 'services' sector constitutes one fundamental difference.

This system of incentives and controls has been complemented by a policy of increasing public investment in infrastructure in the problem regions. In the Fourth Plan, the distinction was made between a policy of *accompagnement*, aimed at reinforcing desirable aspects of growth in developing problem regions by the use of social infrastructural investment, and *entrainement*, aimed at inducing growth, using government investment as a propulsive tool. The Plan also emphasised the need to promote self-sustaining growth rather than to just simply alleviate pockets of unemployment and introduced the strategy of growth centres into French regional planning.

The growth centre approach has since been developed as an integral element in French plans for decentralisation and regional development, and in 1966 a policy of building up counter magnets in the form of *métropoles d'équilibrium* throughout France to counterbalance the influence of the Paris region and provide foci for regional development was officially endorsed. The country is divided into nine functional regions based on Paris and eight other centres (Figure 12.3). The latter were chosen on the basis of a range of criteria but with the size of the cities and their central-place status being the major considerations. Excluding Paris, the chosen centres ranged in population size from less than 400 000 in Toulouse to almost 1·5 million in Lyons–St. Etienne. The policy is now to concentrate public investment in these centres creating the urbanisation economies which are at present mainly limited to Paris. It is hoped that these will be attractive to new firms, which, when they come, will create their own localisation economies of linked industries.

The success of this growth centre policy obviously depends on the ability of the new centres to reduce the influence of Paris. Some of the centres in the west are quite small and the Paris zone of influence is extensive. It is unfortunate that a new centre could

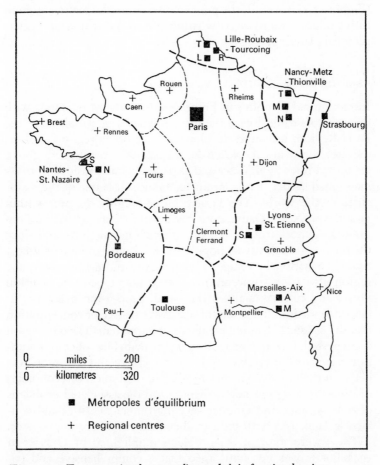

Fig. 12.3   France: regional metropolises and their functional regions

SOURCE   J. R. Boudeville, *Problems of Regional Economic Planning*, Edinburgh University Press (1966).

not have been designated in the south-central area of France to offset this central domination, but the most likely centres such as Clermont-Ferrand and Limoges simply do not possess the necessary initial facilities. The success of the policy also depends on the ability of the centres to transmit growth into their regions, although it is anticipated that the introduction of a series of intermediate regional centres, *centres-relais*, might fulfil this rôle (Figure 12.3). Overall, the policy represents a fascinating attempt to introduce a more discriminating spatial dimension into interregional planning.

FRENCH INTRA-REGIONAL PLANNING

Intra-regional planning in France tends to be synonymous with the attempts to deal with the metropolitan scale problems of the Paris Region, although developments in other regions such as the development of *métropoles d'equilibrium* mentioned above are not without significance and also merit some consideration. As mentioned earlier, Paris dominates France. It is one of the major cities of the world. The Paris region, roughly the area within 50 miles of Notre Dame, now has a population approaching ten million—almost 20% of the total French population—and since the turn of the century its population has been growing at almost twice the national average. Perhaps even more important, the region also has a concentration of economic activity, political power and cultural facilities out of all proportion even to this large proportion. It is from this excessive degree of concentration that the physical planning problems of Paris stem. The city region is congested. Its radial growth along the main lines of communication has placed excessive strain on the centre and the interstices between the radials. The net results are the typical diseconomies of growth—long journeys to work with the associated problems of time wastage and fatigue, very high inner densities and conflicting land uses with industry hemmed in on unsuitable sites.

These were some of the problems highlighted by Gravier in 1947 but it was not until 1960 that a comprehensive and coordinated plan for the region was approved by the government. This plan, *Plan d'Aménagement et d'Organisation Générale de la Région Parisienne* (PADOG),[7] was short-term in perspective dealing with the period from 1960 to 1970. It firstly assumed that the population growth of the area could be limited by cutting the future annual migration into Paris from 100 000 to 50 000. A limit was then proposed on the physical growth of the Paris agglomeration, accommodating population growth through the redevelopment of the structure of the existing city, creating suburban nodes, and the expansion of major towns like Orleans and Rouen some 60 miles or so from Paris. This approach was widely criticised partly on the failure to fully consider Paris in the context of its region, and particularly on the grounds that a total stop on the further growth of the agglomeration was unrealistic. As it was, the innate attraction of Paris led to a much faster rate of population growth than had been assumed and the plan was rapidly overtaken by events.

In 1965, a new plan was produced under the new regional planning body, the District de la Région de Paris. This plan, the *Schéma Directeur d'Aménagement et d'Urbanisme de la Région de Paris*[8] (Figure 12.4) mapped out the general guidelines for the development of the region up to the year 2000. It differed markedly from its PADOG predecessor in that it estimated a much faster rate of population growth with an approximate total figure of 14 million by 2000, including an extra two million jobs. It further accepted that there was a need to plan to accommodate this growth rather than restrict it and this would inevitably involve expansion—but planned expansion—of the agglomeration of Paris.

The aim of the new plan was to rectify the region's present monocentric form creating a new intermediate level of centre. Using the Paris region as a functional planning unit, the plan sought to accommodate the anticipated growth by the renovation of urban centres within the existing agglomeration and the development of new urban centres along preferential axes tangential to the main agglomeration. The former involves the continuation of some of the PADOG proposals, such as the comprehensive renewal scheme at La Défense. The latter, involving the organisation of growth into major centres along broad NW–SE twin corridors at a distance of between 15 and 30 miles from the city, represents a fundamental shift of approach. It is a determined approach to break away from the radial–concentric structure. As such, it involves a rejection of a green belt/new town

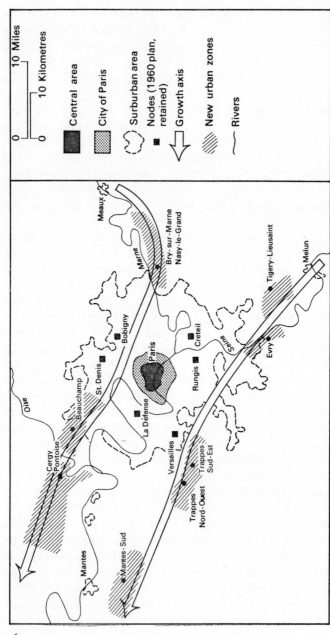

Fig. 12.4 The Schéma plan (1965) for the Paris region

approach which was regarded as unnecessarily constricting on the agglomeration and as possibly intervening with town development programmes outside the region. It also means a rejection of a 'second Paris' solution, or the development of several major axes—which was regarded as an expensive and inefficient solution.

The proposed growth along the axes will be in the form of major sub-regional service and employment centres with populations of 300 000 to 500 000. Three such centres—Cergy-Pontoise, Beauchamp and Bry-sur-Marne—were proposed for the 45-mile northern axis; and five for the 55-mile southern axis. The specific locations were chosen where the main routes from Paris intersect the tangential axes. It is argued that this solution is efficient in terms of transportation investment and, by preserving an open wedge along the Seine Valley, will also guarantee easy access to open space for the bulk of the population. Of course, not everyone is convinced and such a radical solution has raised much opposition. The plan has been strongly criticised especially on the question of the excessive costs involved and on the likely impact on development in the more distant problem regions. Although the plan has since been reviewed, it nevertheless represents a courageous attempt to deal with these major regional problems.

Elsewhere in France there was little progress in planning at the intra-regional level until comparatively recently. In most regions in the 1950's the extent of regional planning was limited to the work of the regional expansion committees which were mainly concerned with the diagnosis of regional problems—although there were some interesting exceptions. During the same period, a limited number of quasi-public development corporations were set up to implement redevelopment programmes. One such organisation was the *Compagnie Nationale d'Aménagement de la Région du Bas-Rhône et du Languedoc* (CNARBL), which after much study initiated the Lower Rhône–Languedoc programme to tap water from the Rhône to irrigate a vast area of southern France freeing it from an economy narrowly based on vine culture. The programme soon developed a much wider range of projects concerned with many aspects of the life of the region.

More recently, the new sub-regional agencies (OREAM), established to produce plans for the development of the major *métropoles d'équilibrium* have begun to produce results. To date they have produced a series of *livres blancs* (white books) on demographic and economic prospects as a basis for planning, and some have produced *schémas d'aménagement* which constitute more concrete plans for the development of their areas. The OREAM Marseilles for example, following interesting exercises in public consultation, has now produced plans[9] to accommodate a population increase of up to 140% in its 2600 square mile area by the year 2000. However the agencies are purely study teams with no executive powers and the powers of implementation rest with the central government and local authorities.

THE FUTURE

France has now developed a sophisticated if perhaps somewhat complex planning system for dealing with its regional problems. But this system is not without problems. In spite of its elaborate structure, it is still highly centralised with the regional bodies, CODER and CAR, having only limited powers and the main power and control remaining in the hands of central government. This issue provoked a referendum in 1969, when proposals for greater regional autonomy, involving the creation of more representative and powerful regional assemblies, were put forward. In the event, the referendum was clouded by other issues and the proposals were rejected. But this is only a temporary halt and greater regional autonomy to counter the excessive centralisation on Paris seems to be only a matter of time.* A positive step in this direction could be to reduce the number of regions. Boudeville believes that the population of the French *régions de programme* should be in the order of four to five million. Yet only Paris, Rhône–Alpes and Nord fit into this scale, and ten regions have populations of less than 1·5 million. It could be

* Indeed, modest steps have recently (1972) been taken towards regional reform with some widening of the functions and composition of the regional bodies. But this is more concerned with streamlining the existing regional structure rather than changing it and each region will continue to be administered by a Government-appointed prefect.

argued that this present balkanisation is one of the major factors favouring the continuing domination of Paris.

2 Dutch regional planning

The Netherlands is a thriving and prosperous nation occupying an important strategic position in Western Europe. It is also a small country. In spatial terms it is considerably smaller than either the United Kingdom or France—indeed it is no larger than the largest regions in these countries. Yet despite its overall prosperity and small size, it still presents a striking diversity of problems. Within the country there are varying shades of prosperity and even prosperity itself brings problems.

In this small country a factor of vital importance is the growth and distribution of population. Round about the year 1800 a growth of one million in population took 50 years, now it only takes six years and by the year 2000, it may only be four years. Hence it has been estimated that the 1971 population of 13 100 000 may increase to 20 000 000 by the end of the century.[10] The impact of population growth is further complicated by its high concentration in a small economically prosperous area in the west of the country which for many years has acted as a magnet for migrants from the more rural peripheral provinces to the north, east and south. In 1971, the three provinces of North Holland, South Holland and Utrecht, the Dutch 'Randstad', accounted for 46% of the total population on only 21% of the total land area. There are many reasons for this higher level of economic activity in the western provinces but of particular importance is their juxtaposition to the major trading axes of the North Sea and the Rhine, and their continued historical ascendancy in the administrative and cultural spheres.

For many years, Dutch planners have realised the need for an enlargement of the scale of planning to meet the problems now and in the future of this most densely populated country, and their advances in developing administrative structures, inter-regional planning frameworks, and both allocative and innovative forms of intra-regional planning offer important lessons of more general relevance. (Useful references on aspects of Dutch regional planning include those by Burke,[11] Hall,[12] Heywood[13] plus official Dutch government publications.)

To reconcile the competing claims on its scarce resources, the Dutch nation has evolved a hierarchical planning structure which is carried out at three levels—national, provincial and municipal—with each level being generally regulated by the policies laid down by those above it.

At the national level, responsibility for spatial planning policy falls to the Minister of Housing and Spatial Planning. He is advised and assisted by the National Physical Planning Agency which carries out much of the day-to-day work of policy preparation; a National Physical Planning Committee which is an interdepartmental consultative body; and an Advisory Physical Planning Council which functions as a channel of communication between the government and the community. Economic planning however comes under a separate ministry, the Ministry of Economic Affairs, and thus considerable onus lies upon inter-ministerial co-ordination.

At the intermediate level there are eleven provinces (Figure 12.5). These provinces, developed from the seventeenth-century United Provinces, are autonomous administrative units which have, over the course of time, gradually gained influence and are now of considerable importance for effective regional planning. In outline, the organisational structure of provincial planning closely resembles the national level. The provinces are authorised to adopt regional plans which can cover all or parts of their areas. This plan preparation is carried out by Provincial Physical Planning Agencies in consultation with Provincial Physical Planning Committees. The municipal authorities must also be consulted and the plan must be approved by the elected regional decision-making body, the Provincial Council.

The municipality constitutes the third level of planning. There are in total some 975 municipal councils in the Netherlands. They are obliged to draw up an allocation plan for the whole of the municipal territory that is not built up and may also do the same for built-up areas. They may also draw up a structure plan for their area, indicating future development. Neither plan should transgress the regional plan. However, should the municipality feel strongly opposed to the restraints set by the province, then it may appeal directly to the Crown, which can overrule the regional plan. In this respect, a recent development of some importance has been the grouping of several municipalities into

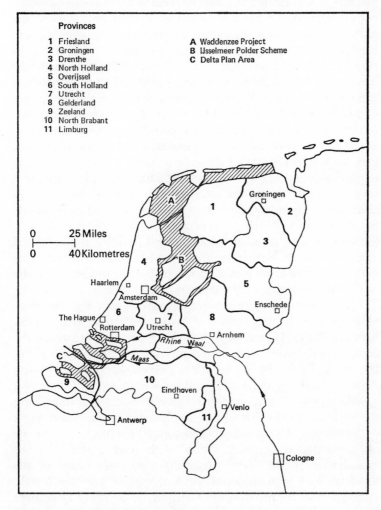

Fig. 12.5   The Netherlands: provinces

Agglomeration Boards which tend to be more effective planning units.

It is possible to identify two elements in Dutch inter-regional planning. Historically, the first element is an industrial location policy, carried out by the Ministry of Economic Affairs and initiated to meet the same problems encountered in other Western European countries (namely, the fact that certain regions of the country lag behind in economic development). In the Netherlands, it is the northern rural provinces (Groningen, Drenthe, Friesland and part of North Holland) and the more industrialised province of Limburg in the south which suffer from economic malaise. In the latter there was a risk of structural unemployment following the closure of the coal mines; whereas in the north, the general problem is one of static or even shrinking employment opportunities owing to the mechanisation of agriculture, as a consequence of which farm labourers are obliged to look for jobs elsewhere. The policy response has been one of 'stimulation and reconversion' with the concentration of government support, through the provision of infrastructural facilities and industrial incentives, in specific primary and secondary nuclei in the problem regions. This policy has met with considerable success especially in the southern part of the country.

The second and more recent element of inter-regional planning involves the preparation of National Physical Plans by the National Physical Planning Agency in an attempt to structure the competing demands on the scarce physical resources of the country, especially in the West. In the Second Report on Physical Planning in the Netherlands (1966), the government proposed a possible physical structure for the year 2000 aimed at improving the irregular distribution of the population over the various parts of the country. The broad urbanisation pattern proposed was one of 'concentrated deconcentration' with some stabilisation of urbanisation in the West conserving the 'green heart' of the Randstad and with dispersal directed especially to the North, certain parts of the province of Overijssel, the Southern IJsselmeer Polders and the province of Zeeland.

302

Table 12.1. *Possible population distributions (millions).*

Part of the Netherlands	1965	Continuation at present trend		With increased dispersal
North	1·3	2·3		3·0
East	2·2	4·0		4·3
West	5·7	8·5	} 13·2	11·5
South	2·6	4·7		
South-West	0·3	0·5		0·7
Southern IJsselmeer Polders	—	—		0·5
	12·1	20·0		20·0

SOURCE: *Second Report on Physical Planning in the Netherlands (1966).*

The more detailed structural scheme distinguished a four-tier hierarchy of physical planning units (Figure 12.6). Yet, despite the innate attraction and theoretical sophistication of the approach, the Second Report constitutes more an indicative proposal rather than an effective national framework for spatial planning. Nevertheless, even broad guidelines as to how current trends could be accommodated in the light of existing policies are of considerable relevance, especially to regional planners.

INTRA-REGIONAL PLANNING

It is also possible to identify two forms of Dutch intra-regional planning—provincial planning and regional development planning. *Provincial planning* is primarily allocative regional planning concerned with maintaining the smooth functioning of the existing system over time in accordance with evolving policies. This involves several rôles. Provincial planning must firstly bridge the gap between national and municipal planning, allowing the consideration of regional priorities in the formulation of national investment decisions and vice versa. In the Netherlands this is done through a series of regular consultations between the various planning levels and is also aided by provincial regulation of two major items of expenditure—roads and town centre redevelopment.

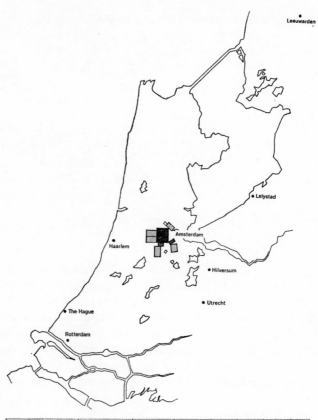

Physical planning unit	Road type	Public transport	Service standard	Garden facilities
A (Population 5000)	Residential street	Regional bus	Shops for general daily requirements at short distance; loss of time in buying reduced to a minimum; simple neighbourhood centre building.	Public garden
B (Population 1500)	Local roads	Regional bus or slow train	Shopping centre as for A, but larger assortment; neighbourhood centre for social services.	Community park
C (Population 60 000)	Main roads	Express train and town bus	Combination of shopping centre with other facilities in the services sector (cafe-restaurant cinema, etc.); cultural centre.	City park
D (Population 250 000)	Urban motorways	Express train and town rail system on free track	Larger and more varied centre than for C; more shops; specialization within the branch (fur shop and trousers shop) and according to assortment (technical bookshop); theatre, concert hall, museum, operahouse.	City region park (woods, parks, lakes etc.).

Fig. 12.6   The Netherlands (Randstad): heirarchy of settlements

A second rôle involves the co-ordination of municipal planning—reconciling local conflicts and avoiding the duplication of expensive infrastructural investment. On paper this is achieved through the preparation and implementation by the Provincial Council of the regional and sub-regional plans—documents which hopefully take a wider view of issues than the individual municipalities. Unfortunately this can sometimes result in major provincial–municipal disagreements as exemplified by the conflicts between the major cities of Amsterdam and Rotterdam and their provinces over restrictions on their growth potentials along the North Sea Canal and in the Rhine Delta respectively. In such situations, the strength of democratic authority may not be sufficient for the provincial bodies and in reality the municipality often wins the day. It has been argued that this may reflect the physical orientation of the regional plans and their failure to appreciate economic forces, and the greater financial and political resources of the larger municipal authorities.[14]

Finally, provincial planning can also bee seen as an input into national planning. This is certainly the case in the Netherlands where the existence of a series of regional plans greatly facilitated the preparation of the Second National Physical Plan.

The second form of intra-regional planning, *Regional Development Planning*, predates the provincial form and is somewhat of a Dutch speciality for which the nation is rightly famous. Regional development planning is innovative involving the moulding of change on a large scale. It is concerned with integrated development schemes, schemes of great impact which require planning at the regional scale to ensure the greatest possible benefit for all activities in the region. In the Netherlands, the IJsselmeer Polders scheme to reclaim the Zuyder Zee, the Delta Plan to close the Rhine–Maas Delta, and the Waddenzee project to reclaim large areas of land between the West Frisian Islands and the north coast, all fit into this category.

The varying objectives of such schemes have been discussed by Van den Berg.[15] Originally, the main objective was one of economic growth (the Zuyder Zee reclamation scheme was proposed as early as 1848 to foster commerce, shipping and agriculture). But it was the threat to the Dutch people of the ravages of both sea and river inundations which in the end proved to be the most forceful objective and the most powerful political argument. Over time however multiple objectives have developed including water supply, the improvement of communications and land reclamation and its subsequent use for agriculture, industry and housing.

Of the three schemes, reclamation of the IJsselmeer Polders has progressed furthest. Of the area of 870 000 acres closed to the North Sea, 300 000 have already been reclaimed and three polders have been settled. A further 250 000 will be reclaimed by 1980 with the rest remaining as a fresh-water reservoir. In contrast to the older polders which are being developed primarily for agriculture, rather more space in the newer reclaimed areas will be set aside for recreation, industrial sites and new residential areas. Thus the 1965 structure plan for the South IJsselmeer Polders[16] was made to fit in with the aim of national planning—releasing pressure from the crowded and growing cities of Amsterdam and Utrecht. Within this broad structure a detailed hierarchy of centres is planned.

These major multi-purpose projects are carried out by semi-autonomous regional development agencies under the auspices of the Department of Water Management. Although such an approach might be viewed as undemocratic it does have the advantages of achieving impressive results in a relatively short period of time unhindered by inter-departmental and provincial–municipal conflicts. Further, as the projects proceed, reclaimed land is returned to the control of adjacent provinces.

The Dutch approach to regional planning has much to commend it. The possession of an intermediate level of provincial planning with statutory powers and an elected provincial council would seem to be a major administrative asset; the national physical plan provides useful guidelines for regional planning and the regional development agencies fulfil a valuable innovative rôle. But there are also problems. At all levels there appears to be a failure to integrate economic and physical planning. This lack of effective horizontal co-ordination is particularly clear at the national level and it has been suggested 'that on the national planning level all financial, economic and technical means should be concentrated in one ministry'.[17] Provincial planning could also be more effective; at present it is politically and financially rather weak and is in consequence squeezed from above and below.

3 Regional planning in a European community

In addition to dealing with their problem regions within a national framework, some countries are now having to allow for the effects of integration into major international blocs such as the EEC. It is possible that such integration may aggravate existing regional problems or even create new ones. With the recent expansion of the EEC from the original six—France, Germany, Holland, Belgium, Luxembourg and Italy—to nine, with the addition of the UK, Eire and Denmark, this factor is particularly relevant to a discussion of UK regional problems.

INTEGRATION AND REGIONAL PROBLEMS

In assessing the effects of economic integration it is important to differentiate between the immediate impact effects and the long-run dynamic effects. The impact effects result from given supply and demand conditions and often reveal themselves most clearly via price changes (the expected rise in UK food prices on joining the Common Market provides an example of this effect). The dynamic effects result from changes in the underlying conditions of supply and demand arising from opportunities for rationalisation, economies of scale, specialisation and centralisation in a supra-national market—250 million people in the enlarged EEC.

Three long-run effects may have a particular significance for regional problems. In the first place, the elimination of internal tariffs and the adoption of common policies for transport will lead to the creation of a large and competitive market. This will stimulate greater efficiency favouring the most efficient enterprises which can best take advantage of the economies of scale. This will inevitably lead to increased *specialisation*, bringing greater prosperity to some regions, but also aggravating the problem of the depressed industrial and agricultural areas. (In Belgium, the winds of EEC competition have had a traumatic impact on the admittedly inefficient coal industry of the Borinage.) An open market will also tend to lead to an *equalisation of factor prices* with capital and labour flowing from locations where earnings are low to those where earnings are high until some equilibrium position is reached. The level of factor earnings will be determined by the most productive enterprises in the prosperous regions. The weaker enterprises in the problem areas which had only survived by paying lower rates will have to either improve their efficiency or, more likely, decline. This introduces a third major effect, the tendency for increasing *centralisation* of economic activity in the prosperous centre of the wider community to the detriment of the partners on the fringe. The centre reaps the advantage of scale economies and the net effect may be the replacement of national centre–periphery disparities with a wider community centre–periphery. In Western Europe, the impact of this effect could be to concentrate economic activity in the Rhine–Rhône axis or the so-called 'Golden Triangle'.

THE EEC AND UK REGIONAL PROBLEMS

As a country on the periphery of Europe, the effects of EEC membership, especially those of increased centralisation and specialisation, on regional problems, are of considerable importance in the UK. It would seem likely that, in the absence of controls, economic activity will tend to gravitate towards the centre of the market it is mainly aiming to supply. For although, as noted in Chapter 6, the micro-location of industry is becoming more flexible, the macro-location is tending to a greater concentration on a limited number of areas. What will be the impact on the UK of this centralisation in the Golden Triangle of Western Europe—will it become the Northern Ireland of the EEC? The areal extent of this Golden Triangle tends to vary according to the nationality of the delineator. Accepting the implicit British bias it can perhaps be roughly identified as the area bounded by Birmingham, Amsterdam, the Ruhr, Milan and Paris, although it isn't a static phenomenon.

Clark, Wilson and Bradley[18] ingeniously attempted to identify which regions in Western Europe were the most attractive to industry and the likely effects of both economic integration in the EEC and transport developments on the most favoured regions, using a quantitative approach based on the concept of

308

economic potential. The latter is derived from Stewart's[19] form of demographic potential and has also been used by Clark[20] in an estimate of the economic potentials in Britain. The countries of Western Europe were subdivided into major regions, and the economic potential of a focal point in each region was defined by summing regional incomes around it—each regional income having been first divided by the 'distant costs' of reaching it. The distance costs included tariffs, and land and sea transport costs. The areas with the highest economic potential were assumed to be those most attractive to industrial location. The validity of the approach rests of course on the assumptions that firms are attracted by the large markets and scale economies of the areas of dense population, and that the capacity of a region to act as a market and supplier of inputs is directly related to regional income and inversely to the distance costs from other markets.

Using this method, contours of equi-potential were constructed for Western Europe for several different situations. Prior to the Treaty of Rome, clearly identifiable centres of equally high potential could be identified in South East England, the Paris region and the Rhine–Ruhr area. These areas were in marked contrast to the Benelux countries where major troughs of depression were apparent. Other attractive regions in the UK included the Midlands, the South East and North West regions; although potential fell quickly in the peripheral regions to the north and west.

But with the advent of Customs Union and the elimination of trade barriers between the original 'Six', the model revealed a marked shift in potential with the formation of a single central region of high potential concentrated in the Rhine Valley, Eastern Belgium and South East Netherlands, from which potentials diminished with distance on all sides. The net result was to relegate the whole of the UK to a European periphery of low potential. The enlargement of the EEC to include the UK, Eire, Norway* and Denmark, is shown to bring about some improvement in the relative UK position, as is the impact of increased containerisation and the building of a channel tunnel. Yet even with these improvements, the concentric pattern persists with Britain lying outside the areas of greatest potential.

* Norway was included in the model.

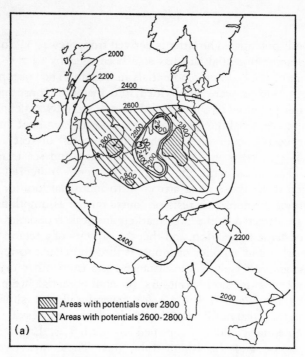

Areas with potentials over 2800
Areas with potentials 2600-2800

(a)

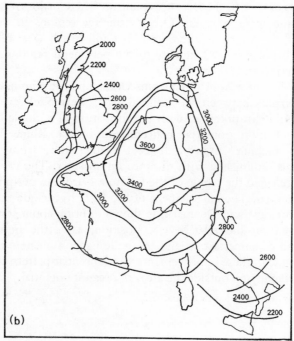

(b)

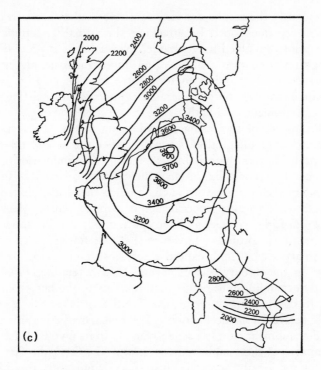

Fig. 12.8   Economic Potential in a European Community

    a Pre-Treaty of Rome

    b Post-Treaty of Rome

    c Enlarged Community

SOURCE: Clark, C., Wilson, F., and Bradley, J., Industrial location and economic potential in Western Europe, *Regional Studies,* **3,** 2, pages 197–212, (1969).

Obviously the results are very sensitive to the approach used and can be questioned by attacking the structure, inputs and assumptions involved in the model. Nevertheless it provides an interesting attempt at analysis of an important issue, and at the least suggests that unless there is some form of positive intervention there may be considerable aggravation of existing UK regional problems and perhaps the creation of new ones.

The impact of increasing specialisation in the UK resultant from economic integration is equally difficult to assess, although it is probable that the existing efficient growth industries of the UK economy would be the ones most likely to benefit.[12] In the secondary sector, industries such as petro-chemicals, electronics and heavy electrical engineering might hope to benefit. Mechanical engineering, vehicles and aerospace might also be 'moderate gainers'. It is probable however that the tertiary sector and quaternary sector (high expertise services) might stand to gain most. In the tertiary sector, several British retailing firms are already expanding into continental markets to the benefit of the UK. In the quaternary sector, the South East is established as a world centre for finance, banking, insurance, marketing, research and development, and has several factors in its favour. It has the advantages of the established contacts of 'the City', the fact that the internationally accepted quaternary language is English, a strong tradition of scientific research and that elusive asset, the 'quality of the English way of life'. Offset against such advantages are the low degree of 'Europeanness' of the UK capital, the barrier of the English Channel (necessitating some reliance on public transport), the low salary for brainpower in the UK, and the rapidly inflating prices for office accommodation, all of which may over time constitute major constraints.

Whatever the particular effects of increased specialisation and centralisation, the likely general effect on the UK will be to relatively favour the already prosperous regions and especially the South East at the expense of the already ailing problem regions. The peripheral areas, Northern Scotland, Wales and Northern Ireland may face particularly difficult problems. But given better air and sea links, the North East and Central Scotland are both well placed for export to the Continent, and may enjoy better long-term prospects in the market than some people seem to fear.

The dynamic effects of economic integration on all countries in the Community are in themselves a major reason for policy at an EEC level. The aims of economic and perhaps ultimately political unity will not be furthered if some regions suffer badly from such union. As in the UK national context, widening regional disparities may encourage separatist tendencies and there are therefore important political motives for intervention. The Treaty of Rome setting out why the original Six countries wanted to create the EEC, includes the following reason, 'to ensure their harmonious development by reducing the differences between the existing regions'. This view was reiterated by the communiqué on the 1972 Common Market Summit, 'The Heads of State or of Government agreed that a high priority should be given to the aim of correcting in the Community, the structural and regional imbalances which might affect the realisation of Economic and Monetary Union.' There is also a need to intervene to co-ordinate the variety of national regional policies to prevent the development of situations where governments are actively outbidding each other to attract foreign investment.

For reasons such as these, the EEC is today more than ever aware of the need to work towards a co-ordinated regional policy. But this is not synonymous with the replacement of national regional policies. M. Borschette, a Community Commissioner recently said:

'the Commission and the Community recognise it is unlikely that a single regional policy could ever apply in all its details in all regions of the Community. We know that each region is a special case, often requiring special treatment. We also know that it is primarily for national governments to produce the ideas for dealing with these special problems. It is not our task to seek to intervene with the efforts of national governments directed towards this end. But we think that a common Regional Policy is necessary to supplement national efforts.'

The rôle of Community regional policy can therefore be seen as one of co-ordinating and 'topping up' the efforts of individual countries as and when necessary.

Three major elements in Community policy to date can be identified. Firstly the Commission has sought to create an awareness of regional problems organising studies and sponsoring conferences on the theory, techniques and practice of regional planning. A particular interesting development in this field was the commissioning by the EEC of the study into the feasibility of promoting an industrial development pole at Bari-Taranto in the heel of Southern Italy.

In the second place, the Commission has sought to co-ordinate the regional measures of the various member countries in an attempt to prevent excessive and wasteful competition between countries seeking to attract foreign, especially American, investments. In this area there has been notably less success. However, in 1971, a new set of guidelines were proposed which would limit industrial investment aid to a maximum of 20% of the total cost for any project in the so-called 'central area' of the Community. The central area includes the more developed areas. There would be no such limitation in the peripheral areas. Yet even if such proposals to control direct aid were successful the situation would still be open to abuse through the use of indirect aids such as the generous provision of social and economic infrastructure. The problem of co-ordinating regional measures presents a thorny problem.

The third and rather more successful element of EEC regional policy is the provision of capital to regions, 'topping up' the various national regional measures. Several community institutions, financed by subscriptions from the member states, have been established with this purpose in mind. By 1971, the European Investment Bank had loaned over 1500 million dollars for regional development, primarily to Southern Italy; the European Social Fund had aided the training and resettlement of over a million workers, again mainly from Italy; the European Coal and Steel Community had allocated loans of over 1000 million dollars to coal and steel modernisation projects largely in Germany and Belgium; and the European Agricultural Fund had provided major grants towards the rationalisation of farming, with approximately 80% of the total going to France. However the 1972 Community Summit gave a fresh impetus to a common Community regional policy initiating several new developments. It requested the

Community to establish a Regional Development Fund before the end of 1973. This fund will no doubt be the principal vehicle for mobilising the Community's own resources, directed at the medium and long term development of the less developed and declining regions in the member states. But its establishment raises several questions as to the amount of money available, the method of distribution and areas to be aided. Certainly the fund will need to be substantial if it is to be effective in providing grants and interest rebates on loans to industrial schemes, service activities and infrastructure projects in the problem regions. In addition, a recent European Commission Green Paper on regional policy[23] has also proposed the establishment of a Regional Development Committee to fulfil the vital role of co-ordinating the regional policies of member states and to provide a framework for Community regional policies.

COMMUNITY POLICY AND THE UK

Most members of the Community have a range of regional measures similar to those operating in the UK—revolving around financial and taxation advantages to enterprises prepared to set up in problem regions; although the actual amounts allocated by the countries do vary widely with, for example, Britain spending ten times more than France. At present, the extent to which Britain may have to amend her regional policies is not yet clear. Variable cost subsidies, such as REP, which are more peculiar to the UK and might have clashed with Community policy are, wisely or otherwise, being phased out. Other measures which might cause problems are the tax-linked subsidies, such as accelerated depreciation, which to the Commission smack of 'under-the-counter' incentives, the extent of which are difficult to control. The extent of Britain's assisted areas has also come under attack, although it is probable that of these, only the Intermediate Areas will revert to the community central area in the near future, with the consequent 20% limit to state aid on new investment programmes. (Here it should be noted that although most of the British state aid does not at present reach the 20% limit, the Commission intends to systematically reduce the limit in the future.)

315

On the positive side, Britain will soon begin to benefit from the small existing Community regional aid programme, with investors being able to get loans from the European Investment Bank and the redundant to get aid from the Social Fund. In the future, Britain will also no doubt be one of the prime beneficiaries of the new regional initiatives. Perhaps herein lies the most difficult task for future Community regional policy—that of convincing nations, such as France and Germany, that it is in their interests that their neighbours, such as Britain and Italy, should have a larger share of Community finances.

4 Summary

In both France and the Netherlands the incidence of socio-economic disparities between different areas of the country and the need to co-ordinate physical, economic and social development at a supra-urban scale have necessitated an intermediate level of planning. For this purpose the highly centralised France has been divided into 21 planning regions. In the Netherlands, the eleven provinces provide the regional framework. As in the United Kingdom the duality of problems has led to a duality in regional planning. Within the regions there has been an emphasis on spatial plans to 'deconcentrate' the capital cities—Paris and the polycentric Randstad. There have also been interesting developments in innovative planning using semi-independent regional development bodies. Between regions, both countries, but especially France, have developed industrial location policies. They have also sought to introduce a more discriminatory spatial dimension—as represented in the French policy of *métropoles d'équilibrium* and the Dutch national physical plans. But as in the United Kingdom the regional level of planning is still lacking in power and autonomy, with France still heavily centralised around Paris and the Dutch provinces unable to combat national and municipal pressures.

In a wider context, it is possible that within the expanded European Economic Community certain regional problems may be aggravated by the market trends of increasing centralisation, specialisation and equalisation of factor prices. Peripheral areas of the Community, including large areas of Britain, may be particularly vulnerable, and this may necessitate a reappraisal and more vigorous pursuance of regional planning in the member countries and a more extensive European regional policy.

References

1 Allen, K., and MacLennan, M. C., *Regional Problems and Policies in Italy and France,* Allen and Unwin (1970).
2 Boudeville, J. R., *Problems of Regional Economic Planning,* Edinburgh UP (1966).
3 Hansen, N. M., *French Regional Planning,* Indiana UP (1968).
4 Hall, P., *The World Cities,* Weidenfeld and Nicolson (1966). See also: Gravier, J., *La question régionale,* Flammarion, Paris (1970).
5 Gravier, J. F., *Paris et le Désert Français,* Paris (1958).
6 Hackett, J. and A. M., *Economic Planning in France,* Allen and Unwin (1963).
7 France, Ministère de la Construction, *Plan d'Aménageemnt et d'Organisation Générale de la Région Parisienne* (1960).
8 France, Premier Ministre. *Délégation Générale du District de la Région de Paris, Schéma Directeur d'Aménagement et d'Urbanisme de la Région de Paris* (1955).
9 OREAM: Marseilles, *Schéma d'Aménagement de l'Aire Métropolitaine Marseillaise* (1970).
10 *Second Report on Physical Planning in the Netherlands,* Government Printing Office of the Netherlands, The Hague (1966).
11 Burke, L., *The Greenheart Metropolis,* Macmillan (1966).
12 Hall, P., *The World Cities, op cit.*
13 Heywood, P., Regional planning in the Netherlands and England and Wales, *Journal of the Town Planning Institute,* December 1970.
14 Dunham, D. M., The Processes of Spatial Planning in the Netherlands, in Dunham, D. M., and Hilhorst J. G. M. (eds.), *Issues in Regional Planning,* Mouton (1971).
15 Van den Berg, G. J., Changing Regional Planning Goals in a Changing Country, *Town and Country Planning Summer School,* Keele (1966).
16 Rijkswaterstraat Communications, **6,** *Structure Plan for the Southern IJsselmeer Polders* (1965).
17 Steigenga, W., 'Recent Planning Problems in the Netherlands', *Regional Studies,* page 106, **2** (1968).
18 Clark, C., Wilson, F. and J., and Bradley, J., Industrial location and economic potential in Western Europe, *Regional Studies,* **3,** 2, pages 197–212 (1962).

19 Stewart, J. Q., Empirical mathematical rules concerning the distribution and equilibrium of population. *Geog. Review,* **37** (1947).

20 Clark, C., Industrial location and economic potential, *Lloyds Bank Review,* **82,** pages 1–17 (1966).

21 For an interesting discussion and further references, See: Wise, M. J., Britain on the Brink of Europe, in Chisholm, M., (ed.), *Resources for Britain's Future,* David and Charles (1972).

22 See: Europe Community Information Service, Community Topics, 33: *Regional Policy in an Integrated Europe* (1969); Lind, H., *Regional Policy in Britain and the Six,* and Flockton, C., *Community Regional Policy,* Chatham House/PEP European Series, 15 (1970). McCrone, G., *Regional Policy in Britain,* Chapter XI, Allen and Unwin (1969).

23 *Report on the Regional Problems in the Enlarged Community,* Commission of the European Communities, May 1973.

Conclusion: retrospect and prospect

There is a growing awareness of the need for regional planning in many countries of the world. In some this awareness has provoked positive action. This has certainly been the case in the United Kingdom which today has a more extensive system of regional planning than most. But this development of British regional planning has not been smooth, and at first was somewhat intermittent. In the early years of this century, the functional problems of urban regions arising from rapid population growth, increasing urbanisation and increasing standards of living and personal mobility highlighted the need for intra-regional planning; similarly, the 'economic malaise' of the depressed industrial and rural regions aroused concern over regional variations and the need for the inter-regional allocation of resources to remedy the imbalance. But at this stage, the motivation for regional planning was founded more on emotion than considered argument and the achievements were minimal. The Barlow Report (1940) gave a welcome stimulus, which was reflected in major regional planning developments in the immediate post-war period (1945–51). Unfortunately this initiative was soon dissipated in the 1950's, and it was not until the last decade that regional planning reappeared in earnest. Now, supported by economic as well as social and political arguments, it is tempting to conclude that regional planning has finally arrived on the British scene. Inter-regional planning has an extensive armoury of incentives and controls designed to effect industrial relocation

319

to assisted areas and these appear to be having some effect. In addition specific regional and sub-regional plans are being produced for many areas of the country. But while it is true that progress has been made and that the need for regional planning is now widely accepted—even in government circles—it still only represents a start and there are many fundamental problems yet to be resolved.

Firstly, there is a need to define regions which are satisfactory for planning at this intermediate level. The problem is to find areas suitable for inter-regional resource allocation and intra-regional planning providing a framework for more local plans. The solution may be to compromise taking just one set of regions such as the 21 French planning regions. Alternatively a multi-level hierarchical division of a country into planning regions may be more suitable.

A second problem relates to the hazy nature of regional goals and objectives. There is a lack of general guidelines on the most desirable future inter- and intra-regional distributions of population and employment. As compared with France, the UK national planning framework is weak. In particular, there is a marked absence of policies on spatial priorities at the national level. Should the nineteenth-century settlement pattern be preserved, or should new areas such as Solway and Severnside be opened up? In the early 1960's, there were several suggestions for a national framework for future population distribution, and the Central Unit for Environmental Planning was established in the mid 1960's to consider such problems. But the net result to date is the production of the *Long Term Population Distribution Study*[1] which merely suggested the need to investigate the feasibility of Severnside, Humberside and Tayside as future reception centres for national population growth. At the intra-regional level, there is similarly a need for more guidance on a whole range of strategic issues such as the relative merits of concentration and dispersal and the associated problems of new urban developments versus the rehabilitation of existing communities.

A third problem concerns the relationship between the principles of regional analysis and the practice of regional planning. The principles outlined in earlier chapters provide a valuable insight into regional growth and change and the spatial structure

320

of regions; yet there is a wide gap between theoretical possibilities and the *ad hoc* rule-of-thumb practice. There are of course examples where the gap is narrowing, but there are also some examples of the misuse of concepts (the growth pole theory is a point in question). One explanation of this gap in many countries could be the poor state of the regional information system, for a good regional data base is essential for effective planning.

Contemporary UK regional policies and strategies tend to suffer from a certain rigidity of approach and this constitutes a fourth problem. In inter-regional planning this rigidity has been reflected in the approach to the delineation of assisted areas, which until quite recently followed a 'blanket' approach based on rather narrow criteria. The emphasis on attracting private manufacturing industry, with only a minor rôle for the public sector and service industry, provides another example. Even the industrial location policies themselves could be more flexible relating more closely to the needs of particular industries and regions (perhaps the advent of the Regional Industrial Development Executives may provide the necessary stimulus here). In intra-regional planning there has been a similar rigidity with a tendency for a rather narrow approach, often with a strong physical emphasis. There is a need for an integrated approach considering the interrelationships of a wide range of factors—physical, economic, social and the like—at the regional level, with a multi-alternative dynamic view of future situations.

Finally, there is the problem of administration. This constitutes a major constraint on effective regional planning in many countries and certainly in the United Kingdom. Reform of the regional machinery raises many questions of boundaries, functions and powers. What is the most suitable framework for co-ordinating local plans? How much of the administration of inter-regional planning can be devolved to the regional level? With regard to the latter it would seem that whatever the degree of regional autonomy, the inter-regional allocation of resources would still require some degree of co-ordinated central control. Chapter 11 outlined a range of possibilities for regional reform and with local government reorganisation and the Commission on the Constitution due to report, there may be some major changes quite soon. But even this is only a stage in a continuing process, and any system must be adaptable to future changes.

However, despite the problems, significant progress has been made in regional planning in this country and abroad. But the problems should not be ignored. They can provide a valuable guideline to future research priorities. Research is needed into technical areas—such as the rôle of growth centres, industrial location factors in practice and regional information systems; and into institutional areas—such as the relationship between regional planning and adjacent planning levels and the most satisfactory form of regional machinery. All of this requires more regional planners and improved educational programmes. In this respect it is interesting to note the views of the Programme Director, Regional Development, at the United Nations Research Institute for Social Development, who clearly indicates that the demand for regional planners is not homogeneous.[2] He identifies the need for five different types of regional planners—inter-regional and intra-ragional planners, plus regional statisticians, locational planners and regional futurologists.

Yet, however skilful the approach of the regional planner and however efficient the regional machinery, regional problems will persist for many years to come. But the failure to tackle them now, and with vigour, will result in even greater social, economic and political problems in the future.

References

1 Department of the Environment, *Long term population distribution in Great Britain—a study*, HMSO (1971).
2 Kuklinski, A. R., *Education for Regional Planners*, in Dunham, D., and Hilhorst, J. G. M. (eds.), *Issues in Regional Planning*, Mouton, The Hague (1971).

APPENDIX A
UK regional statistics: major published sources

This summary of the major published sources of regional statistics makes no attempt to be comprehensive. It seeks merely to outline some of the sources of relevance to regional planning. The general sources, although composed mainly of secondary sources derived from the original statistics, provide a useful framework. The selection of supplementary sources provide a basis for more detailed investigation of particular aspects of the regional environment. The regions referred to in the sources are primarily the eleven UK Economic Planning Regions.

General Sources

Abstract of Regional Statistics (Central Statistical Office)—published annually since 1965. It is a compilation of 80 tables of economic and social statistics for the Economic Planning Regions of England and Wales, plus GLC. Major categories are:

1 Area and Climate	7 Production
2 Population	8 Construction and Investment
3 Social Services	9 Distribution
4 Education	10 Transport
5 Employment	11 Incomes
6 Energy	12 Household Surveys

An Analysis of Regional Economic and Social Statistics.
(Hammond, E., Univ. of Durham, Rowntree Research Unit, 1968). This is a very useful publication bringing together a large body of regional information, and combining material formerly published in a wide variety of scattered sources together with original material.

323

Approximately 200 tables are grouped into the following categories:

1	Population	5	Health
2	Employment/Industry	6	Environment
3	Housing	7	Social
4	Education		

Digest of Scottish Statistics (Scottish Statistical Office)—published twice annually.

Digest of Welsh Statistics (Welsh Office)—published annually.

Numerous Regional and Sub-Regional Studies, Plans, Reports and Strategies, all of which contain a wealth of information specific to the particular region. (See Appendix C).

List of Principal Statistical Series Available (Central Statistical Office)—a general guide to published economic, financial and regional statistics.

Supplementary Sources

1 *Population*

Census of Population (General Register Office). This is the most important single source on population, and has been taken every 10 years from 1801, with the exception of 1941 (War) and 1966 (10% sample census). Census data provides a great deal of information, available for all levels from the national and regional to the smallest possible enumeration unit, on the following topics (1961 Census): England and Wales/Scotland

Preliminary	Migration
Usual Residence	Education
Age/Marital/General	Socio-Economic Factors
Birthplace	Workplace
Housing	Household Composition
Immigration	Greater London
Occupation	Fertility
Industry	Place Names
Qualifications	

Publication of the full results of the 1971 Census will be complete in 1974.

Other useful sources on population are:

Statistical Review Part II (General Register Office), published annually. This includes mid-year population totals for regions, conurbations and local authorities.

Quarterly Return—December (General Register Office)—includes population totals subdivided into age/sex groups and population projections for regions and conurbations.

Long Term Population Distribution in Great Britain—A Study. (Report by an Inter-Dept. Study Group of the Dept. of the Environment 1971). This is a very useful study including long term population trends and projections for 10 Economic Planning Regions (excluding N. Ireland) and 61 Sub-Regions (Ministry of Housing and Local Government subdivision).

Statistics for Town and Country Planning, Series III—Population and House-holds No. 1 'Projecting growth patterns in regions'. HMSO (1970). The tables in this publication produce estimates of changes by regions and subdivisions.

Social Trends (Central Statistical Office)—published annually since 1970, provides much useful information 'about people' and includes many regional breakdowns.

2 *Employment*

Department of Employment Gazette—published monthly. This is the major source on employment. At the regional level there is monthly information on employment (placings and vacancies) and unemployment (form and duration), and annual information on number of employees (age/sex/SIC/Min. List Heading), activity rates, seasonal unemployment and new employment. Data breakdowns by employment exchange are unpublished.

New Earnings Survey (Dept. of Employment)—1971 and annually, relates to earnings from employment by industry, occupation, region, etc.

3 *Production*

Census of Production (Board of Trade)—taken in 1948, 1951, 1954, 1958, 1963, 1968. The Census provides numbers of establishments, total sales and volume of employment for 130 industries at the regional level. Provisional results only are available for 1968.

4 *Distribution*

Census of Distribution (Board of Trade)—taken in 1950, 1957, 1961, 1966, 1971. The Census provides estimates of the numbers of retail establishments, sales and employment by kind of business, for areas with populations over 20,000. Unfortunately, the sample basis of the 1957 and 1966 censuses limits the disaggregation of sales and employment data to the regional level. Provisional results only are available for 1971.

5 Agriculture

Agricultural Statistics (Ministry of Agriculture, Food and Fisheries)—information is obtained by counties once a year on a census basis with sample enquiries at other times within the year.

6 Education

Statistics of Education (Department of Education and Science)—published annually and include a wide variety of regional data, such as staff/student ratios, distribution of pupils in different types of schools.

7 Transport

Highway Statistics (Department of the Environment (Transport))—published annually, provide data on the mileages of road, expenditure on roads and the number of vehicles with current licences for counties and county boroughs in England and Wales.

Roads in England and Wales (Department of the Environment (Transport))—also published annually, includes information on traffic volumes on major roads and future estimates of expenditure on major road schemes.

8 Income and Expenditure: Individual and Community

Report of the Commissioners of Inland Revenue (Inland Revenue Board)—regional surveys of personal income are published annually, and more detailed county surveys are published quinquennially.

Family Expenditure Survey (Department of Employment). The sample size of this very useful survey was increased to 11 000 households in 1967, and is now suitable for regional analysis. At the regional level the survey includes data on weekly income by household and average weekly household expenditure on over 100 goods and services.

Local Government Financial Statistics (Department of the Environment (Housing and Local Government))—includes summaries of local authority finances.

9 Land Use—Housing/Derelict Land

Local Housing Statistics (Department of the Environment (Housing and Local Government))—published quarterly. These statistics include

326

data on all new housing (private/local authority/new towns) sub-divided into completions, housing under construction, and housing approved but not yet started, and information on slum clearance schemes and improvement grants. All data can be aggregated from the local authority upwards.

Derelict Land Survey (Department of the Environment (Housing and Local Government))—annual survey of acreages of derelict land, land restored and land proposed for treatment, for counties and county boroughs.

Statistics for Town and Country Planning, Series II—Floorspace (Department of the Environment)—published quarterly. A comprehensive source of commercial floorspace statistics, compiled from rating valuations, and broken down to local authority level.

APPENDIX B

Summary of British government regional measures (mid–1972)

Measures		*Assisted Areas*		
	Special development areas	*Development areas*	*Intermediate areas*	*Elsewhere**
Measures directed at the individual firm				
Regional Development Grants. (On SIC II to XX) Available to firms already established in the assisted areas as well as to incoming firms, on:				
New Machinery, Plant and Mining Works	22%	20%	Nil	Nil
Building Works (other than Mining Works).	22%	20%	20%	Nil
Tax Allowances: Initial (first-year tax allowances)				
New Machinery and Plant	100%	100%	100%	100%
New Industrial Buildings.	44%	44%	44%	44%
Tax Allowances: Annual (calculated on balance of costs after deducting initial allowance)				
New Machinery and Plant	Nil	Nil	Nil	Nil
New Industrial Buildings.	4%	4%	4%	4%

Measures	Assisted Areas			
	Special development areas	Development areas	Intermediate areas	Elsewhere*
Selective Assistance:				
Loans: Available on preferential terms for general capital purposes for projects providing additional employment; on non-preferential terms for projects that maintain or safeguard employment.	Yes	Yes	Yes	N/A
Interest Relief Grants: Available towards the interest costs of finance provided from private sources which provide additional employment.	Yes	Yes	Yes	N/A
Removal Grants: Available on up to 80% of certain expenses involved in moving any undertaking from any part of Britain to an assisted area (i.e. expenses of removal of plant and machinery, stock, travel and accommodation by management, and termination of employment payments).	Yes	Yes	Yes	N/A
Government Factories for rent or for sale: Rents are usually at favourable rates and there may (subject to a 'cost per job' limit) be a rent free period for the first two years of occupation.	Yes	Yes	Yes	N/A
Some factories may be available for sale with the repayment of capital and interest spread over a period of up to 15 years at a fixed rate of interest.	Yes	Yes	Yes	N/A
Regional Employment Premium: The Premium is available to any employer with a manufacturing establishment, and is payable at the rate of £1.50 per week for each man, 75p per week for each woman or				

Measures	Assisted Areas			
	Special development areas	Development areas	Intermediate areas	Elsewhere*

boy, and 47½p per week for each
girl employed (to be phased out over
a period from September 1974).

	Yes	Yes	N/A	N/A

Locational Controls:
  Industrial Development Certificates
  (IDC's) are required for developments
  of greater than 15,000 sq. ft. (and
  greater than 10,000 sq. ft. in the
  South East Economic Planning
  Region), with the exception of the
  Special Development Areas and
  Development Areas.

    IDC's not required

  Office Development Permits (ODP's)
  are required for office developments
  of more than 3,000 sq. ft. in Greater
  London and 10,000 sq. ft. in the rest
  of the South East Economic Planning
  Region and the urban parts of the
  East and West Midlands Regions

    ODP's not required

Measures directed at labour mobility and re-employment

Training:
  Where an employer provides training
  for workers to fill new jobs, the
  Department of Employment may pay
  him weekly grants over an approved
  period at the rate of £15 per man
  and £12 per woman.

  There are also other schemes
  providing grants for training
  apprentices and technicians; the
  purchasing of machinery and

Measures	*Assisted Areas*			
	Special development areas	*Development areas*	*Intermediate areas*	*Elsewhere**
equipment needed for additional off-the-job training; and assistance with training older workers.	Yes	Yes	Yes	N/A
Government Training Centres are also sited in most assisted areas.				
Transferred Workers:				
Key workers Scheme: for key workers transferring to install plant or machinery, train local employees or form a nucleus for a new labour force, grants are available towards the costs of settling in (£6), lodgings (up to £4.55 per week), furniture removals and house buying fees).	Yes	Yes	Yes	N/A
Resettlement Transfer Scheme: for workers who live in assisted areas and move home to get a job, or who undertake training and then have to move to use their skills, a rehousing grant of £600 is available.	Yes	Yes	Yes	N/A

General measures

Environmental Improvement: Grants are available to local authorities towards the costs of clearing derelict land.	85%	85%	75%	50%
Under the Housing Act, 1971, the public contribution towards the cost of housing improvement is extended to 75% of approved expenditure.	75%	75%	75%	50%
Contracts Preference Schemes: Under the General Preference Scheme, a firm in an assisted area will receive preference to firms from other areas,				

Measures	Assisted Areas			
	Special development areas	Development areas	Intermediate areas	Elsewhere*
where price, quality, delivery date and other considerations are equal.	Yes	Yes	N/A	N/A
Under the Contracts Preference Scheme, a firm from an assisted area, which has been unsuccessful in its original tender may still be given an opportunity to tender for up to 25% of the contract, provided that it can meet the accepted price.	Yes	Yes	N/A	N/A

* *Note:* The range of measures available in Northern Ireland are similar to those available in the British Special Development Areas, although rather more generous. A limited range of measures (Regional Development Grants, Tax Allowances, Resettlement Grants and grants for environmental improvement) are also available in the North Midlands Derelict Land Clearance Area for a two-year period (1972–74).

Major UK regional and sub-regional planning studies

This appendix lists the major post-war (predominantly post-1965) Regional and Sub-Regional Planning Studies. The studies are grouped according to major regional divisions. The list seeks to be a representative rather than a comprehensive bibliography of such studies undertaken within this period.

Scotland

Report of the Committee of Inquiry into the Scottish Economy (Toothill Report), Scottish Council. Cmnd. 1835. HMSO 1962.
The Scottish Economy 1965–70. Cmnd. 2864. HMSO 1966.
Clyde Valley Regional Plan, a Report prepared for the Clyde Valley Regional Planning Committee by Abercrombie and Matthew, HMSO 1946.
Central Scotland: A Programme for Development and Growth, Cmnd. 2206, HMSO 1963.
The Lothians Regional Survey and Plan; **1**: *Economic and Social Aspects.* **2**: *Physical Planning Aspects,* Scottish Development Department, HMSO 1966.
The Central Borders: A Plan for Expansion, **1**: *Plan and Physical Study,* **2**: *Economic and Geographical Report,* Scottish Development Department, HMSO 1968.
Grangemouth—Falkirk Regional Survey and Plan, **1**: *Economic and Social Issues,* **2**: *Physical Planning Aspects,* Scottish Development Department, HMSO 1968.
A Strategy for South-West Scotland, Scottish Development Department, HMSO 1970.

Tayside: Potential for Development, Scottish Development Department.
HMSO 1970.
North East Scotland: A Survey of its Development Potential, Scottish
Office Department, HMSO 1969.
Moray Firth: A plan for growth, The Jack-Holmes Planning Group for
the Highlands and Islands Development Board, 1968.
Cairngorm Area, Report of the Technical Group, HMSO 1967.

Northern Ireland

An Economic Survey of Northern Ireland, Isles and Cuthbert,
HMSO 1957.
Report of the Joint Working Party on the Economy of Northern Ireland
(Hall Report), Cmnd. 1835, HMSO 1962.
Economic Development in Northern Ireland (Wilson Report), Cmnd.
479, HMSO 1965.
The Belfast Regional Survey and Plan, Prof. Robert Matthew,
HMSO 1963.
Area Development in Northern Ireland, Northern Ireland Economic
Council, HMSO 1969.
Development Programme (1970–75), Government of Northern Ireland,
1970.

Wales

Wales: The Way Ahead, Secretary of State for Wales, Cmnd. 3334,
HMSO 1967.
Strategy for Rural Wales, Welsh Council, 1971.
Strategy for North West Wales, Welsh Council, 1971.

Northern Region

The North East: A Programme for Development and Growth,
Cmnd.3206, HMSO 1963.
Challenge of a Changing North, Northern Economic Planning Council,
HMSO 1966.
Outline Strategy for the North, Northern Economic Planning Council,
1969.
Cumberland and Westmorland: A Sub-Regional Study, Department of
Economic Affairs, HMSO 1965.
Teesside Survey and Plan, 1: *Policies and Proposals,* 2: *Analysis Parts
1 and 2,* Wilson, H., and Wolmersley L., Scott Wilson Kirkpatrick
and Partners, HMSO 1969 (Vol 1), 1971 (Vol 2).

North-West

The North West: A Regional Study, Department of Economic
Affairs, HMSO 1965.
The Problems of Merseyside (An *Appendix* to 'The North West: A
Regional Study'), 1965.
Strategy II: The North West of the 1970's, North West Economic
Planning Council, 1968.
Strategic Plan for the North West: Issues Report, SPNW,
December 1971.
North East Lancashire Plan: A Report on Sub-Regional Development,
Lancashire County Council, Blackburn and Burnley County Borough
Councils, 1972.

Yorkshire and Humberside

A Review of Yorkshire and Humberside, Yorkshire and Humberside
Economic Planning Council, HMSO 1966.
Yorkshire and Humberside Regoinal Strategy, Yorkshire and Humberside
Economic Planning Council, HMSO 1970.
Area Studies: Halifax and the Calder Valley, 1968; *Huddersfield and
the Colne Valley;* 1969; *Doncaster,* 1969, Yorkshire and Humberside
Economic Planning Council, HMSO.
Humberside: A Feasibility Study, Central Unit for Environmental
Planning, HMSO 1969.

East Midlands

The East Midlands Study, East Midlands Economic Planning Council,
HMSO 1966.
Opportunity in the East Midlands, East Midlands Economic Planning
Council, HMSO 1969.
Leicester and Leicestershire Sub-Regional Planning Study, Leicester City
Council and Leicestershire County Council, 1969.
Nottingham and Derbyshire Sub-Regional Study, Nottinghamshire County
Council, Derbyshire County Council, Nottingham City Council,
Derby County Borough Council, 1969.

West Midlands

The West Midlands: A Regional Study, Department of Economic
Affairs, HMSO 1965.

335

The West Midlands: Patterns of Growth, West Midlands Economic
Planning Council, HMSO 1967.

A Development Strategy for the West Midlands, Report of the West
Midland Regional Study, Birmingham, 1971.

The West Midlands: An Economic Appraisal, West Midland Economic
Planning Council, HMSO, 1971.

Coventry–Solihull–Warwickshire: A Strategy for the Sub-Region, Coventry
City Council, Solihull County Borough Council, Warwickshire
County Council, 1971.

East Anglia

East Anglia: A Study, East Anglia Economic Planning Council,
HMSO 1968.

Small Towns Study, East Anglia Consultative Committee and East
Anglia Planning Council, Shire Hall, Cambridge, 1972.

South East

Greater London Plan, 1944, A Report prepared on behalf of the
Standing Conference on London Regional Planning by Professor
Abercrombie, HMSO 1945.

The South East Study, 1961–1981, Ministry of Housing and Local
Government, HMSO 1964.

A Strategy for the South East, South East Economic Planning
Council, HMSO 1967.

Strategic Plan for the South East, South East Joint Planning Team,
HMSO 1970.
> *Studies:* **1**: *Population and Employment;* **2**: *Social and Environmental
> Aspects;* **3**: *Transportation;* **4**: *Strategies and Evaluation;* **5**: *Report
> of Economic Consultants Ltd.*

Report of the Monitoring Group on Strategic Planning in the South-East,
Department of the Environment, HMSO 1973.

South East: A Study of Sub-Divisions, South East Economic Planning
Council, 1969.

South East Kent Study, South East Economic Planning Council,
HMSO, 1969.

*South Hampshire Study: Report on the Feasibility of Major Urban
Growth,* Colin Buchanan and Partners, HMSO, 1966.
> *Supplementary* **1**: *The area, its people and activities; Supplementary* **2**:
> *Methods and policies.*